Praxis® II

Elementary Education: Content Knowledge Practice Questions

Mometrix

TEST PREPARATION

DEAR FUTURE EXAM SUCCESS STORY

First of all, **THANK YOU** for purchasing Mometrix study materials!

Second, congratulations! You are one of the few determined test-takers who are committed to doing whatever it takes to excel on your exam. **You have come to the right place.** We developed these practice tests with one goal in mind: to deliver you the best possible approximation of the questions you will see on test day.

Standardized testing is one of the biggest obstacles on your road to success, which only increases the importance of doing well in the high-pressure, high-stakes environment of test day. Your results on this test could have a significant impact on your future, and these practice tests will give you the repetitions you need to build your familiarity and confidence with the test content and format to help you achieve your full potential on test day.

Your success is our success

We would love to hear from you! If you would like to share the story of your exam success or if you have any questions or comments in regard to our products, please contact us at **800-673-8175** or **support@mometrix.com**.

Thanks again for your business and we wish you continued success!

Sincerely,
The Mometrix Test Preparation Team

TABLE OF CONTENTS

Practice Test #1

English

1. Research indicates that developing oral language proficiency in emergent readers is important because:

a. Proficiency with oral language enhances students' phonemic awareness and increases vocabulary.
b. The more verbally expressive emergent readers are, the more confident they become. Such students will embrace both Academic and Independent reading levels.
c. It encourages curiosity about others. With strong oral language skills, students begin to question the world around them. The more they ask, the richer their background knowledge.
d. It demonstrates to students that their ideas are important and worth sharing.

2. Arthur writes a paper. One classmate identifies ideas and words that resonated with her when she read it. Another describes how reading the paper changed his thinking. A third asks Arthur some questions about what he meant by certain statements in the paper. A fourth suggests that a portion of the paper needs more supporting information. Which of the following is taking place?

a. A portfolio assessment
b. A writing workshop
c. A holistic scoring
d. A peer review

3. Which text should a teacher choose in order to practice the skills of previewing and reviewing information?

a. A poem
b. A chapter from the students' science class textbook
c. A library book of each student's own choosing
d. A short story from language arts class

4. "Language load" refers to:

a. The basic vocabulary words a first grader has committed to memory.
b. The number of unrecognizable words an English language learner encounters when reading a passage or listening to a teacher.
c. The damage that carrying a pile of heavy books could cause to a child's physique.
d. The number of different languages a person has mastered

5. The first-grade teacher wants her class to understand that stories have a certain order. She reads them a story, then orally reviews how each event that happened in the story caused the next event to happen. To reinforce the lesson, the teacher should:

a. Give each child a piece of drawing paper that has been folded in half and then in half again, creating four boxes, along with a piece that has not been folded. The teacher should then ask the students to draw a cartoon about the story. Each of the first four boxes will show the events in order. The second page is to show how the story ends.
b. Give each child a piece of drawing paper and ask the students to draw the most important scene.
c. Give each child a piece of drawing paper and ask the students to draw the story's beginning on the front of the page and ending on the back.
d. Give each child a piece of drawing paper that has been folded in half and then in half again, creating four boxes, along with a piece that has not been folded. The teacher should then ask the students to draw a cartoon about anything they want. She reminds them to put their story cartoons in proper order.

6. Which of the following typically combines signal phrases, parenthetical references, and page numbers for documenting sources in literature?

a. A list of works cited formatted to MLA guidelines
b. In-text citations in a research paper following MLA style
c. Informational notes with MLA-style formatting
d. A bibliography following APA citation style

7. Following instruction time, Ms. Pitman provides each student with a small sign that can be hung around the waist or neck. Ten children in her class receive signs displaying a single weekly vocabulary word. Five students get signs with the following: *dis-*, *re-*, *pre-*, *un-*, and *mis-*. The remaining students have signs with the following: *-ing*, *-ed*, *-s*, *-less*, and *-ful*. What is the best choice for a follow-up class activity based on this information?

a. The students are arranged into groups to demonstrate tangibly that certain parts of the English language have fixed functions.
b. Each student must use his or her sign to brainstorm a list of possible words that include those letters.
c. Each time a bell is rung, students must find a new partner with whom he or she can combine signs to make a new word.
d. Ask each student to explain what his or her sign means and how it functions in the English language.

8. At the beginning of each month, Mr. Yi has Jade read a page or two from a book she hasn't seen before. He notes the total number of words in the section and the number of times she leaves out or misreads a word. If Jade reads the passage with less than 3% error, Mr. Yi is satisfied that Jade is:

a. Reading with full comprehension
b. Probably bored and should try a more difficult book
c. Reading at her independent reading level
d. Comfortable with the syntactical meaning

9. Activity settings are aspects of the sociocultural context in which students participate in instructional activities. Of five activity settings, one is participant identity, or who the students are. Of the other four, which is most related to motivation?

a. When the activity is done
b. Why the activity is done
c. Where the activity is done
d. How the activity is done

10. If a student has a writing assignment, which of the following is true regarding his or her audience?

a. The student need not identify the audience because it is the teacher.
b. The student should consider the readers' purpose for reading and response to the writing.
c. The student should know his or her writing purpose and not be concerned with a reader's purposes.
d. The student can develop an audience profile but assume the main audience is the teacher.

11. Which of the following is correct regarding phonological awareness in kindergarteners?

a. Children with delayed language development have benefited from phonological awareness training.
b. Researchers into instruction in phonological awareness advise against using SLPs and their methods.
c. Phonological awareness in kindergarteners requires changing phonemes in words to change meaning.
d. Phonological awareness instruction for kindergarteners involves only the individual phoneme level.

12. Sight words are:

a. Common words with irregular spelling
b. Words that can easily be found on educational websites
c. Any word that can be seen, including text words, words on signs, brochures, banners, and so forth
d. There is no such thing; because oral language is learned before written language, all words are ultimately based on sound. The correct term is sound words and includes all words necessary to decode a particular text.

13. A second-grade teacher wants to help her students enrich their vocabulary. She's noticed that their writing journals are filled with serviceable but unexciting verbs such as "said" and "went," and general rather than specific nouns. The most effective lesson would involve:

a. Suggesting students use a thesaurus to replace common words with more unusual words
b. Suggesting students add an adjective to each noun
c. Brainstorming a list of verbs that mean ways of talking or ways of going, then adding them to the word wall along with some nouns that specify common topics
d. Suggesting students look up the meanings of boring words and consider another way to express them

14. Which of the following students may need extra instruction and evaluation with respect to oral language skills?

a. Rosa: whose first language is Spanish. Rosa speaks with a distinct accent and can be difficult to understand when speaking about a new or unfamiliar topic.
b. Greer: who avoids oral assignments when possible. He avoids speaking up in class and only responds when called upon.
c. Ashley: who often has trouble answering questions in class. Her responses are often off-topic. She also struggles with oral presentations, seeming to present a string of unrelated facts.
d. Brett: who frequently becomes loud and disruptive whenever group work is assigned. He often becomes involved in heated discussions with classmates when discussing ideas.

15. Which of the following factors affects ELL students' English-language literacy development?

a. A Chinese student's L1 is not written alphabetically like English is.
b. A Spanish student's L1 is more phonetically regular than English is.
c. Neither one of these has any effects on L2 literacy development.
d. Both factors affect L2 literacy development but in different ways.

16. The term "common words" means:

a. One-syllable words with fewer than three letters. Some examples are *it*, *an*, *a*, *I*, *go*, *to*, and *in*. They are the first words an emergent writer learns.
b. One-syllable words with fewer than five letters. Some examples include *sing*, *goes*, *sit*, *rock*, *walk*, and *took*.
c. Words that are ordinary or unexceptional; because they tend to flatten a piece of writing, they should be avoided.
d. Familiar, frequently used words that do not need to be taught beyond primary grades.

17. Which of the following linguistic domains does NOT play a role in decoding unfamiliar words when reading?

a. Syntactic
b. Semantic
c. Graphophonic
d. Pragmatic

18. Which of the following statements is most accurate regarding writing style?

a. Diction and style are not related.
b. The focus of style is on formatting.
c. Writer purpose guides the writing style.
d. Style is added later in the writing process.

19. What statement is most accurate regarding the context(s) wherein students develop literacy?

a. Students develop literacy by reading, writing, listening, and speaking.
b. Students develop literacy by reading, writing, and listening to speech.
c. Students develop literacy by reading and writing only.
d. Students develop literacy only by reading.

20. The most effective strategy for decoding irregular sight words is:

a. Segmenting sight words into syllables. Beginning readers are understandably nervous when encountering a long word that isn't familiar. Blocking off all but a single syllable at a time renders a word manageable and allows the reader a sense of control over the act of reading.
b. Word families. By grouping the sight word with similar words, patterns emerge.
c. A phonemic approach. When students understand the connection between individual words and their sounds, they will be able to sound out any sight word they encounter.
d. None; irregular sight words cannot be decoded. Readers must learn to recognize these as whole words on sight.

21. Editing involves:

a. Correcting surface features such as sentence fragments, spelling, and punctuation
b. Fine-tuning the underlying structure of the piece to make the theme stand out
c. Reconsidering ideas, adding or subtracting information, and changing the underlying structure
d. Adding illustrations, charts, and other useful addenda

22. Which of the following is NOT a method of peer editing?

a. Pairs of students analyze each others' sentences for variety.
b. Groups of students ask questions of the author to make the writing more clear.
c. Students work together to perform a final edit.
d. Students decide whether another student's essay is good writing or poor writing.

23. Which of the following MOST accurately summarizes the relationship between reading fluency and reading comprehension?

a. As students develop greater reading comprehension, their reading fluency also improves.
b. When students develop greater reading fluency, their reading comprehension improves.
c. The relationship between reading fluency and reading comprehension is a reciprocal one.
d. Reading fluency and reading comprehension are two separate, mainly unrelated skill sets.

24. Phonological awareness activities are:

a. Oral
b. Visual
c. Tactile
d. Semantically based

25. William Shakespeare wrote during which historical and literary period?

a. Medieval
b. Renaissance
c. Restoration
d. Enlightenment

26. Which of the following sentences is an appeal to emotion?

a. Using a cell phone while driving is dangerous, as you have to steer with one hand.
b. It is really stupid to use a cell phone when you drive because it is so dangerous.
c. Statistics conclusively show that using a cell phone while driving is dangerous.
d. Many places have driving laws that ban the use of a cell phone while driving.

27. To determine the subject matter of a section within a text chapter, what should the teacher tell the student to do?

a. Read the section heading
b. Read the chapter glossary
c. Read the index in the text
d. Read through the section

28. A class is reading *The Heart Is a Lonely Hunter*. The teacher asks students to write a short paper explaining the story's resolution. She is asking them to locate and discuss the story's:

a. Outcome
b. Highest or most dramatic moment
c. Plot
d. Lowest point

29. Which of the following linguistic domains relates primarily to the meanings of words?

a. Graphophonic
b. Semantic
c. Syntactic
d. Pragmatic

30. Abi, a fifth-grader, is reading aloud to his teacher during one-on-one reading time. His teacher uses this time to evaluate ongoing fluency and comprehension skills. Following today's reading, Abi's teacher determines that he needs practice with words that begin with digraphs. Which of the following sets of words would most likely be part of this assignment?

a. Chicken, Shells, That
b. Were, Frame, Click
c. Sponge, Think, Blank
d. Packed, Blistered, Smoothed

31. To support student vocabulary development, which of the following most accurately describes the instructional materials teachers should use?

a. Teachers should only use literature and expository texts to support student vocabulary development.
b. Teachers should use newspapers, magazines, etc., in addition to literature and expository textbooks.
c. Teachers should use trade books, content-specific texts, and technology for vocabulary development.
d. Teachers should use a broad variety of instructional materials, including all of the above and others.

32. A fifth-grader has prepared a report on reptiles, which is something he knows a great deal about. He rereads his report and decides to make a number of changes. He moves a sentence from the top to the last paragraph. He crosses out several words and replaces them with more specific words. He circles key information and draws an arrow to show another place the information could logically be placed. He is engaged in:

a. Editing
b. Revising
c. First editing, then revising
d. Reviewing

33. When students are taught to use effective reading comprehension strategies, one of the benefits is that they learn to think about how they think when they read, a process or skill known as which of the following?

a. Schemata
b. Scaffolding
c. Metacognition
d. Metamorphosis

34. Which exercise would be best for building fluency in young students?

a. Allowing students to draw pictures that illustrate the texts they read if they are unable to write their responses
b. Using daily games and lessons to reinforce phoneme-identification skills
c. Placing the students into groups to read aloud to one another
d. Reading to the students every day from a variety of texts

35. Which of the following correctly sequences children's typical developmental phases in writing?

a. Beginning sounds emerge; letter-like symbols; scribbling; letter strings; initial, middle, and final sounds; consonants represent words; standard spelling; transitional phases
b. Letter-like symbols; beginning sounds emerge; letter strings; scribbling; initial, middle, and final sounds; transitional phases; standard spelling; consonants represent words
c. Scribbling; letter-like symbols; letter strings; beginning sounds emerge; consonants represent words; initial, middle, and final sounds; transitional phases; standard spelling
d. Letter strings; beginning sounds emerge; initial, middle, and final sounds; consonants represent words; letter-like symbols; transitional phases; standard spelling; scribbling

36. Which of the following choices is NOT an element of metacognition?

a. A reader's awareness of themselves as a learner
b. A reader's understanding of a variety of reading strategies
c. A reader who is conscious about remembering what has been read
d. A reader who can read with prosody

37. An ESL student whose L1 is Chinese tends to omit plural endings and articles before nouns. Of the following, which is the most likely explanation for this?

a. The student has not yet learned these English grammatical forms.
b. These English grammatical forms are notoriously difficult to learn.
c. Incompatible nature and rules of the L1 are transferring to the L2.
d. The student does not understand how the L1 and L2 forms relate.

38. Which choice describes an appropriate alternative to round robin reading?

a. All students read together, simultaneously speaking the text aloud.
b. Students break into pairs assigned by the teacher to take turns reading the text while the teacher circulates among the pairs to guide and assess the students.
c. The teacher reads aloud to the students before engaging in a class discussion about what they have learned.
d. Students work on independent assignments while the teacher listens to students read individually.

39. What is the best way for teachers to help students develop larger reading and writing vocabularies?

a. Give students weekly vocabulary lists to memorize for tests.
b. Assign students to search texts for new vocabulary words.
c. Give students many opportunities for reading and writing.
d. Assign students new-word quotas to include in writing.

40. A class reads an essay about the benefits to youth of pet ownership. The author's position is very clear: she believes young people should be given the responsibility of taking care of pets. The author cites facts, research studies, and statistics to strengthen her position. This type of writing is called:

a. Expository
b. Narrative
c. Persuasive
d. Didactic

Mathematics

1. The ratio of employee wages and benefits to all other operational costs of a business is 2: 3. If a business's total operating expenses are $130,000 per month, how much money does the company spend on employee wages and benefits?

a. $43,333.33
b. $86,666.67
c. $52,000.00
d. $78,000.00

2. Given that x is a prime number and the greatest common factor of x and y is greater than 1, compare the two quantities.

Quantity A	Quantity B
y	the least common multiple of x and y

a. Quantity A is greater.
b. Quantity B is greater.
c. The two quantities are the same.
d. The relationship cannot be determined from the given information.

3. If 1 inch on a map represents 60 feet and one yard is equal to 3 feet, how many yards apart are two points if the distance between the points on the map is 10 inches?

a. 1,800
b. 600
c. 200
d. 2

4. The vertices of a polygon are $(2, 3)$, $(8, 1)$, $(6, -5)$, and $(0, -3)$. Which of the following describes the polygon most specifically?

a. Parallelogram
b. Rhombus
c. Rectangle
d. Square

5. Which of these tables properly displays the measures of central tendency that can be used for nominal, interval, and ordinal data?

a.

	Mean	Median	Mode
Nominal			x
Interval	x	x	x
Ordinal		x	x

b.

	Mean	Median	Mode
Nominal			x
Interval	x	x	x
Ordinal	x	x	x

c.

	Mean	Median	Mode
Nominal	x	x	x
Interval	x	x	x
Ordinal	x	x	x

d.

	Mean	Median	Mode
Nominal			x
Interval	x	x	
Ordinal	x	x	x

6. What is the correct solution for x in the following system of equations?

$$\begin{cases} x - 1 = y \\ y + 3 = 7 \end{cases}$$

a. $x = 6$
b. $x = 5$
c. $x = 4$
d. $x = 8$

7. Katrina wants to solve this math problem: "If there are 30 days in a month and today is the 12th, how many days until the end of the month?" What should be her first problem-solving step?

a. Devise a plan for solving the problem
b. Carry out the plan she created
c. Look back to check that her answer is correct
d. Understand what the problem is asking

8. A random sample of 90 students at an elementary school were asked these three questions:

Do you like carrots?
Do you like broccoli?
Do you like cauliflower?

The results of the survey are shown below. If these data are representative of the population of students at the school, which of these is most probable?

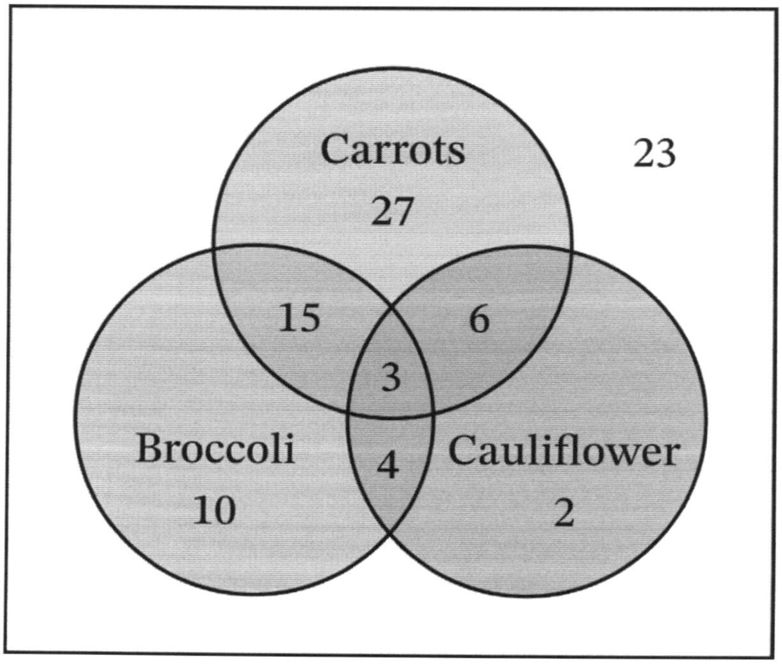

a. A student chosen at random likes broccoli.
b. Given a student chosen at random likes carrots, they will also like at least one other vegetable.
c. Given a student chosen at random likes cauliflower and broccoli, they will also like carrots.
d. A student chosen at random does not like carrots, broccoli, or cauliflower.

9. Robert buys a car for $24,210. The price of the car has been marked down by 10%. What was the original price of the car?

a. $25,900
b. $26,300
c. $26,900
d. $27,300

10. Which of the following formulas may be used to represent the sequence 8, 13, 18, 23, 28, ...?

a. $a_n = 5n + 3; n \in \mathbb{N}$
b. $a_n = n + 5; n \in \mathbb{N}$
c. $a_n = n + 8; n \in \mathbb{N}$
d. $a_n = 5n + 8; n \in \mathbb{N}$

11. Which of the following learning goals is most appropriate for a fourth-grade unit on geometry and measurement?

a. The students will be able to use a protractor to determine the approximate measures of angles in degrees to the nearest whole number.
b. The students will be able to describe the process for graphing ordered pairs of numbers in the first quadrant of the coordinate plane.
c. The students will be able to determine the volume of a rectangular prism with whole number side lengths in problems related to the number of layers times the number of unit cubes in the area of the base.
d. The students will be able to classify two-dimensional figures in a hierarchy of sets and subsets using graphic organizers based on their attributes and properties.

12. Hannah spends at least $16 on 4 packages of coffee. Which of the following expresses this relationship in terms of the cost of a package of coffee, *p*?

a. $16 \geq 4p$
b. $16 < 4p$
c. $16 > 4p$
d. $16 \leq 4p$

13. A cylindrical carrot stick is sliced with a knife. Which of the following shapes is NOT a possible cross section?

a. Circle
b. Rectangle
c. Ellipse
d. Triangle

14. Adam rolls a standard six-sided die. What is the probability he rolls a number greater than or equal to 5?

a. $\frac{1}{6}$
b. $\frac{1}{5}$
c. $\frac{1}{4}$
d. $\frac{1}{3}$

15. A teacher is working with her students on a unit on subtraction. She notices that most students are much more successful when working the problems with manipulatives rather than working the problems with numerals. In which stage of development are most of her students operating?

a. Formal operations stage
b. Concrete operations stage
c. Pre-operations stage
d. Sensory motor stage

16. During February, the sixth-grade teachers at an elementary school decide to work together to teach a unit about the heart. The English teacher will have the students write essays about how the heart functions. The science teacher will teach the basic parts of the heart. The art teacher will have the students build models of the heart. The math teacher will have the students determine the amount of blood that flows through the heart in everyday units of capacity. Which of the following concepts are the teachers implementing?

a. Differentiated instruction
b. Formative assessment
c. Thematic units
d. Collaborative learning

17. Which of the following correctly compares the given rational numbers?

a. $0.2 > 0.0499 > 0.007$
b. $0 < -2 < 7$
c. $\frac{1}{5} > \frac{1}{4} > \frac{1}{3}$
d. $-1 < -4 < -10$

18. On his morning run, a jogger records his distance from his front door in meters as a function of time in seconds. If x represents time in seconds, which of the following equations represents the jogger's distance from his front door as a function of time?

Time	0	3	4	6	7
Distance	5.2	25.0	31.6	44.8	51.4

a. $y = 3x + 25$
b. $y = 25.0x + 5.2$
c. $y = 18.4x + 3$
d. $y = 6.6x + 5.2$

19. Which of the following equations is a linear equation?

a. $y = x^2 + 4$
b. $y = \frac{2}{x^3}$
c. $2x - 3y = 5$
d. $x = (y + 2)^2$

20. Which of the following correctly explains one method that may be used to determine the size of each angle in a regular polygon of more than four sides?

a. Draw all possible diagonals of the polygon. The sum of the angles of the polygon is equal to the product of the number of triangles formed and 180°. Finally, divide this sum by the number of sides of the polygon.
b. Choose one vertex of the polygon and draw diagonals from that vertex to all nonconsecutive vertices. The sum of the angles of the polygon is equal to the area of the triangles formed. Finally, divide the sum by the number of triangles formed.
c. Draw all possible diagonals of the polygon. The sum of the angles of the polygon is equal to the product of the number of triangles formed and 180°. Finally, divide the sum by the number of triangles formed.
d. Choose one vertex of the polygon and draw diagonals from that vertex to all nonconsecutive vertices. The sum of the angles of the polygon is equal to the product of the number of triangles formed and 180°. Finally, divide this sum by the number of sides of the polygon.

21. Mr. Gomez is a sixth-grade teacher presenting a unit on compound probability. He places ten marbles labeled with the digits 0 through 9 in a bowl on his podium. He draws a marble, records the number, and then places the marble back in the bowl. He repeats the process. What is the probability that he drew two 5s in a row?

a. $\frac{1}{10}$
b. $\frac{1}{5}$
c. $\frac{1}{100}$
d. $\frac{1}{50}$

22. Mr. Carver is teaching his students about deductive reasoning and states the premises listed below. Which of these students has reached a valid conclusion?

Premise 1	All primates are mammals.
Premise 2	All lemurs are primates.

a. Mia states, "All primates are lemurs."
b. Carlos states, "All lemurs are mammals."
c. Xavier states, "All whales are mammals."
d. Gavin states, "All monkeys are primates."

23. Which of the following accurately describes the set of integers?

a. The set of counting numbers
b. The set of counting numbers, plus zero
c. The set of numbers that may be written as the ratio of $\frac{a}{b}$, where $b \neq 0$
d. The set of counting numbers, zero, and the negations of the counting numbers

24. Jackson can decorate a cake in 3 hours. Eli can decorate the same cake in 2 hours. If they work together, how long will it take them to decorate the cake?

a. 0.8 hours
b. 1.2 hours
c. 1.5 hours
d. 1.8 hours

25. Given that the two horizontal lines in the diagram below are parallel, which of the following statements is correct?

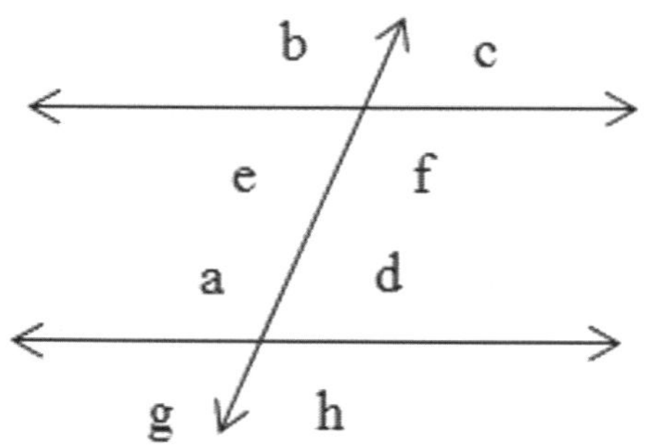

a. Angles b and g are complementary.
b. Angles d and c are supplementary.
c. Angles a and e are supplementary.
d. Angles e and h are congruent.

26. What scale factor was applied to the larger triangle to obtain the smaller triangle below?

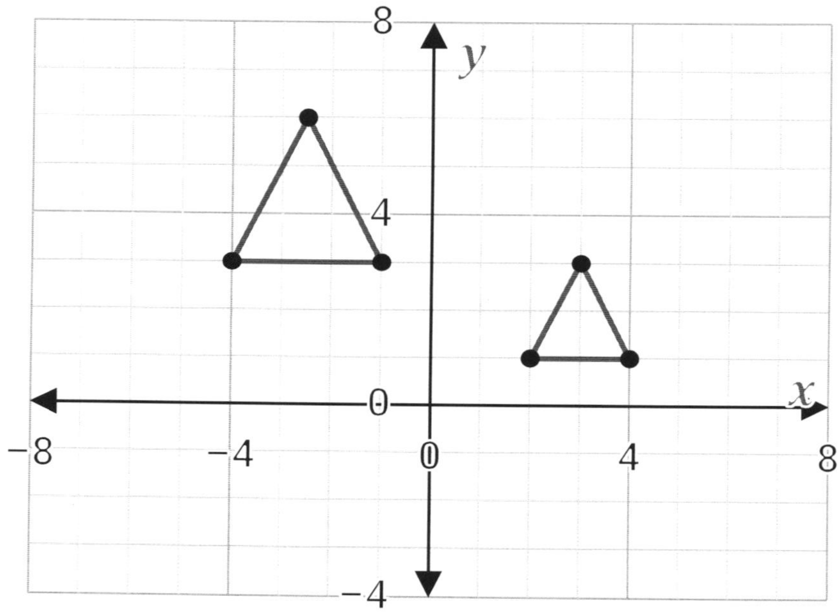

a. $\frac{1}{4}$
b. $\frac{1}{3}$
c. $\frac{1}{2}$
d. $\frac{2}{3}$

27. Given the boxplots below, which of the following statements is correct?

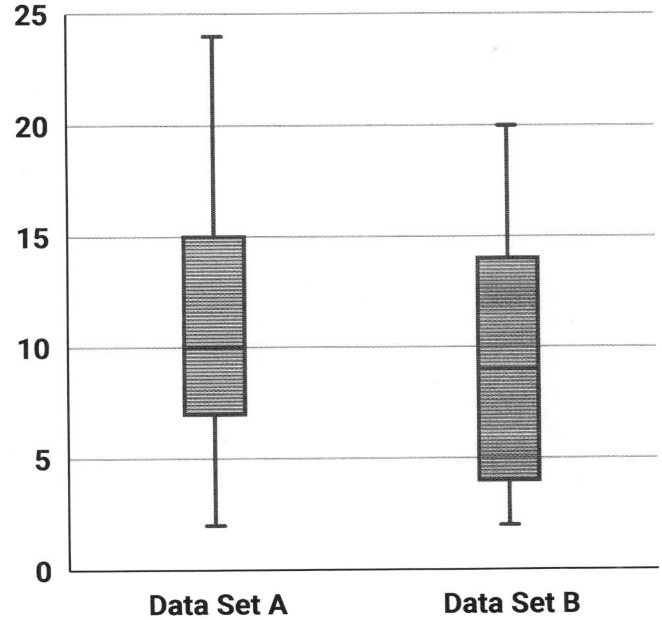

a. Data Set A has a larger range and a larger median.
b. Data Set A has a smaller range and a larger median.
c. Data Set A has a larger range and a smaller median.
d. Data Set A has a smaller range and a smaller median.

28. A sheriff's office in a small town creates a chart of violent crimes in the area for the year of 2005. Based on the chart below, which prediction for 2006 seems the most appropriate?

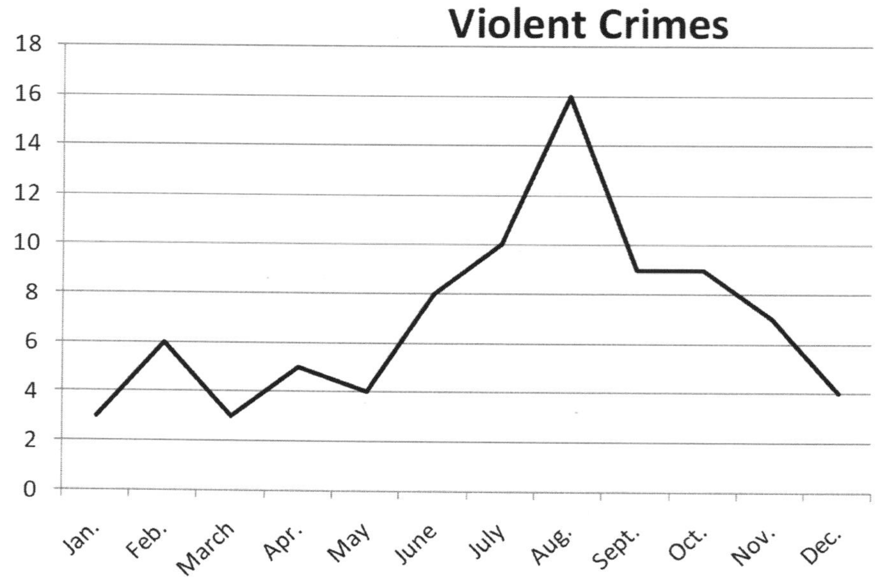

a. The winter months are likely to see a spike in violent crime rates.
b. Holiday months will likely see an increase in personal theft.
c. Violent crimes will be greatest when the weather is the warmest.
d. The number of violent crimes per month will continue to grow throughout the year.

29. In a town of 35,638 people, about a quarter of the population is under the age of 35. Of those, just over a third attend local K–12 schools. If the number of students in each grade is about the same, how many fourth graders likely reside in the town?

a. Fewer than 100
b. Between 200 and 300
c. Between 300 and 400
d. More than 400

30. To which of the following sets of numbers does –4 NOT belong?

a. The set of whole numbers
b. The set of rational numbers
c. The set of integers
d. The set of real numbers

31. Solve the inequality: $|x + 6| < 9$

a. $(-15, -3)$
b. $(-15, 3)$
c. $(3, -3)$
d. $(6, -9)$

32. A triangle with vertices $A(-4,2)$, $B(-1,3)$, and $C(-5,7)$ is reflected across $y = x + 2$ to give $\Delta A'B'C'$, which is subsequently reflected across the y-axis to give $\Delta A''B''C''$. Which of these statements is true?

a. A 90° rotation of ΔABC about $(-2,0)$ gives $\Delta A''B''C''$.
b. A reflection of ΔABC about the x-axis gives $\Delta A''B''C''$.
c. A 90° rotation of ΔABC about $(0,2)$ gives $\Delta A''B''C''$.
d. A translation of ΔABC two units down gives $\Delta A''B''C''$.

33. A decimal can be converted to a percentage by:

a. Moving the decimal point two places to the right
b. Dividing by 100
c. Doubling the number
d. Moving the decimal point one place to the left

34. Which of the following is true regarding children's development of the concept of symbolic representation?

a. When young children engage in make-believe and pretend play, this is symbolic representation.
b. Children do not develop this ability until they are old enough to engage in fully abstract thinking.
c. Children first show this concept by reading, writing, and connecting written with spoken language.
d. When young children first begin counting on their fingers, they have not yet developed this concept.

35. Which of the following transformations has been applied to ΔABC?

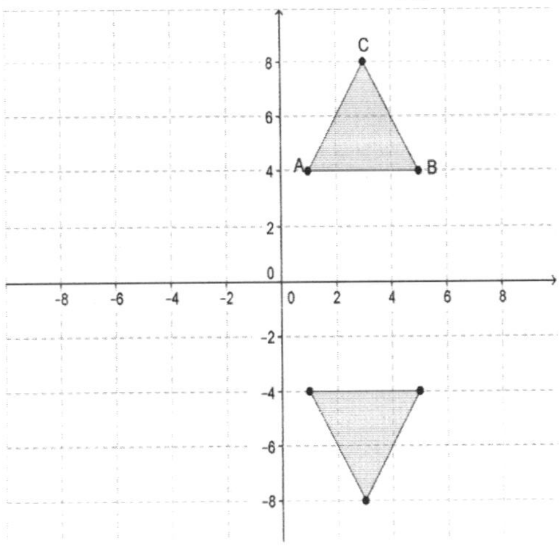

a. Translation
b. Rotation of 90 degrees
c. Reflection
d. Dilation

36. Attending a summer camp are 12 six-year-olds, 15 seven-year-olds, 14 eight-year-olds, 12 nine-year-olds, and 10 ten-year-olds. If a camper is randomly selected to participate in a special event, what is the probability that he or she is at least eight years old?

a. $\frac{2}{9}$
b. $\frac{22}{63}$
c. $\frac{4}{7}$
d. $\frac{3}{7}$

37. Carlos spends $\frac{1}{8}$ of his monthly salary on utility bills. If his utility bills total \$320, what is his monthly salary?

a. \$2,440
b. \$2,520
c. \$2,560
d. \$2,600

38. Which of the following solids has the smallest volume?

a. A cube with side length 5 cm
b. A rectangular prism with height 5 cm, length 3 cm, and width 7 cm
c. A cylinder with height 4 cm and radius 3 cm
d. A cone with height 10 cm and radius 3 cm

39. Eric has a beach ball with a radius of 9 inches. He is planning to wrap the ball with wrapping paper. Which of the following is the best estimate for the number of square feet of wrapping paper he will need? Use 3.14 for π.

a. 4.08
b. 5.12
c. 7.07
d. 8.14

40. A dress is marked down by 20% and placed on a clearance rack, under a sign reading "Take an extra 25% off already reduced merchandise." What fraction of the original price is the final sale price of the dress?

a. $\frac{2}{5}$
b. $\frac{9}{20}$
c. $\frac{3}{5}$
d. $\frac{11}{20}$

Science

Refer to the following for question 1:

A biome featuring scrubby plants and small evergreen trees has a hot, dry summer followed by a wetter winter. The following food chain exists in the biome:

$$tree \rightarrow caterpillar \rightarrow frog \rightarrow snake \rightarrow hawk \rightarrow vulture \rightarrow worm$$

1. Which biome is this?

a. Taiga
b. Coniferous forest
c. Chaparral
d. Savanna

2. Which of these was NOT an immediate consequence of the Age of Exploration?

a. The development of more accurate navigation instruments
b. The introduction of new foods and other goods to Europe
c. The decline of England as a world power
d. The discovery of new lands where people might seek a better life

3. What causes the motion of glaciers?

a. Gravity
b. Erosion
c. Wind
d. Temperature change

4. What term is used to describe two waves that are out of phase as they come together to produce a new wave?

a. Incomplete interference
b. Distorted interference
c. Constructive interference
d. Destructive interference

5. Which structures on a leaf surface open to release water vapor during transpiration and close during drought?

a. Pith
b. Stomata
c. Guard cells
d. Sepals

6. The electrolysis of water is an example of which of the following?

a. An adiabatic process
b. A chemical change
c. A synthesis reaction
d. Reverse osmosis

7. When using a light microscope, how is the total magnification determined?

a. By multiplying the ocular lens power by the objective being used
b. By looking at the objective you are using only
c. By looking at the ocular lens power only
d. By multiplying the objective you are using by two

8. Why do balloons filled with helium float while balloons filled with air do not float?

a. Balloons filled with air are larger than balloons filled with helium, which makes them heavier preventing them from floating.
b. Helium is less dense than air, which allows balloons filled with helium to float.
c. Helium balloons travel on higher air currents and balloons filled with air travel on lower air currents.
d. Air causes balloons to generate static electricity so the balloon will be attracted to the ground.

9. Which of the following sources of fresh water is generally NOT available for human consumption?

a. Rivers
b. Estuaries
c. Aquifers
d. Glaciers

10. When heat is removed from water during condensation, which of the following are formed.

a. Atoms
b. Covalent bonds
c. Intermolecular bonds
d. Ionic bonds

11. The amount of potential energy an object has depends on all of the following except its

a. Mass
b. Height above ground
c. Gravitational attraction
d. Temperature

12. Which statement accurately describes a state of matter?

a. Solids take the shape of their container
b. Gases maintain a fixed shape
c. Liquids will expand to fill the volume of a container
d. Gases expand to fill an entire space

13. Which of the following situations would result in the generation of new crust?

a. Two crustal plates converge.
b. Two crustal plates move apart.
c. Two crustal plates slide past one another.
d. A crustal plate is pushed down into the mantle.

Refer to the following for question 14:

A chemistry experiment is performed to determine the effect of a nonvolatile solute on the boiling point of water. Three trials are performed in which 10 mg, 20 mg, and 30 mg of salt are added to 500 mL of distilled water. Each solution is heated on a hot plate, and the elevated boiling points are recorded.

14. What is the purpose of conducting this experiment?

a. To test a hypothesis
b. To collect data
c. To identify a control state
d. To choose variables

15. A long nail is heated at one end. After a few seconds, the other end of the nail becomes equally hot. What type of heat transfer does this represent?

a. Radiation
b. Conduction
c. Convection
d. Entropy

16. Which of the following would increase the reaction rate of a chemical reaction?

a. Low kinetic energy
b. Low temperature
c. High concentration of reactants
d. High activation energy

17. Which of the following is an example of a trace fossil?

a. A mouse jaw
b. A footprint
c. A shark tooth
d. A cast of a skull

18. When two tectonic plates are moving laterally in opposing directions, this is called a(n):

a. Transform boundary
b. Compressional boundary
c. Oppositional boundary
d. Lateral boundary

19. If an atom's outer shell is filled, what must be true?

a. It reacts with other atoms through chemical reactions.
b. It exchanges electrons to form bonds with other atoms.
c. It has 32 electrons in its outer shell.
d. It is a stable atom.

20. What type of substance is least likely to be soluble in water?

a. Ionic
b. Polar
c. Hydrophilic
d. Non-polar

21. Which of the following describes the physical or non-biological part of the carbon cycle?

a. Phytoplankton use carbon dioxide and other nutrients to produce carbohydrates and oxygen.
b. Cold water dissolves atmospheric carbon dioxide, stores it, and releases it back out to the atmosphere as needed.
c. Carbon dioxide is dissolved in sea water and is broken up to free carbon for use by marine life.
d. Warm, surface water dissolves carbon dioxide where it is converted to nitrogen and phosphorus for use by marine life.

22. In a food chain, where does energy go after the secondary consumer dies?

a. Back to the Sun
b. To the producers
c. Into the air, becoming wind
d. To decomposers

23. When you walk barefoot on a hot sidewalk, what process is primarily responsible for heat transfer from the sidewalk to your foot?

a. Conduction
b. Convection
c. Radiation
d. None of the above.

24. Where is the type of RNA that carries and positions amino acids for further assembly located in the cell?

a. Cytoplasm
b. Nucleus
c. Ribosome
d. Mitochondria

25. What other planet in the solar system experiences a greenhouse effect similar to that observed on Earth?

a. Mercury
b. Venus
c. Neptune
d. Saturn

26. The energy radiated by stars is produced by:

a. Neutronicity
b. Nuclear fusion
c. Nuclear fission
d. Gravitational confinement

27. If a glass rod is rubbed with a cloth made of polyester, what will the resulting charge be on each material?

a. The charge on the glass rod is positive and the charge on the cloth is negative.
b. The charge on the glass rod is negative and the charge on the cloth is positive.
c. The charge on the glass rod is neutral and the charge on the cloth is positive.
d. The charge on the glass rod and the cloth both become neutral.

28. What do all animals belonging to the Echinodermata phylum have in common?

a. They use multiple appendages for locomotion.
b. They use tube feet for locomotion and feeding.
c. They have an exoskeleton made of chitin.
d. They must shed their outer layer of skin to grow.

29. Which of the following creates an electromagnet?

a. Rapidly spinning and rotating electrons inside an iron bar
b. An iron bar moving inside a coil of wire that contains a current
c. The movement of electrons through a complete circuit
d. Convection currents within the liquid core of Earth's interior

30. Which of the following is a proposed explanation for the formation of black holes?

a. High-energy collisions
b. Gravitational collapse
c. Accretion of matter
d. A and B

31. A man accidentally drops his wallet in a swimming pool. He can see his wallet at the bottom of the pool. He jumps in to retrieve it, but the wallet is not where it appeared to be. What is the reason for the optical illusion?

a. The reflection of sunlight off of the water disrupted his view.
b. Light is refracted as it enters the water, changing the wallet's apparent location.
c. The current at the bottom of the pool caused the wallet to move.
d. The heat from the Sun has impaired the man's vision.

32. The precision of a number of data points refers to:

a. How accurate the data is
b. How many errors the data contains
c. How close the data points are to each other
d. How close the actual data is to the predicted result

33. How does adding a solute to a liquid solvent affect the vapor pressure of the liquid?

a. The vapor pressure increases by an amount proportional to the amount of solute.
b. The vapor pressure increases by an amount proportional to the amount of solvent.
c. The vapor pressure decreases by an amount proportional to the amount of solute.
d. The amount of solute present in a liquid solvent does not have any effect on vapor pressure.

34. What drives weather systems to move west to east in the mid-latitudes?

a. The prevailing westerlies
b. The prevailing easterlies
c. The trade winds
d. The doldrums

Refer to the following for question 35:

A teacher in Arizona takes her class on a walk through a nearby park to study the flora and fauna of their local desert ecosystem. The students see cacti, snakes, and even evidence of coyote activity.

35. How should the teacher explain to students how these organisms are able to survive in harsh desert conditions?

a. Over thousands of years, these organisms have developed adaptations to survive in arid climates.
b. These organisms migrate out of the desert during the summer months, only living in the desert for a portion of the year.
c. Snakes, cacti, and coyotes work together to find sources of food and water.
d. Snakes, cacti, and coyotes are all aquatic species that live in ponds and rivers during the hot day.

36. In which of the following scenarios is work NOT applied to the object?

a. Mario moves a book from the floor to the top shelf.
b. A book drops off the shelf and falls to the floor.
c. Mario pushes a box of books across the room.
d. Mario balances a book on his head.

37. Which of the following would not be used as evidence for evolution?

a. Fossil record
b. DNA sequences
c. Anatomical structures
d. Reproductive habits

38. Which of the following are formed when the plasma membrane surrounds a particle outside of the cell?

a. Golgi bodies
b. Rough endoplasmic reticulum
c. Secretory vesicles
d. Endocytic vesicles

39. Which of the following words is NOT connected to the process of mountain building?

a. Folding
b. Faulting
c. Transform
d. Convergent

40. Which of the following gases is known as a compound gas?

a. Oxygen
b. Nitrogen
c. Ammonia
d. Hydrogen

Social Studies

1. Which of the following empires still existed following the armistice ending World War I?

a. The Austro-Hungarian Empire
b. The Ottoman Empire
c. The German Empire
d. The British Empire

2. What is the main difference between a primary election and a caucus?

a. A primary election is privately run by political parties, and a caucus is held by local governments.
b. Caucuses are always held on the same day, but the dates of state primaries vary.
c. A caucus is privately run by political parties, and a primary is an indirect election run by state and local governments.
d. Primary elections are all held on the same date, but the dates of caucuses vary.

3. How are members of the Federal Judiciary chosen?

a. They are elected by voters.
b. They are appointed by the president and confirmed by the House of Representatives.
c. They are chosen by a committee.
d. They are appointed by the president and confirmed by the Senate.

4. Which of the following conquistadores unwittingly gave smallpox to the indigenous peoples and destroyed the Aztec empire in Mexico?

a. Vasco Núñez de Balboa
b. Juan Ponce de León
c. Hernán Cortés
d. Álvar Núñez Cabeza de Vaca

5. Which of the following statements is false regarding the Puritans?

a. In terms of their theology, the Puritans were considered Calvinists.
b. Many Puritans agreed with radical views that criticized the Swiss Calvinists.
c. Many of those identified as Calvinists opposed the Puritans.
d. The Restoration and the Uniformity Act reunified the Puritan movement and the Church of England.

6. Of the following economists, who advocated government intervention to prevent and remedy recessions and depressions?

a. Adam Smith
b. John Maynard Keynes
c. Friedrich Hayek
d. Milton Friedman

7. The Supreme Court has nine members. How is this number determined?

a. It is outlined in the Constitution.
b. Congress determines the number.
c. The President determines the number.
d. The Court decides on the number.

8. The first amendment guarantees all below except:

a. Freedom of assembly
b. The right to bear arms
c. Freedom of the press
d. The right to speak freely

9. Which of the following is NOT one of the demographic variables?

a. Fertility
b. Diversity
c. Mortality
d. Migration

10. John Maynard Keynes advocated what?

a. Supply-side economics
b. Demand-side economics
c. Laissez faire economics
d. The Laffer Curve

11. The bubonic plague spread through Europe in which of the following ways?

a. It spread along rivers and through contaminated drinking water.
b. It was carried by birds that migrated south during the winter.
c. It spread along trade routes, carried by infected animals and people on ships.
d. It was carried by travelers on religious pilgrimages.

12. Which of the following was NOT an immediate effect of rapid urban growth in the 1800s?

a. Poor sanitation conditions in the cities
b. Epidemics of diseases in the cities
c. Inadequate police and fire protection
d. Widespread urban political corruption

13. Which of the following is the best example of a factor resulting from Europe's Commercial Revolution that contributed to the 1700s' Industrial Revolution?

a. The rediscovery of concrete
b. New advances in making iron
c. The steam engine's invention
d. Increases in population growth

14. A group that grew in numbers as a result of the Industrial Revolution was:

a. Small farmers.
b. Unskilled workers.
c. Skilled craftsmen.
d. The rural population.

15. The primary expense for most state and local governments is:

a. Emergency medical services
b. Transportation services
c. Police and fire departments
d. Education

16. Of the following, which person or group was NOT instrumental in advancement of civil rights and desegregation during the 1940s and 1950s?

a. The President
b. The Supreme Court
c. The Congress
d. The NAACP

17. Which of the following is true of social changes and the Industrial Revolution in Europe in the 18th and early 19th centuries?

a. They gave rise to a new middle-class
b. They improved working conditions
c. They were the result of urbanization
d. They were caused by the labor unions

18. Which Supreme Court case enforced the civil rights of citizens to not incriminate themselves?

a. Marbury v. Madison
b. Miranda v. Arizona
c. Youngstown Sheet and Tube Company v. Sawyer
d. United States v. Carolene Products Company

19. Which of the following are true of the demand curve?

I. It is normally downward sloping
II. It is normally upward sloping
III. It is influenced by the law of diminishing marginal utility
IV. It is unaffected by the law of diminishing marginal utility

a. I and III only
b. I and IV only
c. II and III only
d. II and IV only

20. Which of the following was the reason the economy of colonial New England focused mainly on manufacture and trade?

a. The soil and climate conditions in New England were not conducive to year-round farming.
b. The New England colonists were primarily merchants from England and Scotland.
c. Slavery did not exist in the northern colonies.
d. The New England colonists wanted to achieve economic dominance over the Middle Atlantic colonies.

21. Which of the following world religions believes in many gods and goddesses?

a. Confucianism
b. Hinduism
c. Sikhism
d. Islam

22. The president serves as commander-in-chief. What are the president's two limitations in that role?

a. The president cannot declare war or make rules governing the military.
b. The president cannot enforce blockades or declare war.
c. The president cannot enforce quarantines or make rules governing the military.
d. The president cannot enforce blockades or quarantines.

23. When the prices farmers receive for their crops decline in a developing country, this typically results in which of the following?

a. Increased urbanization
b. Increased college enrollment
c. Declining literacy rates
d. Higher prices for those crops in developed countries

24. Which of the following is NOT true about the Crusades?

a. Their purpose was for European rulers to retake the Holy Land (Jerusalem and surrounding areas) from Muslims.
b. The Crusades succeeded at European kings' goal of reclaiming the "holy land."
c. The Crusades accelerated the already incipient decline of the Byzantine Empire.
d. Egypt saw a return as a major Middle Eastern power as a result of the Crusades.

25. Every citizen 18 years of age and older has the constitutional right to vote. What do states govern in the voting process?

a. The registration for and timing of federal elections
b. The administration and timing of federal elections
c. The registration for and administration of federal elections
d. The registration for federal elections only

26. Who may write a bill?

a. Anyone
b. A member of the House
c. A Senator
d. Any member of Congress

27. A teacher tells a class that anybody who gets 100 percent on the next quiz will be excused from doing homework for that day. According to behaviorist terminology relative to motivation theory, this incentive is an example of what technique?

a. Positive reinforcement
b. Primary reinforcement
c. Negative reinforcement
d. Secondary reinforcement

28. Which invention had a major role in communication during the Civil War?

a. Morse Code
b. Telephone
c. Radio
d. Computer

29. Regarding the three basic temperament types identified by psychologists in infants, which of these is true?

a. There is no clear majority among infants having one of the types.
b. The majority of babies are found to be of Difficult temperament.
c. The majority of infants are found to be Slow to Warm Up types.
d. The majority of infants are found to have the Easy temperament.

30. Which of the following are NOT included in a geographical definition of Southeast Asia?

a. Myanmar, Laos, Cambodia, and Thailand
b. Vietnam, the Malay Peninsula, and Brunei
c. East Malaysia, Indonesia, and the Philippines
d. These are all geographical parts of Southeast Asia.

31. The results of increased production of crops and a managed approach to agriculture is called:

a. The industrial revolution
b. The information revolution
c. The agricultural revolution
d. The scientific revolution

32. A researcher is collecting data for her study on parenting. She hypothesized that countries where mothers carry their infants on their person have children who have more secure attachments as toddlers. Which method would be the most helpful in collecting data for this study?

a. Interviewing parents in the United States about their methods of carrying babies.
b. Determining methods of carrying babies and studying the toddlers in several countries.
c. Researching popular methods of carrying infants on the internet.
d. Collecting data on the number of strollers sold in several countries.

33. On a map of Africa, there is a small box around Nairobi. This city is depicted in greater detail in a box at the bottom of the map. What is the name for this box at the bottom of the map?

a. Inset
b. Legend
c. Compass rose
d. Key

34. Land is typically more expensive in urban areas than in rural areas. Which geography concept does this reflect?

a. Location
b. Distance
c. Pattern
d. Interaction

35. Of these materials, which can teachers use to help students develop chronological thinking?

a. Only history books can be used for this.
b. Biographies can also serve this function.
c. Historical literature can be used for this.
d. These are all good chronology materials.

36. A law proposed in Congress but not yet passed is called:

a. A bill
b. A proposal
c. An introduced law
d. A debate

37. What is true regarding survey findings about family differences among American socioeconomic and racial groups?

a. Cultural and demographic factors influence disagreement styles more than parental stress does.
b. Low-socioeconomic young children have no more development/behavior problems than others.
c. Data have shown more violence in African-American families, followed by Latino and then white families.
d. Socioeconomically disadvantaged children have more problems and receive more help for these.

38. Which of the following is NOT considered among the causes of the French Revolution?

a. Famines causing malnutrition and starvation
b. War debt, court spending, and a bad monetary system
c. Resentment against the Catholic Church's rule
d. Resentment against the Protestant Reformation

39. What does *due process* mean?

a. It's important for every citizen to follow the laws of their state and country.
b. Any accused person may confront the accuser and provide a defense.
c. Capital punishment is appropriate if a person is convicted of murder.
d. An accused person is considered guilty until proven to be innocent.

40. Inflation has what effects?

a. Harms all members of an economy
b. Helps all members of an economy
c. Harms no members of an economy
d. Harms some members of an economy, helps others

Answer Key and Explanations for Test #1

English

1. A: Proficiency with oral language enhances students' phonemic awareness and increases vocabulary. Understanding that words are scripted with specific letters representing specific sounds is essential to decoding a text. Students cannot effectively learn to read without the ability to decode. An enhanced vocabulary supports the act of reading; the larger an emergent reader's vocabulary, the more quickly he will learn to read. He will be able to decode more words, which he can organize into word families and use to decode unfamiliar words.

2. D: This description matches that of a typical peer review, so (D) is correct. In a peer review, writers read a peer's paper and then identify values in it, describe it, ask questions about it, and suggest points for revision. These types of feedback have been identified by experts as helpful for writing. (A) and (C) are incorrect because these types of reviews are not typically collaborative. For a portfolio assessment (A), the teacher collects finished work products from a student over time, eventually assembling a portfolio of work. Holistic scoring (C) is a method of scoring a piece of writing for overall quality (evaluating general elements such as focus, organization, support, and conventions) rather than being overly concerned with any individual aspect of writing. While a writing workshop (B) may be collaborative, it may or may not include a peer review session, and the main motivation for attending a writing workshop is generally not for the peer feedback but for professional guidance, as from a coach or editor, and to build a professional network.

3. B: Previewing and reviewing are skills that assist in learning detailed or large amounts of information. Using these concepts, students learn skills such as skimming and outlining to get an idea of what the text is about before actually reading it. After reading, the students learn to review the information they learned and compare it to their initial previews. This method is particularly helpful when individuals are reading in order to learn new information, as they would be when reading their science texts.

4. B: Language load is the number of unrecognizable words an English language learner encounters when reading a passage or listening to a teacher. Language load is one of the barriers English language learners face. To lighten this load, a teacher can rephrase, eliminate unnecessary words, divide complex sentences into smaller units, and teach essential vocabulary before the student begins the lesson.

5. A: The teacher should give each child a piece of drawing paper that has been folded in half and then in half again, creating four boxes, along with a piece that has not been folded. The teacher should then ask the students to draw a cartoon about the story. Each of the first four boxes will show the events in order. The second page is to show how the story ends. When a child is able to visually see the way a familiar story has unfolded, that child can find causal or thematic connections in the action that increases her comprehension of the story overall. Asking the class to draw a single picture or to draw the beginning and end doesn't sufficiently demonstrate the importance of order to meaning. While some first-graders may be able to create their own cartoon stories that demonstrate a logical series of events, many first-graders are not yet ready to organize thought into a linear progression.

6. B: The Modern Language Association (MLA) system for documenting literary sources defines in-line citations in a paper as combining signal phrases, which usually include the author's name and give information from a source using a paraphrase or quotation; parenthetical references following the material cited, generally at the end of the sentence; and, except for internet sources that are unpaginated, page numbers. Neither the MLA nor the American Psychological Association (APA) require signal phrases or parentheticals in bibliographies or lists of works cited, so choices A and D are incorrect. The MLA defines a list of works cited as an alphabetized list found at the end of a research paper that gives the information sources referenced in the paper. Informational notes would not necessarily include all these elements, and their purpose is not necessarily to document a source, so choice C is incorrect. Such notes can be used to add important material without interrupting the paper's flow, to supply comments about sources, or to make references to multiple sources.

7. C: One-half of the class receives signs showing vocabulary words, which are probably used as root words. The remaining students are split into two general groups: those with prefixes on their signs and those with suffixes. The best approach is to get the students moving, listening, and talking in order to solidify their understanding of how roots, suffixes, and prefixes work together to make new meanings out of various root words. This approach also allows the students to participate in a game in a group context, making the activity more fun and engaging.

8. C: When reading independently, students are at the correct level if they read with at least 97% accuracy.

9. B: Of the five activity settings referred to in the question, why the students participate—or why the activity is done (B)—is the one most closely related to motivation, so choice B is correct. The other three options, when the activity is done (A), where the activity is done (C), and how the activity is done (D), are all influences on learning that vary according to cultural, social, and economic factors.

10. B: Students should always target an audience, perform an audience analysis, and develop an audience profile to determine what they should include in or omit from their writing. Even though the assigning teacher may be the only one to read the writing, students still need to identify an audience (A) and should not write as if the teacher is the main audience (D). In addition to knowing their purpose for writing before beginning, students should also consider what purpose their writing will meet for their readers (C) and how it is likely to be used.

11. A: Multiple research studies have found that teaching phonological awareness skills to kindergarteners with delayed language development has enhanced their language development. Researchers also recommend involving speech-language pathologists (SLPs) and their instructional methods as effective in teaching phonological awareness skills (B). Phonological awareness involves being able to recognize and change phonemes (speech sounds) without any reference to meanings (C) of words, syllables, or morphological units. Researchers and others instructing kindergarteners in phonological awareness skills have provided training at both the individual phoneme level (identifying and differentiating phonemes, matching initial and final phonemes, deleting phonemes, blending phonemes, etc.) and above (D) the phoneme level (syllable, word, and rhyme awareness).

12. A: Sight words occur in many types of writing; they are high-frequency words. Sight words are also words with irregular spelling. Some examples of sight words include *talk, some,* and *the.* Fluent readers need to recognize these words visually.

13. C: The most effective lesson would be brainstorming a list of verbs that mean ways of talking or ways of going, then adding them to the word wall along with some nouns that specify common topics. Second graders aren't developmentally ready for a thesaurus; most will believe that any words in a particular list are interchangeable. For example, a student who wrote *my little sister walks like a baby* might find the verbs *strut, sidle,* and *amble* in the thesaurus. None of these verbs would be an appropriate substitution. Supplementing a noun with an adjective often results in flat writing: *There's a tree in my yard* might become *There's a nice tree in my big yard.* Adjectives such as *pretty, fun, cute, funny,* and so forth don't add much in terms of meaning, but they are the adjectives younger writers reach for first. A more specific noun is both more meaningful and more interesting. *There's a weeping willow in my yard* is evocative.

14. C: Oral language skills can be distinguished from specific speech characteristics exhibited by some children. Many students like Rosa, whose first language is not English, will speak with an accent and may be less clear when speaking about a topic that is unfamiliar. In fact, even those who are not English Language Learners may exhibit difficulty speaking on new topics. Greer may avoid oral assignments or speaking in class for a number of reasons, such as self-consciousness. This student could be helped by evaluating oral language skills in a one-on-one environment or by introducing peer scaffolding to help reduce anxiety. Brett's demeanor in group assignments may also be due to social characteristics rather than oral skills; it would be important to evaluate his skills in various contexts. Ashley, however, shows marked problems communicating orally both in class discussion and in prepared assignments. She would benefit from specific instruction related to presenting ideas orally.

15. D: The concept in question is known as language transfer, also known as L1 interference, in which language features from the first language affects the acquisition of a second language. This is particularly noteworthy in language features that exist in one language, but not in the other. For instance, in English, plural nouns are usually marked by adding *-s* to the end of the word, whereas Chinese does not make use of a plural indicator. This grammatical feature, therefore, is commonly difficult to accurately acquire. Regarding the options in the question, the Chinese written language is ideographic rather than alphabetic (A)—that is, its written symbols represent concepts visually rather than being letters representing speech sounds. Also, the fact that Spanish is much more phonetically regular than English (B) (i.e., many more words are pronounced the same way as they are spelled than in English) contributes different effects to ELL students' English-language literacy development. Therefore, choice C is incorrect.

16. D: Common words are familiar, frequently used words that do not need to be taught beyond primary grades. Common or basic words are the first tier of three-tier words. These words are widely used across the spoken and written spectrum. Some examples are *walk, go, wish, the, look, happy,* and *always.* This essential vocabulary is taught early in a reader's instruction, and beyond that, it need not be taught.

17. D: Decoding unfamiliar words when reading primarily involves understanding the structure, meaning, and the relationship between letters and sounds. Syntactic (e.g. syntax) refers to word order and sentence structure, which is necessary to interpret the meaning of phrases in context. Semantics refers to word meaning and has a very direct role in decoding meaning when encountering word roots. Graphophonic refers to written words and how the written form corresponds to the oral form of a word. To adequately read and recognize unfamiliar words, a reader needs to be able to sound out and possible recognize patterns that they have encountered elsewhere. With each of these systems activated, readers are able to succeed when encountering many unfamiliar words. However, the pragmatic domain, which deals with the use of language in social contexts and the rules for effective communication, does not directly contribute to the process of decoding written words.

18. C: Because writer purpose affects all the aspects of a particular piece of writing, the style of writing should fit the purpose, so choice C is correct. Choice A is incorrect as any language choices that are part of diction will also be part of style. Choice B is incorrect because style includes all the elements of written language and does not have a particular focus on formatting. Style is not added later in the writing process, so choice D is incorrect.

19. A: Students develop literacy within multiple contexts by learning to listen to, speak, read, and write language. Therefore, it is inaccurate to say that only reading, writing, and listening (B) are activities for developing literacy. Literacy development is not confined to reading and writing (C) as some non-educators may believe. Some may even have the mistaken impression that reading is the only activity important for literacy development (D). However, literacy develops through all activities using language.

20. D: None; irregular sight words cannot generally be decoded. Readers must learn to recognize these as whole words on sight. They either have irregular spelling or do not follow typical phonic patterns, so an attempt at decoding may ultimately mislead the reader. Segmenting them into syllables or using a phonemic approach are ineffective strategies to aid a reader in recognizing a sight word because these approaches depend on rules a sight word doesn't follow. Word families group words that share common patterns of consonants and vowels. The spelling of those words is, therefore, regular because they follow a predictable pattern. Sight words that are irregular, do not follow a predictable pattern, and must be instantaneously recognized for writing fluency. Decoding is not useful.

21. A: Editing is the final step in the writing process and involves correcting surface features such as sentence fragments, spelling, and punctuation. The writer has already decided the ideas or events are in proper order, have been sufficiently described, and are clear. Now the writer turns his or her attention to surface features, "scrubbing" errors in spelling, punctuation, and syntax from the writing.

22. D: Students should not decide whether another student's essay is good writing or poor writing. Peer editing should consist of suggestions for improvement and never involve judgmental decisions about quality.

23. C: Researchers and educators have found that reading fluency and reading comprehension have a reciprocal relationship: the more fluently a student can read, the more able the student's brain is to process the meaning of text. For example, developing automaticity of word identification enhances comprehension. Conversely, the better a student can understand the text, the more fluently she or he can read it. Therefore, while (A) and (B) are both true, each represents only half of the relationship whereas (C) indicates the relationship's mutual nature. (D) is incorrect as reading fluency and reading comprehension are interrelated components in deriving meaning from text and not separate.

24. A: Phonological awareness refers to an understanding of the sounds a word makes. While phonological awareness leads to fluent reading skills, activities designed to develop an awareness of word sounds are, by definition, oral.

25. B: Shakespeare (1564-1616) wrote during the Renaissance (B), which is generally considered to encompass the 15th and 16th centuries. The medieval (A) era, also known as the Middle Ages, was earlier, ending in the late 15th century, and included authors like Geoffrey Chaucer, Dante Alighieri, the author of *Sir Gawain and the Green Knight,* and Sir Thomas Malory. The Restoration (C) period in English literature followed the Renaissance, starting in the middle of the 17th century and ending before the 18th century. It included authors like John Dryden, who wrote poetry, satire, and criticism. The Enlightenment (D) occurred in the 18th century and included the authors Jonathan Swift, Alexander Pope, Dr. Samuel Johnson, and James Boswell.

26. B: The sentence is choice B appeals to the reader's emotions by stating simply that it is "really stupid" to use a cell phone while driving; it does not provide any evidence or logic to support the statement but relies on the emotion behind calling something stupid. Thus, choice B is correct. That steering one-handed makes driving more dangerous is a logical, common-sense argument, so choice A cannot be considered purely an appeal to emotion and is incorrect. Supporting evidence such as statistics is an appeal to logic, so choice C is incorrect. Citing the fact that many laws ban the use of cell phones while driving appeals to logic in that it supports the idea that this behavior is dangerous, and it appeals to authority in that it borrows some credibility from government. It is also not an appeal to emotion, so choice D is incorrect.

27. A: Students need to know why and how to use text features to inform their reading. Reading headings above sections within chapters (A) help students determine the main subject matter of each section. Reading the glossary for a chapter (B) gives students definitions of terms used in the chapter. Reading the index in a text (C) is a way to locate page numbers of references to subjects or authors in the text. Whether they will be reading the entire section or not, students need not read through the whole thing (D) only to determine its subject matter when its heading will typically indicate this. Headings inform students of topics in advance if they will be reading the section; if they are doing research or choosing what to read, headings can help them decide.

28. A: Story action can be analyzed in terms of rising action, story climax, falling action, and resolution. Rising action consists of those events that occur before and lead up to the story's most dramatic moment, or climax. The climax occurs toward the end of the book, but rarely, if ever, right at the end. Following the climax, the consequences of that dramatic moment are termed "falling action." The story reaches resolution with the outcome of the falling action.

29. B: Semantics is the branch of linguistics that deals with meaning. The semantic system in language includes all aspects of language use that carries meaning. Semantics include words, phrases, sentences, and further contexts that help to convey meaning. Semantics are involved in both receptive and expressive language processes. Choice A is incorrect because the graphophonic system is largely related to the sounds of a language and their written representations. Graphophonics study the relationship between phonics and orthography (writing system). Choice C is incorrect because the syntactic system refers primarily to sentence structure, word order, and other elements of grammar. Syntax does impact meaning, but in a more indirect way than semantics. Choice D is incorrect because pragmatics refers to practical application of language in a variety of contexts. For example, pragmatics is interested in language shifts between social and academic contexts. In reading, this involves being aware of how writers use language to convey moods and draw out more subtle implications.

30. A: It is important to evaluate specific reading skills, such as phonemic awareness, in a variety of contexts. Reading aloud with Abi allowed his teacher to notice that he consistently misread words beginning with digraphs. Digraphs are sounds in which two distinct letters, when combined, produce a single third sound (e.g., when *s* and *h* produce the *-sh* sound). Blends are words in which two letters produce a third sound which is a combination of both sounds put together (e.g., *b* and *l* combined to make *bl*). The only set of words consisting only of digraphs is choice A.

31. D: Teachers should use a broad variety of instructional materials to support student vocabulary development, including not only literature and expository texts (A) but also newspapers, magazines

(B), trade books, content-specific texts, technology (C), and other sources of vocabulary words to provide students with the richest and most authentic array of contexts possible for the greatest quantity and quality of exposure to and learning of vocabulary.

32. B: Revision (literally, *re+vision*) is the act of "seeing again." When revising, writers examine what they have written in order to improve the meaning of the work. Fine-tuning word choices, moving information to another location, and adding or deleting words are all acts of revision.

33. C: Thinking about thinking, or understanding our own cognitive processes, is known as metacognition, so choice C is correct. Explicitly teaching effective reading comprehension strategies does more than deepen student understanding of reading. It also promotes the higher-order, abstract cognitive skill of metacognition. Choice A is not correct, as schemata are mental constructs we form to understand the world. Reading instructors may refer to experience or background knowledge as "schemata" because students fit what they read to their existing knowledge. Choice B is incorrect because scaffolding (in reading instruction) is temporary support that is given to students as needed while they learn and gradually reduced as the students become more independent. Educators may also describe students' connections of text to prior experience as scaffolding. Metamorphosis (D) is not relevant to reading instruction.

34. B: Reading fluency combines accuracy, speed, and inflection while reading aloud. As children are learning to read, they work on all of these skills simultaneously with writing, thinking, viewing, listening, and comprehension. By using daily games or specific lessons, a teacher can directly affect students' ability to read the individual sounds in words (phonemes). As students identify more sounds correctly, they will read more accurately. Practicing reading aloud can increase fluency, but only if the child's reading partner is able to correct and encourage him or her to read more accurately. By reading aloud to the students, a teacher models correct speed and inflection, but this will affect the students' skills less directly than lessons and games in phonetics.

35. C: *Scribbling*: Children create random symbols, not printing, but significantly, they represent ideas with written or drawn marks. *Letter-like symbols*: Forms resembling letters alternate with numbers, seldom with spacing. *Letter strings*: Some letters are legible, typically capitals, but they are still not spaced; students mostly do not match letters to sounds yet, but they are developing phonological awareness. *Beginning sounds emerge*: Children still may not space between words but begin distinguishing letters from words. Words match pictures, particularly with topics children choose. *Consonants represent words*: Children begin spacing between words, mixing uppercase and lowercase letters, punctuating, and expressing ideas through written sentences. *Initial, middle, and final sounds*: Children may correctly spell familiar names, environmental print, and some sight words, but otherwise spell phonetically; writing is much more readable. *Transitional phases*: Children's writing approximates conventional spelling. *Standard spelling*: Children spell most words correctly; they develop an understanding of word roots, compound words, and contractions, increasing the correct spelling of related words. (J. Richard Gentry, PhD, 1982, 2006, 2010)

36. D: Prosody is not an element of metacognition. Metacognition means a reader's awareness of their own reading processes as they improve reading comprehension. Other elements of metacognition include awareness of areas in the text that the reader does not comprehend and an understanding of how the text is structured.

37. C: Omitting articles (for example, *a/an, the, these*) and plural endings is common among learners of the English language when these parts of grammar work differently in the learner's native language. This is the case with Chinese, so choice C is correct. Articles and plural endings may be covered early by a given curriculum, so it is not reasonable to assume that the student has not learned them, so choice A is incorrect. While the subtleties and precise patterns around article usage and plural usage can be difficult to learn, this by itself is not an explanation for omitting articles and plurals altogether, so choice B is incorrect. Likewise, choice D is incorrect because, though it is true that the student likely does not understand how articles and plurals in English relate to any corresponding forms in their native language, they do not need to understand this in order to use the English forms.

38. B: The intention of round robin reading is to provide practice reading aloud with appropriate fluency. This practice is also used to cover a large quantity of text with the entire class during the class period. By pairing the students, each child will get more practice reading aloud. He or she will also be more likely to stay engaged when working with only one partner, as there will be less time and fewer opportunities to become distracted. The teacher can then circulate amongst the groups to encourage focus and concentration, as well as provide guidance on fluency and comprehension of the text. As long as the students are paired carefully, this strategy is most likely preferable to the round robin method.

39. C: The best way for teachers to help students develop larger reading and writing vocabularies is simply to provide them with as many opportunities as possible for reading and writing. The more they read and write, the bigger their reading and writing vocabularies will grow, more effectively than from having to memorize vocabulary lists and being tested on them weekly (A). Having students search for new vocabulary words in texts (B) does not let them actually read, which is superior for learning new words within meaningful contexts as well as developing all other reading skills. Students learning new words in isolation will not learn their appropriate use. Rather than assigning minimum numbers of new words to include in their writing (D), teachers should give students actual opportunities to write, which both develops all writing skills and increases writing vocabulary. Also, choice B involves reading vocabulary but not writing vocabulary, and choice D involves writing vocabulary but not reading vocabulary, in addition to the fact that neither one involves actual reading and writing.

40. C: The author is hoping to persuade or convince readers to either request a pet and/or the primary care of their pet by providing them with facts as well as by using rhetorical devices such as dispelling opposing arguments.

Mathematics

1. C: When you have a ratio, you can find the fraction that each part of the ratio is of the whole by dividing a part by the sum of the parts. Since the ratio of wages and benefits to other costs is 2: 3, the amount of money spent on wages and benefits is $\frac{2}{2+3} = \frac{2}{5}$ of total operational costs.

$$\frac{2}{5} \times \$130{,}000 = \$52{,}000$$

2. C: If x is a prime number and the greatest common factor of x and y is greater than 1, the greatest common factor of x and y must be x. The least common multiple of two numbers is equal to the product of those numbers divided by their greatest common factor. So, the least common multiple of x and y is $\frac{xy}{x} = y$. Therefore, the two quantities are the same.

3. C: Start by setting up a proportion to solve: $\frac{1\text{ inch}}{60\text{ feet}} = \frac{10\text{ inches}}{x\text{ feet}}$. When the numbers are cross-multiplied, you get $x = 600$. Now we need to convert 600 feet to yards. There are 3 feet in 1 yard, so divide 600 by 3 to find the number of yards between the two points: $600 \div 3 = 200$. Therefore, the two points are 200 yards apart.

4. D: Since all the answer choices are parallelograms, determine whether the parallelogram is also a rhombus, a rectangle, or both. One way to do this is by examining the parallelogram's diagonals. If the parallelogram's diagonals are perpendicular, then the parallelogram is a rhombus. If the parallelogram's diagonals are congruent, then the parallelogram is a rectangle. If a parallelogram is both a rhombus and a rectangle, then it is a square. A plot of the quadrilateral would be:

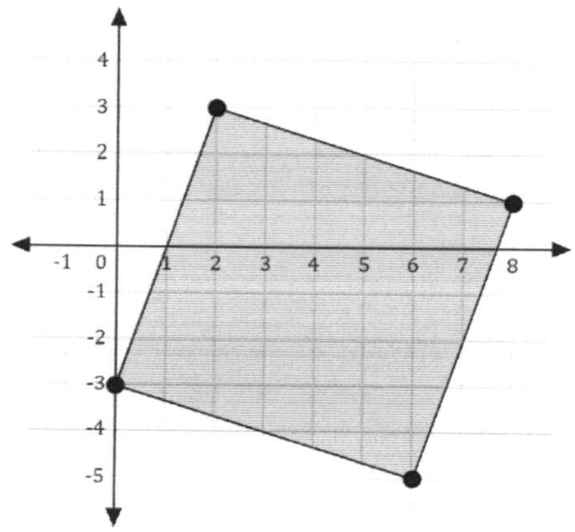

To determine whether the diagonals are perpendicular, find the slopes of the diagonals of the quadrilateral:

Diagonal 1

$$\frac{-5-3}{6-2} = \frac{-8}{4} = -2$$

Diagonal 2

$$\frac{-3-1}{0-8} = \frac{-4}{-8} = \frac{1}{2}$$

The diagonals have slopes that are opposite reciprocals of each other, so they are perpendicular. Thus, the parallelogram is a rhombus. To determine whether the diagonals are congruent, find the lengths of the diagonals of the quadrilateral:

Diagonal 1

$$\begin{aligned}\sqrt{(6-2)^2 + (-5-3)^2} &= \sqrt{(4)^2 + (-8)^2}\\ &= \sqrt{16+64}\\ &= \sqrt{80}\end{aligned}$$

Diagonal 2

$$\begin{aligned}\sqrt{(0-8)^2 + (-3-1)^2} &= \sqrt{(-8)^2 + (-4)^2}\\ &= \sqrt{64+16}\\ &= \sqrt{80}\end{aligned}$$

The diagonals are congruent, so the parallelogram is a rectangle. Since the polygon is a rhombus and a rectangle, it is also a square.

5. A: Nominal data are data that are collected which have no intrinsic quantity or order. For instance, a survey might ask the respondent to identify his or her gender. While it is possible to compare the relative frequency of each response (for example, "most of the respondents are women"), it is not possible to calculate the mean, which requires data to be numeric, or median, which requires data to be ordered. Interval data are both numeric and ordered, so mean and median can be determined, as can the mode, the interval within which there are the most data. Ordinal data has an inherent order, but there is not a set interval between two points. For example, a survey might ask the respondents whether they were very dissatisfied, dissatisfied, neutral, satisfied, or very satisfied with the customer service received. Since the data are not numeric, the mean cannot be calculated, but since ordering the data is possible, the median has context.

6. B: The equation $y + 3 = 7$ is solved by subtracting 3 from both sides to yield $y = 4$. Substituting $y = 4$ into $x - 1 = y$ yields $x - 1 = 4$. Adding 1 to both sides of this equation yields $x = 5$.

7. D: Before you can solve a problem, you must decide what it is asking.

8. B: Determine the probability of each choice.

For choice A, this is the total number of students in the broccoli circle of the Venn diagram divided by the total number of students surveyed:

$$\frac{10 + 4 + 3 + 15}{90} = \frac{32}{90} \approx 35.6\%$$

For choice B, this is the total number of students in the carrots circle and also in at least one other circle divided by the total number in the carrots circle:

$$\frac{15 + 3 + 6}{15 + 3 + 6 + 27} = \frac{24}{51} \approx 47.1\%$$

For choice C, this is the number of students in the intersection of all three circles divided by the total number in the overlap of the broccoli and cauliflower circles:

$$\frac{3}{3 + 4} = \frac{3}{7} \approx 42.9\%$$

For choice D, this is the number of students outside of all the circles divided by the total number of students surveyed:

$$\frac{23}{90} \approx 25.6\%$$

Since choice B has the highest percentage, it is the choice that is most probable.

9. C: The original price may be represented by the equation $24{,}210 = x - 0.10x$ or $24{,}210 = 0.9x$. Dividing both sides of the equation by 0.9 gives $x = 26{,}900$.

10. A: The sum of 3 and the product of each term number and 5 equals the term value. For example, for term number 4, the value is equal to $5(4) + 3$, or 23.

11. A: Choice (A) is correct because standards for fourth grade state that students will be able to use a protractor to determine the approximate measures of angles in degrees to the nearest whole number. Choices (B), (C), and (D) are stated in the standards for fifth grade.

12. D: Since Hannah spends at least \$16, the relation of the cost of a package of coffee to the minimum cost may be written as $4p \geq 16$. Alternatively, the inequality may be written as $16 \leq 4p$.

13. D: The cross section of a cylinder will never be a triangle.

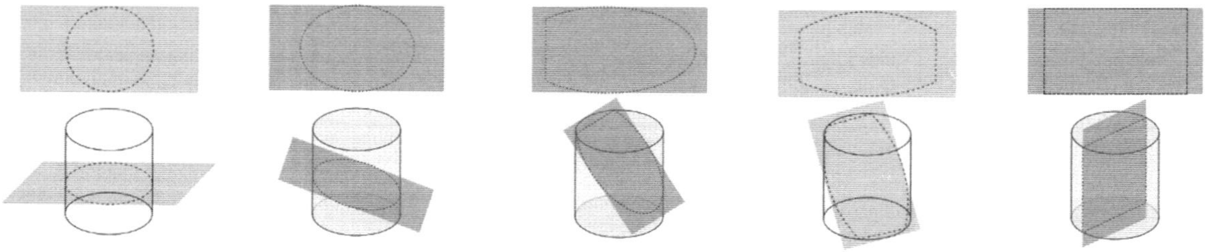

14. D: The number of outcomes in the event is 2 (rolling a 5 or 6), and the sample space is 6 (numbers 1 to 6). Thus, the probability may be written as $\frac{2}{6}$, which simplifies to $\frac{1}{3}$.

15. B: The students are more successful with physical objects. They can understand the concept of conservation. They can grasp subtraction in terms of concrete operations. Typically, 7-11 year olds are in the concrete operations stage. In this stage, the formal code is too abstract for their understanding. Therefore, the correct choice is B.

16. C: Since all of the teachers are implementing a theme about the heart, this is a thematic unit. Collaborative learning typically involves students working in groups. Formative assessments are ways teachers assess learning while working on a unit. Differentiated instruction is the use of multiple methods when teaching a unit. Therefore, the correct answer is choice C.

17. A: In choice A, a comparison of the digits in the tenths place shows that 0.2 is greater than both 0.0499 and 0.007. Then, a comparison of the hundredths place shows that 0.0499 is greater than 0.007. Choice B should read $-2 < 0 < 7$. Choice C should read $\frac{1}{3} > \frac{1}{4} > \frac{1}{5}$. Choice D should read $-10 < -4 < -1$. Therefore, the correct answer is choice A.

18. D: All four answer choices are linear equations in slope-intercept form, $y = mx + b$, where m is the jogger's rate (slope) and b is the jogger's distance from his front door at the beginning of his run (y-intercept). To find the rate, choose any two times (e.g., $x = 0$ and $x = 3$) and divide the change in distance by the change in time: $m = \frac{25.0-5.2}{3-0} = \frac{19.8}{3} = 6.6$. Therefore, the rate is 6.6 meters per second. The starting distance from the door is the distance at $x = 0$, which is $b = 5.2$ meters. The linear equation that represents this situation is $y = 6.6x + 5.2$.

19. C: A linear equation is an equation of the first degree. That means that the highest exponent of any term or variable is one, so it follows that an exponent cannot be variable. Choice C is a linear equation. Choices A and D are quadratic equations. Choice B is neither linear nor quadratic. Therefore, the correct answer is choice C.

20. D: A polygon may be decomposed into triangles by drawing all possible diagonals from one of the vertices. The sum of the degrees of a polygon is equal to the sum of the degrees of the triangles formed. The angle of the polygon is equal to that sum divided by the number of sides. For example, in a hexagon, four triangles are formed. The sum of the interior angles of a hexagon is $4(180°) = 720°$. Each angle of a regular hexagon measures $\frac{720°}{6} = 120°$. Therefore, the correct answer is choice D.

21. C: This is a compound event. Since the marble is replaced after the first draw, the probability of each event is $\frac{1}{10}$. The probability of drawing two 5s in a row is $\frac{1}{10} \times \frac{1}{10} = \frac{1}{100}$.

22. B: If all primates are mammals, and all lemurs are primates, then all lemurs are mammals. All primates are not lemurs. Since neither whales nor monkeys are mentioned in the premises, they cannot be included in the conclusion. The conclusion can only be based on the information given in the premises. Therefore, the correct answer is choice B.

23. D: The set of integers is represented as $\{\ldots, -3, -2, -1, 0, 1, 2, 3, \ldots\}$. The numbers 1, 2, 3, ... are counting numbers, or natural numbers. Thus, the set contains the counting numbers, zero, and the negations of the counting numbers.

24. B: The situation may be modeled with the equation $\frac{1}{3} + \frac{1}{2} = \frac{1}{t}$, which simplifies to $\frac{5}{6} = \frac{1}{t}$. Thus, $t = \frac{6}{5} = 1.2$. If working together, it will take them 1.2 hours to decorate the cake.

25. C: When two parallel lines are cut by a transversal, the consecutive angles formed inside the lines are supplementary.

26. D: The larger triangle has a base length of 3 units and a height of 3 units. The smaller triangle has a base length of 2 units and a height of 2 units. Thus, the dimensions of the larger triangle were multiplied by a scale factor of $\frac{2}{3}$. Note that $3 \times \left(\frac{2}{3}\right) = 2$.

27. A: The ends of Data Set A are farther apart, indicating a larger range. The horizontal line in the middle of a boxplot represents the median, so Data Set A also has a larger median.

28. C: If the rate of violent crimes per month is anything like it is the year before, it will be greatest in the summer months, as there is a spike in the data on the 2005 graph during the summer months. While there is some fluctuation up and down throughout the entire year, these months are well beyond the numbers of the other months and represent the only upward trend in the graph.

29. B: The population is approximately 36,000, so one-quarter of the population consists of about 9,000 individuals under age 35. A third of 9,000 is 3,000, which is the approximate number of students in grades K–12. Since there are thirteen grades, divide 3,000 by 13. There are about 230 students in each grade. So, the number of fourth graders is between 200 and 300.

30. A: The set of whole numbers, $\{0, 1, 2, 3, \ldots\}$, does not contain the number –4. Since –4 is an integer, it is also a rational number and a real number.

31. B: The inequality is solved by writing a double inequality equivalent to the given inequality but without the absolute value bars.

$$-9 < x + 6 < 9$$

Solve the double inequality by subtracting 6 from all three parts.

$$-15 < x < 3$$

The solution set can be written using interval notation.

$$(-15,3)$$

32. C: When a figure is reflected twice over non-parallel lines, the resulting transformation is a rotation about the point of intersection of the two lines of reflection. The two lines of reflection $y = x + 2$ and $x = 0$ intersect at $(0,2)$. So, $\Delta A''B''C''$ represents a rotation of ΔABC about the point $(0,2)$. The angle of rotation is equal to twice the angle between the two lines of reflection when measured in a counterclockwise direction from the first to the second line of reflection. Since the angle between the lines of reflection measures 45°, the angle of rotation which is the composition of the two reflections measures 90°. All these properties can be visualized by drawing ΔABC, $\Delta A'B'C'$, and $\Delta A''B''C''$.

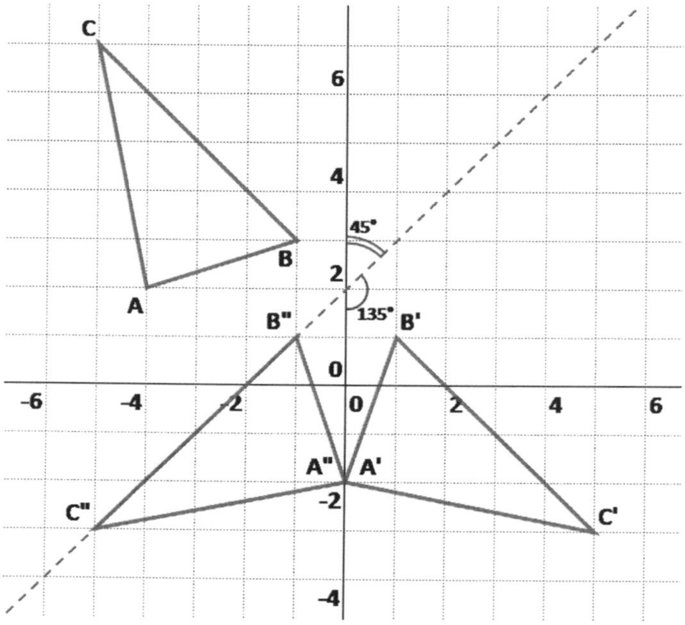

33. A: Moving the decimal point two places to the right is the same as multiplying by 100. For example, the decimal 3.42 is the same as 342%.

34. A: One of the earliest evidences of children's developing the idea of symbolic representation—i.e., the concept that things like numbers, letters, words, and objects can be used to represent other things—is their engaging in make-believe and pretend play (e.g., a toy horse represents a real horse; a block is used to represent a cell phone; a stick becomes a laser sword, etc.). Children develop this ability long before they develop fully abstract thought (B). Make-believe and pretend play develop *sooner than* reading, writing, and the alphabetic principle (C), which also employs the concept of symbolic representation. Another example that young children *have* developed symbolic representation is their counting on their fingers (D).

35. C: The original triangle was reflected across the x-axis. When reflecting across the x-axis, the x-values of each point remain the same, but the y-values of the points will be opposites.

$$(1,4) \to (1,-4) \quad (5,4) \to (5,-4) \quad (3,8) \to (3,-8)$$

36. C: If all possible outcomes are equally likely, then the probability of an event is the number of outcomes in which that event occurs, divided by the number of possible outcomes. A camper who is at least eight years old can be eight, nine, or ten years old, so the probability of randomly selecting a camper at least eight years old is:

$$\frac{\text{number of eight-, nine-, and ten-year-old campers}}{\text{total number of campers}} = \frac{14+12+10}{12+15+14+12+10} = \frac{36}{63} = \frac{4}{7}$$

37. C: His monthly salary may be modeled as $\frac{1}{8}x = 320$. Multiplying both sides of the equation by 8 gives $x = 2{,}560$.

38. D: To determine the smallest volume, it is simplest to calculate the volume of each and then compare:

Solid	Volume Formula	Result
Cube	$V = s^3$	$(5\text{ cm})^3 = 125\text{ cm}^3$
Rectangular Prism	$V = l \times w \times h$	$(5\text{ cm})(3\text{ cm})(7\text{ cm}) = 105\text{ cm}^3$
Cylinder	$V = \pi \times r^2 \times h$	$\pi(3\text{ cm})^2(4\text{ cm}) \approx 113.1\text{ cm}^3$
Cone	$V = \frac{1}{3}(\pi \times r^2 \times h)$	$\frac{1}{3}\pi(3\text{ cm})^2(10\text{ cm}) \approx 94.2\text{ cm}^3$

From this it is clear that the cone has the smallest volume.

39. C: The surface area of a sphere may be calculated using the formula $SA = 4\pi r^2$. Substituting 9 for r and 3.14 for π gives $SA = 4(3.14)(9)^2$, which simplifies to $SA = 1{,}017.36$. So, the surface area of the ball is approximately 1,017.36 square inches. There are twelve inches in a foot, so there are $12^2 = 144$ square inches in a square foot. In order to convert this measurement to square feet, the following proportion may be written and solved for x: $\frac{1}{144} = \frac{x}{1{,}017.36}$. So $x = 7.07$. He needs approximately 7.07 square feet of wrapping paper.

40. C: When the dress is marked down by 20%, the cost of the dress is 80% of its original price. Since a percentage can be written as a fraction by placing the percentage over 100, the reduced price of the dress can be written as $\frac{80}{100}x$, or $\frac{4}{5}x$, where x is the original price. When discounted an extra 25%, the dress costs 75% of the reduced price. This results in the expression $\frac{75}{100}\left(\frac{4}{5}x\right)$, which can be simplified to $\frac{3}{4}\left(\frac{4}{5}x\right)$, or $\frac{3}{5}x$. So the final price of the dress is three-fifths of the original price.

Science

1. C: The chaparral biome features scrubby plants and small evergreen trees and also has a hot, dry summer followed by a wetter winter. This biome is mainly found around the Mediterranean Sea, though there are also chaparrals in Australia, South Africa, and the American Southwest. The taiga is a colder biome found primarily in northern Europe and Asia. The vegetation of the taiga is mainly scattered stands of coniferous trees. A coniferous forest, meanwhile, is a warmer forest composed of trees that have needles and cones rather than leaves. These trees are better suited for a cold climate than are deciduous trees. A savanna is a tropical grassland with only a few trees. Savannas are clustered around the equator.

2. C: Exploration between the 15th and 17th centuries resulted in contact between European cultures and many previously unknown or little-known cultures. Navigation techniques improved, food and other goods were imported, and the New World began to be settled. Rather than declining in influence, England became a more prominent imperial power during this era.

3. A: Glaciers move because they are incredibly heavy, and the force of gravity slowly pulls them lower. Erosion is a result rather than a cause of glacier movement. Although large glaciers may only move a few inches a year or may not move at all, some valley glaciers in Europe move as much as 600 feet annually. The result is a rounded valley and a trail of rock and soil debris known as a moraine. The Great Lakes in the United States were formed by the passage of glaciers long ago.

4. D: Destructive interference describes two waves that are out of phase as they come together to produce a new wave. Out of phase refers to the crest of one and the trough of another arriving together. Interference, when used to discuss wave phenomenon, is the interaction of two or more waves passing the same point, which could be either destructive or constructive. Incomplete interference and distorted interference are not real terms. Constructive interference refers to wave interference that results in higher peaks than the waves singularly because the waves arrive in phase with one another (the crests arrive together).

5. B: Stomata are the pores of the plant that open to release water via transpiration or close during adverse conditions like a drought to prevent the plant from dehydration. Stomata are flanked by guard cells that can respond to stimuli and regulate opening and closing. Pith refers to the central, spongy part of the stem in vascular plants. Sepals are modified leave that protect the flower bud before it opens.

6. B: The electrolysis of water is a chemical change that transforms water into hydrogen and oxygen gases. Synthesis reactions are those that combine reactants to form a product, which is the opposite of what happens when electrolyzing water. Reverse osmosis is a technique often used to purify water by forcing impure water through a semipermeable membrane using a pressure differential.

7. A: When using a light microscope, total magnification is determined by multiplying the ocular lens power times the objective being used. The term "ocular lens" refers to the eyepiece, which has one magnification strength, typically 10x. The objective lens also has a magnification strength, often 4x, 10x, 40x, or 100x. Using a 10x eyepiece with the 4x objective lens will give a magnification strength of 40x. Using a 10x eyepiece with the 100x objective lens will give a magnification strength of 1,000x. The shorter lens is the lesser magnification; the longer lens is the greater magnification.

8. B: The air we breathe is composed of many types of molecules, and is quite heavy compared to helium. The reason helium balloons float is because helium is less dense than the surrounding air. Objects that are less dense will float in objects that are more dense, as a helium balloon does when surrounded by air.

9. B: Fresh water suitable for drinking can be found as surface water and in groundwater, which is obtained through wells. Rivers (surface water) and aquifers (groundwater) are both sources of fresh water that are available to humans. Glaciers and ice caps are indirect sources of fresh water–when they melt, the runoff forms streams and rivers. Water from all of these sources is suitable for drinking with little to no treatment. Estuaries, however, are not sources of fresh water; they are bodies of brackish (moderately salty) water formed where freshwater from a river mixes with salt water from an ocean. This water is not suitable for drinking without treatment such as desalinization.

10. C: A physical change occurs when water condenses. The only thing formed during condensation is new intermolecular bonds. Therefore, no new covalent bonds form (B). The only time new atoms form is during a nuclear reaction (A). The water molecule is not ionizing, so no new ionic bonds form (D).

11. D: The amount of potential energy an object has depends on mass, height above ground and gravitational attraction, but not temperature. The formula for potential energy is $PE = mgh$, or potential energy equals mass times gravity times height. Answers (A), (B), and (C) are all valid answers as they are all contained in the formula for potential energy. Potential energy is the amount of energy stored in a system particularly because of its position.

12. D: The molecules that make up gases are far apart and move about very quickly. Because they have a weak attraction to each other, they expand to take up as much space as possible.

13. B: When two crustal plates move apart, magma welling up could result in the formation of new crust. This has been shown to be occurring on the ocean floor where places of the crust are weaker. The crust spreads apart at these trenches, pushing outward and erupting at the ridges. When two crustal plates converge, sublimation occurs as one plate runs under another pushing it up. Two crustal plates sliding past one another is an example of a transform fault, which does not create new crust. A crustal plate being pushed down into the mantle does not form new crust but perhaps recycles the old one.

14. A: Experiments are conducted in order to test a hypothesis. Collecting data (B), identifying a control state (C), and choosing variables (D) are steps in conducting an experiment designed to test a hypothesis.

15. B: A long nail or other type of metal, substance, or matter that is heated at one end and then the other end becomes equally hot is an example of conduction. Conduction is energy transfer by neighboring molecules from an area of hotter temperature to cooler temperature. Radiation (A), or thermal radiation, refers to heat being transferred through empty space by electromagnetic radiation. An example is sunlight heating the earth. Convection (C) refers to heat being transferred by molecules moving from one location in the substance to another creating a heat current, usually in a gas or a liquid. Entropy (D) relates to the second law of thermodynamics and refers to how much heat or energy is no longer available to do work in a system. It can also be stated as the amount of disorder in a system.

16. C: A higher concentration could increase the reaction rate of a chemical reaction. The rate of reaction is affected by concentration, pressure, and temperature. A higher concentration would allow for more potential collisions that set off the reaction. Low kinetic energy would lead to a lower rate of reaction, as does a lower temperature (usually). The term activation energy refers to the specific threshold that must be overcome for a reaction to occur. If the activation energy is lowered, for example, by a catalyst or enzyme, then the reaction can occur quicker. This rules out high activation energy.

17. B: A trace fossil shows evidence of existence but is not an organism itself. A trace fossil can be contrasted with a body fossil, which has been formed from an organism. Other examples of trace fossils include eggs, nests, burrows, borings, and coprolites (fossilized feces). A mouse jaw and a shark tooth are examples of body fossils. A cast of a skull is a replica and neither a body nor a trace fossil.

18. A: When two tectonic plates are moving laterally in opposing directions, this is called a transform boundary. When there is friction at transform boundaries and pressure builds up, it can result in shallow earthquakes (usually at a depth of less than 25 meters). California's San Andreas Fault is an example of a transform boundary.

19. D: It is a stable atom. If an atom's outer shell is filled, it is a stable atom. The outer shell refers to one of many energy levels, or shells, that electrons occupy around a nucleus. An atom whose outer shell is not filled wants to become stable by filling the outer shell. It fills its outer shell by forming bonds. The atom can do this by gaining electrons or losing electrons in ionic compounds, or if the atom is a part of a molecule, by sharing electrons. If an atom has a full outer shell, such as the noble gases, it does not readily react with other atoms and does not exchange electrons to form bonds. These atoms are known as inert. Therefore, Choices A and B cannot be true. Choice C, it has 32 electrons in its outer shell, is not necessarily true because not all elements have the fourth shell that can hold 32 electrons. Some have fewer shells that hold fewer electrons.

20. D: A non-polar substance is least likely to be soluble in water. A rule of thumb for a substance's solubility is that like dissolves like. Polarity is affected by the types of bonds between atoms and the bonds are affected by the types of atoms. An unequal sharing of electrons leads to polar bonding and polar substances. Water is polar and can dissolve many other polar substances. Hydrophilic molecules are polar and this word means "water-loving". Water also dissolves many ionic substances since they are composed of charged ions and can interact with the polar water molecules. Many organic compounds are non-polar and do not dissolve well in water.

21. B: Cold water dissolves atmospheric carbon dioxide, stores it, and releases it back out to the atmosphere as needed. This describes the physical or non-biological part of the carbon cycle. The carbon and nutrient cycles of the ocean are processed in part by the deep currents, mixing, and upwelling that occurs. Carbon dioxide (CO_2) from the atmosphere is dissolved into the ocean at the higher latitudes and distributed to the denser deep water. When upwelling occurs, CO_2 is brought back to the surface and emitted into the tropical air.

22. D: After a secondary consumer dies, such as a wolf, its body is partially consumed by decomposers, such as bacteria and fungi. Bacteria and fungi live in soil and digest body tissues of dead organisms, converting them into basic nutrients that plants need to grow. Therefore, after secondary consumers die, their energy is consumed by decomposers, who make nutrients available in the soil for producers to use. *Do not confuse nutrients in the soil with energy that producers get from the Sun to make their own food.*

23. A: Heat between objects in contact with each other is transferred by conduction, choice A. Convection is transfer by currents within a body of fluid, and radiation is the transfer of heat between objects *not* in contact, through light rays emitted by the hotter object and absorbed by the cooler one.

24. A: The type of RNA described by the question is transfer RNA (tRNA). The tRNA is found in the cytoplasm and carries and positions amino acids at the ribosome for protein synthesis. There are two other types of RNA. Messenger RNA (mRNA) contains the coding for the amino acid sequence in the protein. The mRNA is first made in the nucleus before traveling through the cytoplasm to a ribosome. Ribosomal RNA (rRNA) is the RNA that is found in the ribosome along with proteins, which allows the mRNA and tRNA to bind for protein synthesis. All three types of RNA originate in the nucleus where they are transcribed from DNA. Mitochondria are organelles that harbor mitochondrial DNA (mtDNA).

25. B: Venus experiences a greenhouse effect similar to that observed on Earth as its dense atmosphere traps the solar radiation and creates a greenhouse effect. The greenhouse gases, including ozone, carbon dioxide, water vapor, and methane, trap infrared radiation that is reflected back toward the atmosphere. While both Venus and Earth experience the greenhouse effect, Venus's greenhouse effect is much more severe. Earth, on the other hand, has many more natural convective processes that help move carbon and other gases around, tempering the effect some. Human activity produces byproducts that contribute to the greenhouse effect. Some practices that increase the amount of greenhouse gases are burning natural gas and oil; farming, which leads to more methane and nitrous oxide; deforestation, which decreases the amount of offset oxygen; and population growth in general, which increases the volume of greenhouse gases. Increased gases mean more infrared radiation is trapped. While the greenhouse effect is not itself debated, the long-term effects tend to be hotly debated among scientists and in political agendas.

26. B: The energy radiated by stars is produced by nuclear fusion. This is the process whereby the nuclei of individual atoms bind together to form heavier elements and release energy outward. By the time this energy, which is created in the star's core, reaches the outer walls of the star, it exists in the form of light.

27. A: The charge on the glass rod is positive and the charge on the cloth is negative when the glass rod is rubbed with a cloth made of polyester. This is an example of static electricity—the collection of electrically charged particles on the surface of a material. A static charge can be quickly discharged, commonly called a "spark," or discharged more slowly by dissipating to the ground. A static charge occurs because different materials have a capacity for giving up electrons and becoming positive (+), or for attracting electrons and becoming negative (−). The triboelectric series is a list of materials and their propensities for either giving up electrons to become positive or to gain the electrons to become negative. Polyester has a tendency to gain electrons to become negative and glass has a tendency to lose electrons to become positive.

28. B: Animals belonging to the phylum Echinodermata have tube feet for locomotion and feeding. About 7,000 species are extant in this phylum, including starfish and sand dollars. Tube feet are an organ system that provides locomotion, respiration, feeding, and sensory functions. Not all echinoderms have appendages. Having an exoskeleton made of chitin is characteristic of arthropods. Not all echinoderms shed their outer layer of skin to grow.

29. B: An iron bar moving inside a coil of wire that contains a current would create an electromagnet. Rapidly spinning and rotating electrons inside an iron bar (A) creates a magnetic field. The movement of electrons through a complete circuit (C) is an electric current. Convection currents within the liquid core of Earth's interior (D) create the Earth's magnetic field.

30. D: Gravitational collapse and high-energy collisions are both proposed explanations for the formation of black holes. Gravitational collapse occurs when the outward pressure exerted by an object is too weak to resist that object's own gravity. Collisions that produce conditions of sufficient density could also, in theory, create black holes. The accretion of matter is considered observational evidence for the existence of black holes.

31. B: Light travels faster in air than it can in water. Water molecules are closer together than air particles are, which causes the light to slow down and bend as it enters the water. The bending of light is called refraction and creates the illusion of the wallet being next to where it actually is.

32. C: The closer the data points are to each other, the more precise the data. This does not mean the data is accurate, but that the results are very reproducible.

33. C: The vapor pressure decreases by an amount proportional to the amount of solute. Raoult's law states that the vapor pressure of a solution containing a non-volatile solute is equal to the vapor pressure of the volatile solvent multiplied by its mole fraction, which is basically the proportion of the solution that is made up by solvent. In a liquid, some of the surface particles have higher than average energy and can break away to become a gas, or evaporate. The pressure of this gas right above the surface of the liquid is called the vapor pressure. Increasing the amount of solute in a liquid decreases the number of solvent particles at the surface. Because of this, fewer solvent molecules are able to escape, thus lowering the vapor pressure.

34. A: The prevailing westerlies drive weather systems to move west to east in the mid-latitudes. The direction refers to that which the wind is coming from. The polar easterlies that travel from the northeast occur between 90-60 degrees north latitude. The ones from the southeast are between 90-60 degrees south latitude. The trade winds refer to those occurring near the equator in the tropics moving east. The doldrums are also in the tropics, but they refer to an area of low-pressure where frequently the winds are light and unpredictable.

35. A: Many organisms, especially organisms that live in harsh conditions such as deserts or frozen icy areas, have developed specific adaptations that allow them to survive. For example, cacti are able to expand to store large amounts of water, coyotes absorb some water from their food, and snakes can escape the heat by hiding within rocks.

36. D: Mario balances a book on his head. In this example, work is not applied to the book because the book is not moving. One definition of work is a force acting on an object to cause displacement. In this case, the book was not displaced by the force applied to it. Mario's head applied a vertical force to the book to keep it in the same position.

37. D: Reproductive habits would not be considered evidence for evolution. Usually, how a species reproduces does not support nor add to the body of evidence for the theory of evolution. Reproductive habits might exemplify how any given organism can adapt to changes in its environment as a way to survive. This does not necessarily show evolution. Fossil record is evidence for evolution as it shows evolutionary change of organisms over time. DNA sequences show that organisms that are related evolutionarily also have related gene sequences. Anatomical structures such as having an internal bony structure provide evidence of descent from a common ancestor.

38. D: Endocytosis is a process by which cells absorb larger molecules or even tiny organisms, such as bacteria, that would not be able to pass through the plasma membrane. Endocytic vesicles containing molecules from the extracellular environment often undergo further processing once they enter the cell.

39. C: Transform is not connected to the process of mountain building. Orogeny, or mountain building, occurs at the Earth's lithosphere or crust. Folding, or deformation, is a process that occurs to make mountains where two portions of the lithosphere collide. One is subducted and the other is pushed upward forming a mountain. This action produces various types of folding. Faulting can be characterized by a brittle deformation where the rock breaks abruptly (compared with folding). Faulting and fault types are associated with earthquakes and relatively rapid deformation. Convergent is a more general term used to describe plates interacting.

40. C: Ammonia is known as a compound gas because its molecules contain atoms of more than one of the chemical elements—nitrogen (B) and hydrogen (D) atoms in the case of ammonia gas. Oxygen (A) as well as nitrogen and hydrogen are elementary gases rather than compound gases because their molecules contain only one chemical element.

Social Studies

1. D: Only the British Empire existed following the armistice ending WWI. The Austro-Hungarian Empire, the Ottoman Empire, and the German Empire were all among the Central powers that lost the war. As empires capitulated, armistices and peace treaties were signed and the map of Europe was redrawn as territories formerly occupied by Central powers were partitioned. For example, the former Austro-Hungarian Empire was partitioned into Austria, Hungary, Czechoslovakia, Yugoslavia, Transylvania, and Romania. The Treaty of Lausanne (1923) gave Turkey both independence and recognition as successor to the former Ottoman Empire after Turkey refused the earlier Treaty of Sèvres (1920), and Mustafa Kemal Ataturk led the Turkish Independence War. Greece, Bulgaria, and other former Ottoman possessions became independent. The Lausanne Treaty defined the boundaries of these countries as well as the boundaries of Iraq, Syria, Cyprus, Sudan, and Egypt.

2. C: Political parties organize their caucus as a private event while an official primary is an indirect election administered by state and local governments. Voters may award delegates to candidates for the national conventions, depending on state laws.

3. D: According to Article III of the Constitution, Justices of the Supreme Court, judges of the courts of appeals and district courts, and judges of the Court of International Trade are appointed by the president with the confirmation of the Senate. The judicial branch of the government is the only one not elected by the people.

4. C: Hernán Cortés conquered the Mexican Aztecs in 1519. He had several advantages over the indigenous peoples, including horses, armor for his soldiers, and guns. In addition, Cortés' troops unknowingly transmitted smallpox to the Aztecs, which devastated their population as they had no immunity to this foreign illness. Vasco Núñez de Balboa was the first European explorer to view the Pacific Ocean when he crossed the Isthmus of Panama in 1513. Juan Ponce de León visited and claimed Florida in Spain's name in 1513. Álvar Núñez Cabeza de Vaca was one of only four men out of 400 to return from an expedition led by Pánfilo de Narváez in 1528 and was responsible for spreading the story of the Seven Cities of Cibola (the "cities of gold").

5. D: Because the Puritans took on a Reformed theology, they were in this sense Calvinists. However, many Puritans endorsed radical views that criticized such Calvinists as John (Jean) Calvin and Huldrych (Ulrich) Zwingli in Switzerland. Not only were Puritans critical of Calvinists despite their mutual Reformed approaches, reciprocally many Calvinists were opposed to the Puritans as well. The Puritan movement changed less in American colonies than in England during the 1660s. Following the Restoration (1660) and the Uniformity Act (1662) in England, nearly all of the Puritan clergy objected and left the Church of England, thereby creating a dramatic change in the movement in that country. Nevertheless, in America, the Puritans who had emigrated from England continued their original Puritan traditions for a longer time, as they had neither the same Anglican Church as in England nor the legislation restoring earlier church status against which the English Puritans had reacted.

6. B: Keynesian economics is based on the notion that governments can effectively stimulate economic growth through taxation, adjustment of interest rates, and the funding of public projects. His economic philosophy contrasts sharply with the free-market philosophies of Smith, Hayek, and Friedman.

7. B: Congress has the authority to shape the judicial branch. The Supreme Court once operated with only six members. Nine has been the standard number since 1869.

8. B: The first amendment to the Constitution states, "Congress shall make no law respecting an establishment of religion, or prohibiting the free exercise thereof; or abridging the freedom of speech or of the press; or the right of the people peaceably to assemble, and to petition the Government for a redress of grievances." The right to bear arms is guaranteed by the second amendment: "A well-regulated Militia, being necessary to the security of a free State, the right of the people to keep and bear Arms, shall not be infringed."

9. B: Diversity is not one of the demographic variables. Demographers, or those who study population, rely on fertility, mortality, and migration to determine the number of people in a region. The general equation is *Total Population = Original Population + Births – Deaths + Immigration – Emigration*. The natural increase, on the other hand, is calculated only with the number of births and deaths. The diversity of a population may be relevant to subsequent research performed by the demographer, but it is not considered one of the essential three demographic variables.

10. B: John Maynard Keynes argued that government could help revitalize a recessionary economy by increasing government spending and therefore increasing aggregate demand. This is known as demand-side economics.

11. C: The bubonic plague spread along trade routes, carried by infected animals and people on ships. After reaching Cyprus in 1347, the epidemic followed trade routes to infect the populations of Italy and France. Then, also through trade routes, it traveled north to Germany, England, and eventually Scandinavia and Russia in 1351.

12. D: Political corruption was not an immediate effect of the rapid urban growth during this time. The accelerated growth of cities in America did soon result in services being unable to keep up with that growth. The results of this included deficiencies in clean water delivery and garbage collection, causing poor sanitation. That poor sanitation led to outbreaks of cholera and typhus, as well as typhoid fever epidemics. Police and fire fighting services could not keep up with the population increases, and were often inadequate. With people moving to the cities at such a fast rate, there were also deficits in housing and public transportation.

13. D: Increases in population growth supplied additional labor forces, helping to enable the Industrial Revolution. These increases were due to the prosperity brought through Europe's Commercial Revolution, which preceded the Industrial Revolution. The rediscovery of concrete, new advances in iron making, and the invention of the steam engine are all examples of developments that occurred during the Industrial Revolution.

14. B: As production shifted to factories, a large number of unskilled workers were needed to operate the machinery that was beginning to put many skilled craftsmen out of work. As farms grew larger and increasingly mechanized, the number of people who owned their own farm began to decrease. The rural population declined as people flocked to the cities in search of employment.

15. D: Free public education has been a US tradition since the 18th century. State constitutions govern the educational issues of each state, although federal, state, and local governments all work together on educational issues.

16. C: The person or group NOT instrumental in advancing civil rights and desegregation immediately after WWII was Congress. As African American soldiers came home from the war, racial discord increased. President Harry Truman appointed a Presidential Committee on Civil Rights in 1946. This committee published a report recommending that segregation and lynching be outlawed by the federal government. However, Congress ignored this report and took no action. Truman then used his presidential powers to enforce desegregation of the military and policies of "fair employment" in federal civil service jobs. The National Association for the Advancement of Colored People (NAACP) brought lawsuits against racist and discriminatory practices, and in resolving these suits, the Supreme Court further eroded segregation. For example, the Supreme Court ruled that primaries allowing only whites would be illegal, and it ended the segregation of interstate bus lines. The landmark civil rights laws were not passed by Congress until the 1960s.

17. A: The Industrial Revolution did create a new working class composed of professionals like doctors and lawyers, industrialists, and businessmen. Formerly, Europe was dominated by royalty and landed gentry over the poor working class. Industrialization allowed many ordinary people to start and run businesses. It did NOT, however, improve working conditions in the 18th and early 19th centuries, but the opposite occurred: Big factories with machines made conditions more dangerous, and child labor caused many deaths, injuries, illnesses, and so on. Women and children were only banned from working in mines in the mid-19th century; housing and work conditions only improved in the late 19th century. Urbanization was the result of industrialization and not vice versa: Mechanization allowed factory construction, and people moved to cities for jobs. Labor unions developed out of the Industrial Revolution, not vice versa, to establish and defend factory workers' rights.

18. B: The Supreme Court ruled that statements made in interrogation are not admissible unless the defendant is informed of the right to an attorney and waives that right. The case of Miranda v. Arizona was consolidated with Westover v. United States, Vignera v. New York, and California v. Stewart.

19. A: As people have more and more of something, they value it less and less. This is the law of diminishing marginal utility, and it is what causes the downward slope of the demand curve.

20. A: Agriculture was not a viable economic model for New Englanders. Although the colonists were mainly from England and Scotland, few were merchants before arriving in the colonies. Slavery existed in the north, although it was less important to the economy than it was in the agricultural south. New England colonists were not actively competing with their neighbors to the immediate south.

21. B: Followers of Hinduism, an indigenous religion of India, believe in one Supreme Reality (Brahman), manifested in many different gods and goddesses that oversee different aspects of life. Confucianism, a Chinese religion, does not address whether there are many gods or one. Followers of Sikhism, an Indian religion originating in Punjab, believe in a single god, Om or Ik Om Kar. Islam, founded by Muhammad in Saudi Arabia, purports a single god, Allah.

22. A: The president of the United States serves as commander-in-chief, but the writers of the Constitution, who feared how authority was used by monarchs, limited the president's power in this role. The president cannot declare war or make rules governing the military, although presidents have traditionally authorized the use of force without war being declared.

23. A: When the prices farmers receive for their crops decline in a developing country, this typically results in increased urbanization. When crop prices decline, farmers can no longer make a living from their land. As a result, they often choose to migrate to cities in search of low-wage employment in the manufacturing or service sectors.

24. B: It is not true that the Crusades ultimately succeeded in retaking the Holy Land (Jerusalem and surrounding areas) from Muslim control. Although the Crusaders achieved temporary victories, such as capturing Jerusalem during the First Crusade (1099) and establishing short-lived Crusader states, these gains were not permanent. Over time, Muslim forces reconquered these territories, and by 1291, the last Crusader stronghold at Acre fell. While the Crusades did not achieve their main goal, they did contribute to the weakening of the Byzantine Empire, which lost territory to the Seljuks and later faced ongoing pressure from other powers. Additionally, the Crusades indirectly helped Egypt reemerge as a significant regional power in the Middle East.

25. C: Nebraska does not require voter registration, but all other states do and have their own process. State and local officials administer federal elections, and though each state has its own method for holding elections, federal elections are always held at the same time.

26. A: Anyone may write a bill, but only a member of Congress can introduce a bill. The President often suggests bills. Bills can change drastically throughout the review process.

27. C: Reinforcement refers to conditioning a behavior to increase in frequency. Punishment is the contrary term that means to condition a behavior to decrease. The terms positive and negative are often confused, but they refer to the stimulus used to either punish or reinforce a behavior. Any stimulus that is added is called *positive,* while any stimulus that is removed is called *negative.* Therefore, you can have any of the four types of conditioning:

	Positive	**Negative**
Reinforcement	Give a child candy to reinforce good manners.	Take away homework when a student does well on quizzes.
Punishment	Spanking a child for talking back.	Taking away a video game for getting in a fight.

The example given in the question is a form of negative reinforcement because it takes away a stimulus (negative) to increase a behavior (reinforcement).

28. A: Samuel Morse invented a code of dots and dashes that became known as Morse Code, and in 1844 the first message was transmitted over a telegraph line. Morse code played an important role in communications during the Civil War.

29. D: Psychologists studying infant behaviors have classified their basic temperaments into Easy, Difficult, and Slow to Warm Up. They find that the majority of babies have the Easy temperament. Thus, option A is incorrect, and babies with Difficult temperaments are not in the majority (B); neither are Slow to Warm Up types (C).

30. D: All of the available answer choices are geographically parts of Southeast Asia. The countries of Myanmar (Burma), Laos, Cambodia, and Thailand are considered Mainland Southeast Asia, as are Vietnam and the Malay Peninsula. Brunei, East Malaysia, Indonesia, and the Philippines are considered Maritime Southeast Asia, as are Singapore and Timor-Leste. The Seven Sister States of India are also considered to be part of Southeast Asia, geographically and culturally. (The Seven Sister States of India are Arunachal Pradesh, Assam, Nagaland, Meghalaya, Manipur, Tripura, and Mizoram, which all have contiguous borders in northeastern India.)

31. C: The agricultural revolution. A dependable food supply is essential to all populations. The agricultural revolution, an organized, almost scientific approach to agriculture, increased the food supply necessary for a growing world population.

32. B: Determining methods of carrying babies and studying the toddlers in several countries would be the best method for gathering data for this study.

33. A: A smaller box in which some part of the larger map is depicted in greater detail is known as an inset. Insets provide a closer look at parts of the map that the cartographer deems to be more important (for instance, cities, national parks, or historical sites). Often, traffic maps will include several insets depicting the roads in the most congested area of the city. Legends, also known as keys, are the boxes in which the symbols used in the map are explained. A legend, or key, might indicate how railroads and boundaries are depicted, for example. A compass rose indicates how the map is oriented along the north-south axis. It is common for cartographers to tilt a map for ease of display, such that up may not be due north.

34. A: In geography, location—specifically, relative location—determines things like land prices based on the characteristics of an area, which are affected by nearby regions. An example of distance (B) is that land that is close to major highways is more expensive, while land far from main thoroughfares costs less. One example of pattern (C) in geography is that where rock folds form mountains (fold regions), the rivers accordingly form trellis patterns. Another example of pattern, in geographically oriented human behavior, is that settlements in mountainous areas form mainly spreading patterns. An example of interaction (D) in geography is when an industrial city needs raw materials from a rural village for production, and the village needs the city both as a market to buy its resources and for its industrial products: their mutual interdependence creates interaction between them.

35. D: Teachers can use not only history books (A); they can also assign students to read well-constructed and well-written biographies (B) of famous figures in history and works of historical literature (C), which set even fictionalized stories within real historical periods and events. Historical narratives written in "storytelling" style are also good for engaging student attention while establishing chronological sequences in history.

36. A: A bill is a proposed law.

37. C: Data collected from 2003 show that more than 15% of African-American families had violent conflicts; over 11% of Latino families did; and fewer than 9% of white families did. While researchers concede that cultural and demographic variables can influence styles of disagreement in families, they find parental stress the strongest influence on whether family conflicts become violent (A). The National Survey of Child and Adolescent Well-Being found that children of socioeconomically disadvantaged families have more developmental and behavioral problems than in other groups (B). However, these children were also less likely to receive help with their problems (D). For example, more than 40% of toddlers and more than 68% of preschoolers in contact with the child welfare system had high levels of developmental and behavioral needs; yet fewer than 23% of these children were receiving services to address those needs.

38. D: Resentment against the Protestant Reformation was not a cause given for the French Revolution. Many causes have been cited for the war. Famines caused malnutrition and even starvation among the poorest people. Escalating bread prices contributed greatly to the hunger. Louis XV had amassed a great amount of debt from spending money on many wars in addition to the American Revolution. Military failures as well as a lack of social services for veterans exacerbated these debts. In addition, the Court of Louis XVI and Marie Antoinette spent excessively and obviously on luxuries even while people in the country were starving, and France's monetary system was outdated, inefficient, and thus unable to manage the national debt. Much of the populace greatly resented the Catholic Church's control of the country. However, there was not great resentment against the Protestant Reformation; there were large minorities of Protestants in France, who not only exerted their influence on government institutions, but undoubtedly also contributed to the resentment of the Catholic Church.

39. B: Due process refers to the right of a defendant to confront accusers and to provide a defense.

40. D: While rising prices may hurt many members of an economy, those same rising prices may benefit other members of the same economy. For example, rising prices may help those who sell goods and services and are able to keep their costs of production low, increasing their profit margin. Meanwhile, rising prices can hurt consumers because their income is now able to purchase fewer goods and services than before.

Practice Test #2

English

1. Which of the following statements is accurate according to research regarding students who are revising and rewriting?

a. Students only correct their mechanical errors in revisions.
b. Students often incorporate new ideas when they rewrite.
c. Students retain their original writing goals during revision.
d. Students' planning in prewriting is unaffected in rewriting.

2. With a teacher's guidance, a class brainstorms main ideas, topics, or concepts from a text. Students choose a select number of these ideas and copy them onto separate index cards. The students then individually review the text, recording any supporting evidence on the notecard with the applicable main idea. This activity would be an excellent pre-lesson for teaching which skill set?

a. Working as a group to interpret a text and write an appropriate and realistic sequel, focusing on interpretive comprehension and creative writing
b. Silent reading as a form of comprehension practice
c. Organizing ideas for writing a cohesive and persuasive essay or research paper that asserts supported arguments with valid supporting evidence
d. Literal and figurative comprehension, as well as contributing to group discussions via oral communication skills

3. A teacher is working with a group of third graders at the same reading level. Her goal is to improve reading fluency. She asks each child in turn to read a page from a book about mammal young. She asks the children to read with expression. She also reminds them they don't need to stop between each word; they should read as quickly as they comfortably can. She cautions them, however, not to read so quickly that they leave out or misread a word. The teacher knows the components of reading fluency are:

a. Speed, drama, and comprehension
b. Cohesion, rate, and prosody
c. Understanding, rate, and prosody
d. Rate, accuracy, and prosody

4. *Carat, carrot, to, two,* and *too* share something in common. They are:

a. Nouns
b. Monosyllabic
c. Homophones
d. Diphthongs

5. Which of the following statements adheres to Information Literacy Standards?

a. Students accessing information must critically evaluate it and its sources before using it.
b. Students accessing information should acquire as much information as possible about their topic.
c. Students accessing information efficiently sacrifice incidental learning.
d. Students accessing information must avoid using it for purposes it was not meant to serve.

6. Third-grade students typically receive their spelling word lists each Monday so that they can practice them at home before the test on Friday. While their teacher is pleased that the students usually receive high grades on spelling tests, she observes that they misspell those same words when writing in journals or doing classwork. How should this teacher modify her instruction?

a. Post a list of vocabulary words when the students are writing to help them recall correct spellings.
b. Integrate spelling words into writing, reading, grammar, phonics, and other activities to help students learn the words in a variety of contexts.
c. Provide more time, such as a two-week period, between tests so that students have more time to study.
d. Review the words before certain activities to increase immediate recall of correct spellings.

7. Of the three tiers of words, the most important words for direct instruction are:

a. Tier-one words
b. Common words
c. Tier-two words
d. Words with Latin roots

8. Which student is most likely to need referral to a reading specialist for assessment, special instruction, or intervention?

a. Annabel: a second-grade student who tends to skip over words or phrases when she reads, affecting her comprehension of the text.
b. Cliff: a kindergarten student who is already reading simple chapter books with his parents at home or in class.
c. Noelle: a first grader who avoids any activity in which she must read, both aloud or silently, preferring to ask an adult to read the text for her first.
d. Barrett: a third grader who often confuses the sounds of certain letters, such as /b/ and /d/ or /v/ and /u/.

9. According to the MLA guidelines for in-text citations in research papers, when can the citation include one author's name and *et al* for any other authors of a single source?

a. When there is more than one author
b. When there are two or three authors
c. When there are three or more authors
d. When there are four or more authors

10. A child in kindergarten is most likely to be referred to a speech-language pathologist if the child does not correctly produce which of the following phonemes?

a. /p/ as in pepper or poppies
b. /ʒ/ as in mirage or measure
c. /v/ as in velvet, valve, or value
d. /s/ as in see, yes, or asking

11. Which of the following best explains the importance prior knowledge brings to the act of reading?

a. Prior knowledge is information the student gets through researching a topic prior to reading the text. A student who is well-prepared through such research is better able to decode a text and retain its meaning.
b. Prior knowledge is knowledge the student brings from previous life or learning experiences to the act of reading. It is not possible for a student to fully comprehend new knowledge without first integrating it with prior knowledge.
c. Prior knowledge is predictive. It motivates the student to look for contextual clues in the reading and predict what is likely to happen next.
d. Prior knowledge is not important to any degree to the act of reading, because every text is self-contained and therefore seamless. Prior knowledge is irrelevant in this application.

12. A fourth-grade teacher had her students write haiku in order to promote the students' __________.

a. reading comprehension
b. vocabulary
c. word identification skills
d. confidence

13. What is a mnemonic device?

a. A saying or image used to help remember a complex concept
b. A tool that increases physical relaxation during a test
c. An old-fashioned torture device involving repeated testing
d. A tool for selecting answers on tests

14. Of the following, which statement is true about instruction in the alphabetic principle?

a. Letter-sound relationships with the highest utility should be the earliest ones introduced.
b. The instruction of letter-sound correspondences should always be done in word context.
c. Letter-sound relationship practice times should only be assigned apart from other lessons.
d. Letter-sound relationship practice should focus on new relationships, not go over old ones.

15. Early in the school year, all members of a group of kindergarten students are able to chant the alphabet. The teacher is now teaching the students what the alphabet looks like in written form. The teacher points to a letter, and the students vocalize the corresponding sound. Alternatively, the teacher vocalizes a phoneme and a student points to it on the alphabet chart. The teacher is using ____________ in her instruction.

a. letter–sound correspondence
b. rote memorization
c. predictive analysis
d. segmentation

16. Components of explicit instruction include:

a. Clarifying the goal, modeling strategies, and offering explanations geared to a student's level of understanding
b. Determining the goal, offering strategies, and asking questions designed to ascertain whether understanding has been reached
c. Reassessing the goal, developing strategies, and determining whether further reassessing of the goal is required
d. Objectifying the goal, assessing strategies, and offering explanations geared toward a student's level of understanding

17. Which choice most appropriately fills the blanks in this statement? "In writing, ________ is the overall choice of language in a piece of writing; ________ is a specialized terminology, used in a discipline, that is not readily understood by readers outside of that discipline."

a. jargon, style
b. vocabulary, diction
c. diction, jargon
d. style, vocabulary

18. Regarding these elements of print awareness in literacy development, which is true?

a. All students with normal development can differentiate printed words from spaces.
b. To identify initial and final letters in words, students must identify words vs. spaces.
c. The only students not automatically knowing left-right directionality are certain ELLs.
d. Being able to identify basic punctuation is not important to reading comprehension.

19. It is the beginning of the school year. To determine which second-grade students might need support, the reading teacher wants to identify those who are reading below grade level. She works with students one at a time. She gives each child a book at a second-grade reading level and asks the child to read out loud for two minutes. Which students will need reading support?

a. Only students who read fewer than 100 words in the time given
b. All students who read fewer than 200 words in the time given
c. All students who read more than 100 words in the time given
d. Only students who read more than 200 words in the time given

20. When working with English language learners, the teacher should:

a. Avoid idioms and slang, involve students in hands-on activities, reference students' prior knowledge, and speak slowly.
b. Speak slowly, use monosyllabic words whenever possible, repeat each sentence three times before moving to the next sentence, and employ idioms but not slang.
c. Use monosyllabic words whenever possible, repeat key instructions three times but not in a row, reference students' prior knowledge, and have students keep a journal of new vocabulary.
d. Have students keep a journal of new vocabulary, reference students' prior knowledge, speak slowly, and involve students in hands-on activities.

21. Which of the following processes used in writing is the most complex?

a. Evaluation
b. Application
c. Comprehension
d. Knowledge recall

22. When a teacher instructs elementary school students in analyzing phonetically-regular words, which of the following would best represent a sequence from simpler to progressively more complex?

a. Long vowels, short vowels, consonant blends, CVC (consonant-vowel-consonant) and other common patterns, individual phonemes, blending phonemes, types of syllables, onsets and rimes
b. Onsets and rimes, short vowels, consonant blends, long vowels, blending phonemes, CVC and other common patterns, types of syllables, individual phonemes
c. Types of syllables, onsets and rimes, CVC and other common patterns, consonant blends, blending phonemes, individual phonemes, long vowels, short vowels
d. Individual phonemes, blending phonemes, onsets and rimes, short vowels, long vowels, consonant blends, CVC and other common patterns, types of syllables

23. Which text(s) are likely to foster the greatest enthusiasm for reading and literature among students?

a. Free choice of reading texts, provided that students complete class assignments, projects, and discussions
b. An all-in-one textbook that includes all reading material for the year, study guides, and sample test questions
c. A variety of texts, including books, magazines, newspapers, stories from oral traditions, poetry, music, and films
d. A small selection of current best-selling books for children, some of which the children may already have read and liked

24. Coarticulation affects:

a. Blending awareness
b. Phonemic awareness
c. Sequencing
d. Aural awareness

25. Some of the students in Mr. Smith's fourth-grade class cannot decode words well enough to read fluently in class. He knows they are well behind grade level and that he needs to provide them with activities that will allow them to be successful, building skills and confidence at the same time. Which activity would be best for this purpose?

a. Enlist the parents' help by sending home a weekly list of sight words that the students can practice and memorize, decreasing the need to decode when they read.
b. Show the students how to create words out of movable alphabet tiles or magnetic letters, building (encoding) words as they sound them out.
c. Provide the children with early childhood readers that contain only very simple words so that the children will not feel badly as they read.
d. Allow those children having trouble to stop each time they reach a challenging word and sound it out carefully, recording it to a list that will be studied for homework.

26. Which of the following involves evaluative reading comprehension?

a. Identifying an author's point of view
b. Explaining the author's point of view
c. Identifying the main idea of the text
d. Predicting what will happen in a text

27. *Since, therefore,* and *accordingly* are examples of which type of signal words?

a. Common, or basic, signal words
b. Compare/contrast words
c. Cause–effect words
d. Temporal sequencing words

28. Which of the following relates primarily to how sounds are represented in a text?

a. Syntactic
b. Semantic
c. Graphophonic
d. Pragmatic

29. Which adult would be most effective in helping a student who frequently mispronounces sounds both in reading and in conversation?

a. A whole language specialist
b. A speech pathologist
c. A paraprofessional
d. A psychologist

30. Of the following, which represents an indirect way in which students receive instruction in and learn vocabulary?

a. Being exposed repeatedly to vocabulary in multiple teaching contexts
b. Being exposed to vocabulary when adults read aloud to them
c. Being pre-taught specific words found in text prior to reading
d. Being taught vocabulary words over extended periods of time

31. A teacher is teaching students using rime analogies to support reading comprehension. Which of the following skills best relates to the use of rime analogies?

a. Students will be able to identify and use metaphors and similes.
b. Students will be able to identify and use similar sounding words.
c. Students will be able to identify and use similarly spelled words.
d. Students will be able to identify and use figures of speech.

32. Scholars have identified three major categories of connections that students make when reading: text-to-self connections, text-to-world connections, and text-to-text connections. Which of the following student statements is an example of a connection of text to the world?

a. These mythic gods have more power but feel and act like humans.
b. This novel is set during a period I learned about in my history textbook.
c. I can relate to how the main character felt about being controlled.
d. The protagonist reminds me of the main character in another story.

33. Learning to construct a reading response would be most beneficial in enhancing which language skill?

a. Oral presentation
b. Comprehension
c. Fluency
d. Learning a second language

34. Which of the following ways of presenting information is best for showing change over time?

a. Tables
b. Maps
c. Graphs
d. Charts

35. A teacher is working with a student who is struggling with reading. The teacher gives him a story with key words missing:

> The boy wanted to take the dog for a walk. The boy opened the door. The ____ ran out. The ___ looked for the dog. When he found the dog, he was very ______.

The student is able to fill in the blanks by considering:

a. Syntax. Oftentimes, word order gives enough clues that a reader can predict what happens next.
b. Pretext. By previewing the story, the student can deduce the missing words.
c. Context. By considering the other words in the story, the student can determine the missing words.
d. Sequencing. By putting the ideas in logical order, the student can determine the missing words.

36. Which statement is most accurate about social contexts of L1 and L2 acquisition?

a. L2 learning can occur equally in varied contexts, from natural to educational, but L1 learning cannot.
b. L1s are only learned in natural contexts, while L2s are learned in educational contexts.
c. Variations in L2 proficiency can result from the different contexts of the learning of L2s.
d. L2s are never learned in natural contexts, as they are not the learners' natural languages.

37. Which of the following choices would be the best comprehensive project for a fourth-grade class at the end of the school year?

a. The students take an open-book, cumulative test that measures the students' understanding of various concepts and genres through multiple choice, short-answer, and short-essay questions.
b. Assign children to a group in which they will read and adapt a short play. Each group will perform its play with costumes and staging while the rest of the class will serve as audience members. Audience members will write short responses to what they have seen, which will be shared with the performers.
c. Each student picks a topic about which they would like to conduct independent research. The students will read a variety of texts from different sources to learn more about the topic and then use that information to create a presentation for the class. The use of technology and media is encouraged in presentations.
d. The students take a field trip to the local university to visit the English Department. The students are permitted to sit in on a class lecture and speak to professors about the program. Students also get a chance to interact with college students and find out what literacy skills are most important for a successful college experience.

38. How should teachers best instruct students in writing?

a. In connection with reading only
b. By itself to focus student attention
c. With relation to reading and speaking
d. Related to listening, reading, and speaking

39. A teacher has a child who does not volunteer in class. When the teacher asks the student a question the student can answer, she does so with as few words as possible. The teacher isn't sure how to best help the child. She should:

a. Leave the child alone. She is clearly very shy and will be embarrassed by having attention drawn to her. She is learning in her own way.
b. Ask two or three highly social children to include this girl in their activities. She is shy, and she probably won't approach them on her own.
c. Observe the child over the course of a week or two. Draw her into conversation and determine if her vocabulary is limited, if she displays emotional problems, or if her reticence could have another cause. Note how the child interacts with others in the class. Does she ever initiate conversation? If another child initiates, does she respond?
d. Refer her to the school counselor immediately. It is clear the child is suffering from either a low IQ or serious problems at home.

40. Which of the following is the source of the silent *b* in the English word *debt*?

a. A Middle English root word
b. An Old English root word
c. A Latin root word
d. A Greek root word

Mathematics

1. Which of the following expressions is equivalent to $-3x(x-2)^2$?

a. $-3x^3 + 6x^2 - 12x$
b. $-3x^3 - 12x^2 + 12x$
c. $-3x^2 + 6x$
d. $-3x^3 + 12x^2 - 12x$

2. McKenzie shades $\frac{1}{5}$ of a piece of paper. Then, she shades an additional area $\frac{1}{5}$ the size of what she just shaded. Next, she shades another area $\frac{1}{5}$ as large as the previous one. As she continues the process to infinity, what is the limit of the shaded fraction of the paper?

a. $\frac{1}{5}$
b. $\frac{1}{4}$
c. $\frac{1}{3}$
d. $\frac{1}{2}$

3. Which of the following represents the net of a triangular prism?

a. 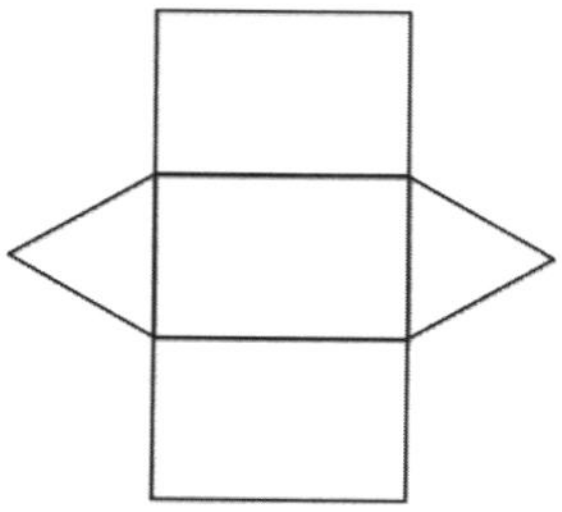

b. 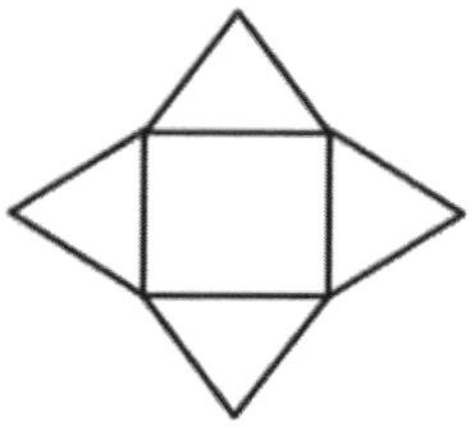

c. 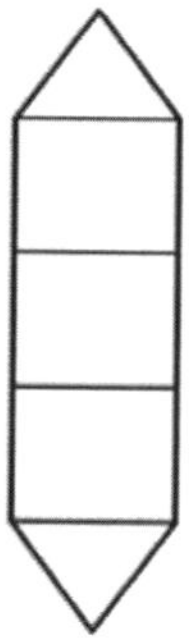

d. 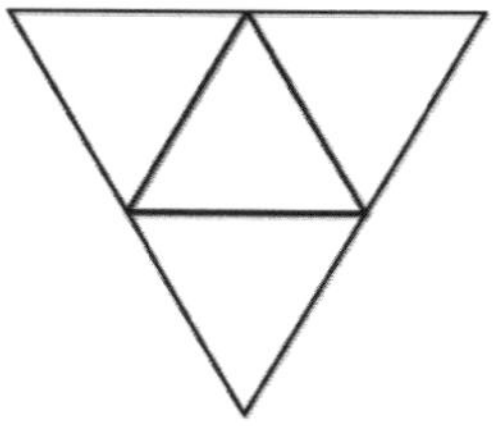

4. Andrew rolls a die. What is the probability he gets a 4 or an even number?

a. $\frac{1}{4}$
b. $\frac{1}{2}$
c. $\frac{2}{3}$
d. $\frac{3}{4}$

5. Which of the following learning goals is most appropriate for a second-grade unit on personal financial literacy?

a. The students will be able to calculate how money saved can accumulate into a larger amount over time.
b. The students will be able to balance a simple budget.
c. The students will be able to identify the costs and benefits of planned and unplanned spending decisions.
d. The students will be able to define money earned as income.

6. Which of the following options represents equivalency between different representations of rational numbers?

a. $16 \div (6-4)^2 = 64$
b. $8 - 2(7-4) = 18$
c. $2^3 \div 2 - 2(2) = 0$
d. $2 + 3(2^2) = 20$

7. Claus has $20 to spend at the local fair. The entrance fee is $2.50, and tickets for the booths are $2 each. Which of the following inequalities represents the number of tickets x that Claus can afford with his $20?

a. $2.50x + 2x \leq 20$
b. $2.50 + 2x \leq 20$
c. $2x \leq 20 + 2.50$
d. $2.50 + 2x \geq 20x$

8. A teacher is assessing the students' understanding of the appropriate units for length, area, and volume. Which of the following only lists units of area?

a. $\text{in}^2, \text{mm}^2, \text{ft}^2$
b. $\text{yd}, \text{yd}^2, \text{yd}^3$
c. mm, cm, m
d. $\text{m}^2, \text{s}^2, \text{km}^2$

9. Ms. Elliott asks her fifth-grade students, "Do you prefer chocolate or vanilla ice cream?" If the probability of her students preferring chocolate ice cream is 0.6, what is the probability of her students preferring vanilla ice cream?

a. 0.6
b. 0.4
c. 0.3
d. 0.5

10. While teaching the concept of addition, a first-grade teacher gives each student two dice to use as manipulatives. Which of the following types of representation is this teacher using to communicate this concept?

a. Concrete
b. Verbal
c. Graphic
d. Pictorial

11. The variables x and y have a linear relationship. The table below shows a few sample values. Which of the following graphs correctly represents the linear equation relating x and y?

x	y
−2	−11
−1	−8
0	−5
1	−2
2	1

a.

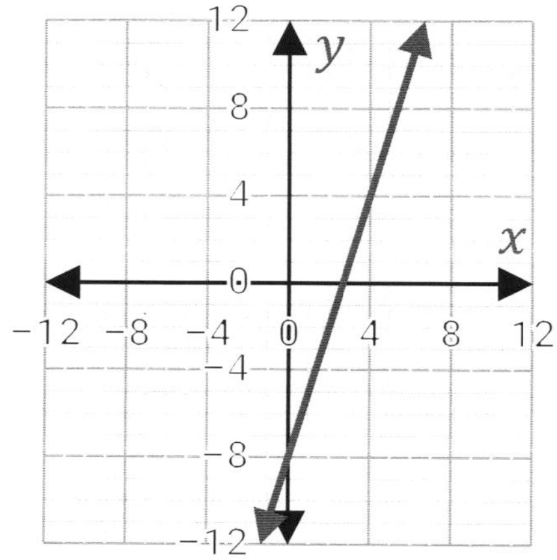

b.

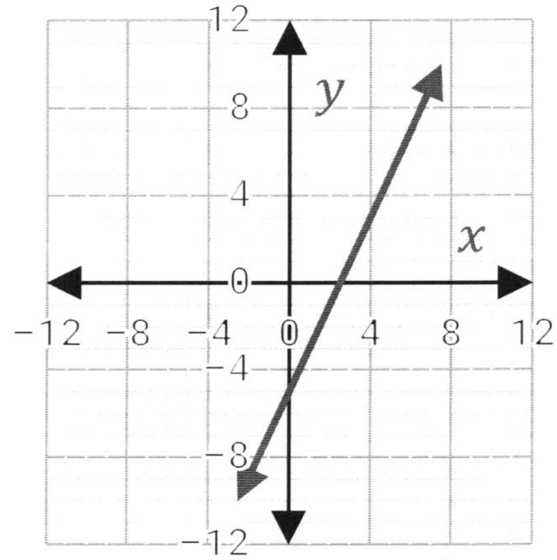

c.

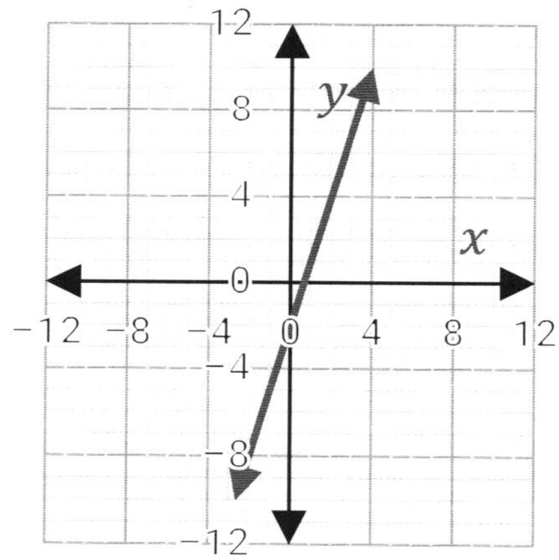

d.

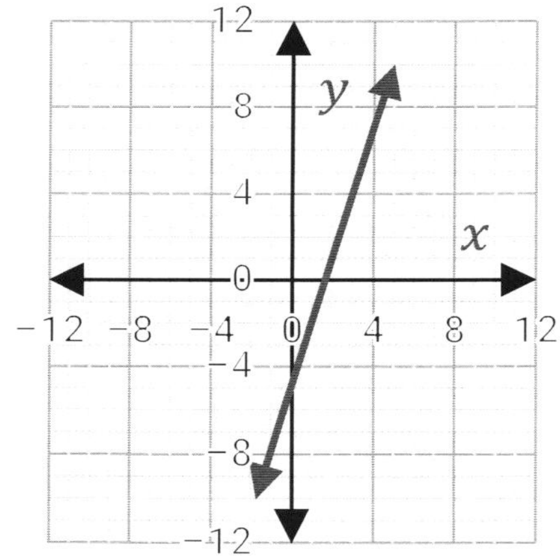

12. What is the midpoint of the line segment below?

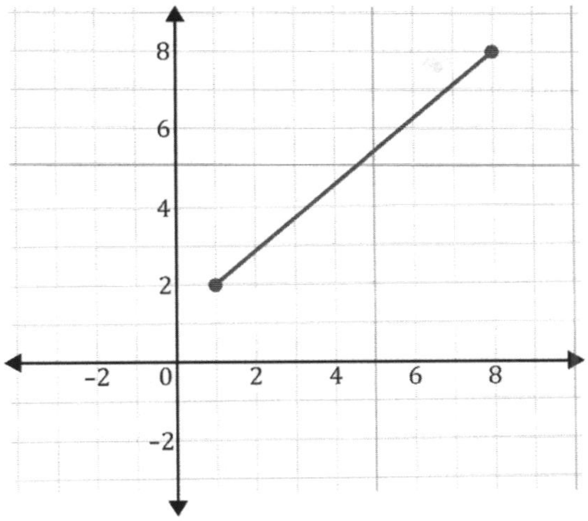

a. (3.5,4)
b. (4,4)
c. (4.5,5)
d. (5,5)

13. Ann must walk from Point A to Point B and then to Point C. Finally, she will walk back to Point A. If each unit represents 5 miles, which of the following BEST represents the total distance she will have walked?

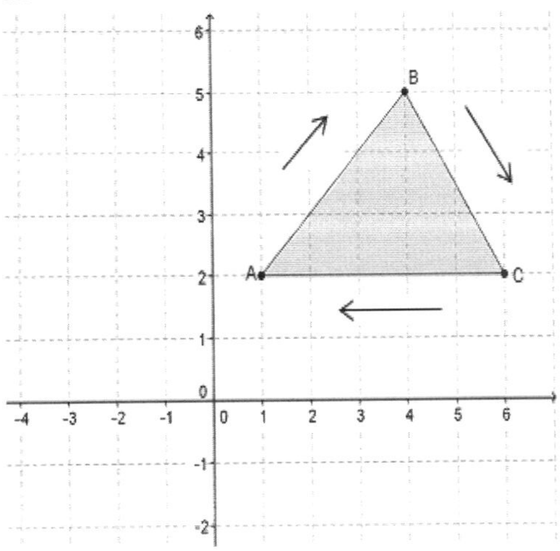

a. 42 miles
b. 48 miles
c. 56 miles
d. 64 miles

14. When planning a unit on linear equations, a teacher would most likely include discussion on which of the following topics?

a. Conjugating to remove irrational denominators
b. Slope of a straight line
c. Order of operations
d. Characteristics of the diagonals of various quadrilaterals

15. Two companies offer monthly cell phone plans, both of which include free text messaging. Company A charges a $25 monthly fee plus five cents per minute of phone conversation, while Company B charges a $50 monthly fee and offers unlimited calling. At what total duration of monthly calls do both companies charge the same amount?

a. 500 hours
b. 8 hours and 33 minutes
c. 8 hours and 20 minutes
d. 5 hours

16. Solve the system of equations.

$$3x + 4y = 2$$
$$2x + 6y = -2$$

a. $\left(0, \frac{1}{2}\right)$
b. $\left(\frac{2}{5}, \frac{1}{5}\right)$
c. $(2, -1)$
d. $\left(-1, \frac{5}{4}\right)$

17. Identify the cross-section polygon formed by a plane containing the given points on the cube.

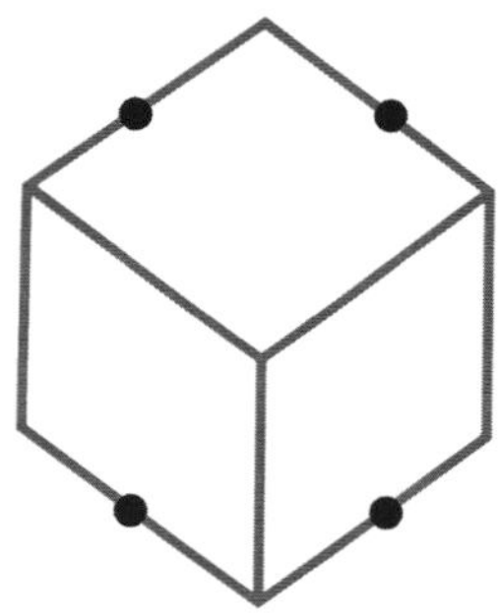

a. Rectangle
b. Trapezoid
c. Pentagon
d. Hexagon

18. In order to analyze the real estate market for two different zip codes within the city, a realtor examined the most recent 100 home sales in each zip code. She considered a house which sold within the first month of its listing to have a market time of one month; likewise, she considered a house to have a market time of two months if it sold after having been on the market for more than one month but before the end of the second month. Using this definition of market time, she determined the frequency of sales by the number of months on the market. The results are displayed below. Which of the following is a true statement for these data?

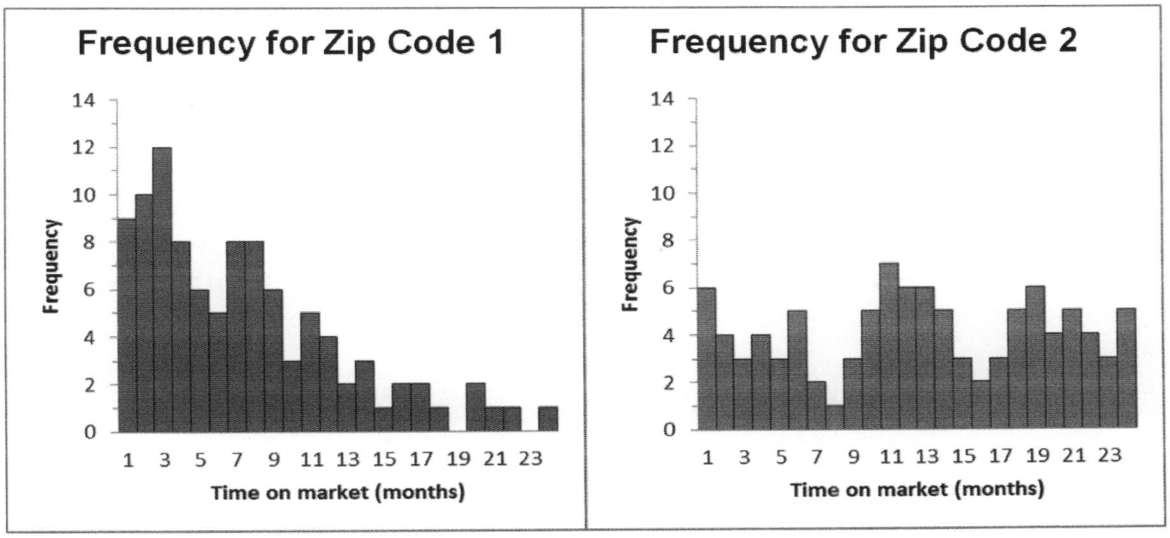

a. The median time a house spent on the market in Zip Code 1 is five months less than Zip Code 2.
b. On average, a house spent seven months longer on the market in Zip Code 2 than in Zip Code 1.
c. The mode time on the market is higher for Zip Code 1 than for Zip Code 2.
d. The median time on the market is less than the mean time on the market for Zip Code 1.

19. Jason decides to donate 1% of his annual salary to a local charity. If his annual salary is $45,000, how much will he donate?

a. $4.50
b. $45
c. $450
d. $4,500

20. Kevin saves $3 during Month 1. During each subsequent month, he plans to save 4 more dollars than he saved during the previous month. Which of the following equations represents the amount he will save during the nth month?

a. $a_n = 3n - 1$
b. $a_n = 3n + 4$
c. $a_n = 4n + 3$
d. $a_n = 4n - 1$

21. A tree with a height of 15 feet casts a shadow that is 5 feet in length. A man standing at the base of the shadow formed by the tree is 6 feet tall. How long is the shadow cast by the man?

a. 1.5 feet
b. 2 feet
c. 2.5 feet
d. 3 feet

22. A coin is tossed 300 times. How many of those tosses can you expect to show heads?

a. 50
b. 100
c. 150
d. 200

23. Mr. Mancelli teaches fifth-grade math. He is making prize bags for the winners of a math game. If he has eight candy bars and twelve packages of gum, what is the largest number of identical prize bags he can make without having any left-over candy bars or packages of gum?

a. 2
b. 4
c. 6
d. 8

24. Which of the following goals is appropriate in the category of algebraic reasoning for first-grade students?

a. Students represent one- and two-step problems involving addition and subtraction of whole numbers to 1,000 using pictorial models, number lines, and equations.
b. Students represent real-world relationships using number pairs in a table and verbal descriptions.
c. Students represent word problems involving addition and subtraction of whole numbers up to 20 using concrete and pictorial models and number sentences.
d. Students recite numbers up to at least 100 by ones and tens beginning with any given number.

25. Which of the following descriptions best fits a hexagonal prism?

a. 8 faces, 18 edges, 12 vertices
b. 6 faces, 18 edges, 12 vertices
c. 8 faces, 16 edges, 8 vertices
d. 6 faces, 14 edges, 10 vertices

26. Addison tosses a six-sided die twelve times and records the results in the table below.

Toss	1	2	3	4	5	6	7	8	9	10	11	12
Results	2	5	1	2	3	6	6	2	4	5	4	3

Which of the following statements is true?

a. The experimental probability of tossing a 6 is greater than the theoretical probability.
b. The experimental probability of tossing a 3 is greater than the theoretical probability.
c. The experimental probability of tossing a 1 is greater than the theoretical probability.
d. The experimental probability of tossing a 2 is greater than the theoretical probability.

27. If $f(x) = \frac{x^3-2x+1}{3x}$, what is $f(2)$?

a. $\frac{1}{3}$
b. $\frac{1}{2}$
c. $\frac{5}{6}$
d. $\frac{5}{2}$

28. What is the distance on a coordinate plane from $(-8, 6)$ to $(4, 3)$?

a. $\sqrt{139}$
b. $\sqrt{147}$
c. $\sqrt{153}$
d. $\sqrt{161}$

29. $A = \{9, 4, -3, 8, 6, 0\}$ and $B = \{-4, 2, 8, 9, 0\}$. What is $A \cup B$?

a. $\{9,8,0\}$
b. $\{9,4,-3,8,6,0,-4,2\}$
c. $\emptyset$
d. $\{9,8,0,2,4\}$

30. On a floor plan drawn at a scale of $1 : 100$, the area of a rectangular room is 30 cm^2. What is the actual area of the room?

a. 30,000 cm^2
b. 300 m^2
c. 3,000 m^2
d. 30 m^2

31. A developer decides to build a fence around a neighborhood park, which is positioned on a rectangular lot. Rather than fencing along the lot line, he fences x feet from each of the lot's boundaries. By fencing a rectangular space 141 yd^2 smaller than the lot, the developer saves \$432 in fencing materials, which cost \$12 per linear foot. How much does he spend?

a. \$160
b. \$456
c. \$3,168
d. The answer cannot be determined from the given information.

Refer to the following for question 32:

The box-and-whisker plot displays student test scores by class period.

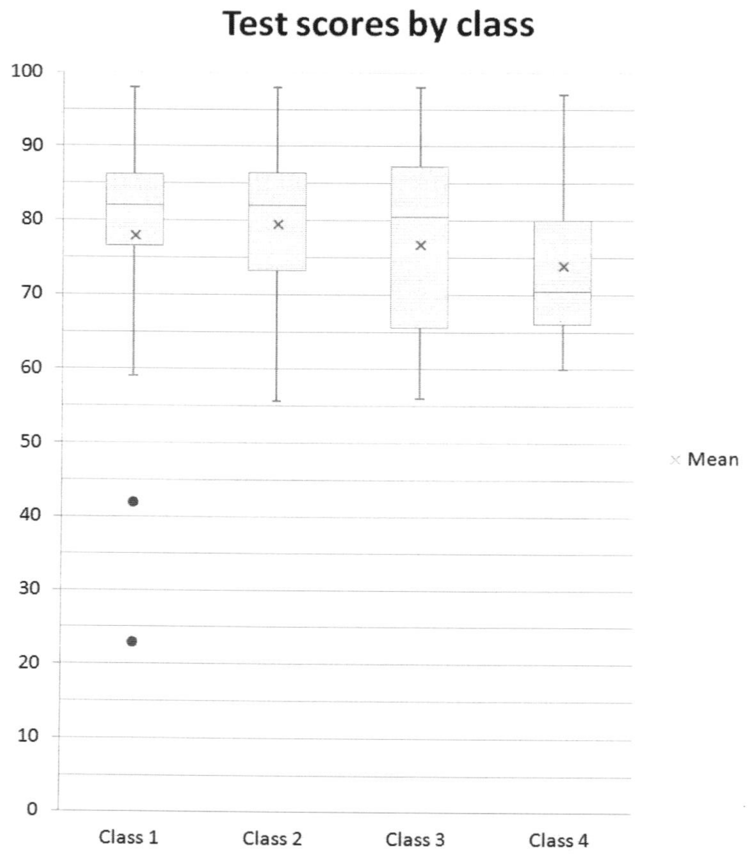

32. Which of the following statements is true of the data?

a. The mean better reflects student performance in class 1 than the median.
b. The mean test score for class 1 and 2 is the same.
c. The median test score for class 1 and 2 is the same.
d. The median test score is above the mean for class 4.

33. A circular bracelet contains 5 charms, A, B, C, D, and E, attached at specific points around the bracelet, with the clasp located between charms A and B. The bracelet is unclasped and stretched out into a straight line. On the resulting linear bracelet, charm C is between charms A and B, charm D is between charms A and C, and charm E is between charms C and D. Which of these statements is (are) necessarily true?

I. The distance between charms B and E is greater than the distance between charms A and D.
II. Charm E is between charms B and D.
III. The distance between charms D and E is less than the distance of bracelet between charms A and C.

a. I, II, and III
b. II and III
c. II only
d. None of these must be true.

34. A gift box has a length of 14 inches, a height of 8 inches, and a width of 6 inches. How many square inches of wrapping paper are needed to wrap the box?

a. 56
b. 244
c. 488
d. 672

35. Eli rolls a six-sided die and tosses a coin. What is the probability that he gets a prime number or tails?

a. $\frac{1}{4}$
b. $\frac{1}{3}$
c. $\frac{1}{2}$
d. $\frac{3}{4}$

36. Ms. Chen is instructing her students on divisibility rules. Which of the following rules can be used to determine if a number is divisible by 6?

a. The last digit of the number is divisible by 2 or 3.
b. The number ends in 6.
c. The number is divisible by 2 and 3.
d. The last two digits of the number are divisible by 6.

37. Marcus is mowing yards and doing odd jobs to earn money for a new video game system that costs $325. Marcus only charges $6.50 per hour. Which of the following equations represents the number of hours Marcus needs to work to earn $325?

a. $6.50x = 325$
b. $6.50 + x = 325$
c. $325x = 6.50$
d. $6.50x + 325 = x$

38. What is the perimeter of the trapezoid graphed below?

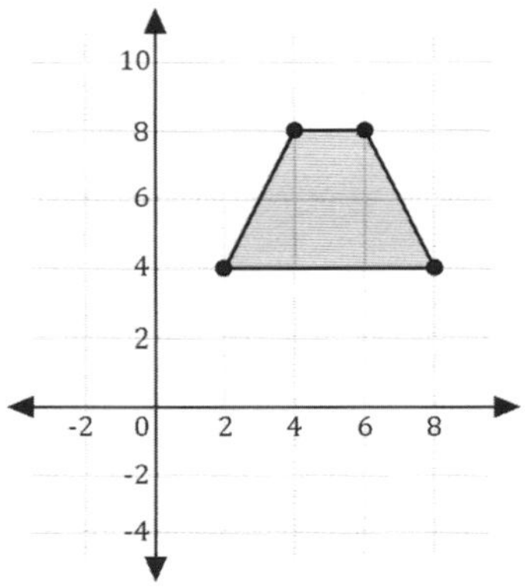

a. $4 + \sqrt{10}$
b. $8 + 4\sqrt{5}$
c. $4 + 2\sqrt{5}$
d. $8 + 2\sqrt{22}$

39. Solve $\frac{x-2}{x-1} = \frac{x-1}{x+1} + \frac{2}{x-1}$.

a. $x = 2$
b. $x = -5$
c. $x = 1$
d. No solution

40. You wish to determine the area of a regular pentagon, and all you know is the length of one side. What additional information is sufficient for you to be able to compute the area?

a. The length of all the other sides
b. The width of the pentagon
c. The length of the apothem
d. No other information needed

Science

1. How do animals of the phylum Mollusca respire?

a. Through gills
b. Through a trachea
c. Through book lungs
d. Through muscle contraction

2. A pulley lifts a 10-kg object 10 m into the air in 5 minutes. Using this information, you can calculate which of the following?

a. Mechanical advantage
b. Efficiency
c. Frictional resistance
d. Power

3. Two companion models, gradualism and punctuated equilibrium, dominate evolutionary theory. Which of the following statements is most consistent with the theory of punctuated equilibrium?

a. Fossils show changes over large periods of time.
b. Fossils showing intermediate characteristics may not necessarily be found.
c. Speciation occurs gradually.
d. Evolution is a slow, steady process.

Refer to the following for question 4:

The illustration below depicts the rock cycle. This cycle illustrates the fact that rocks are not unchanging entities; they undergo changes over time.

THE ROCK CYCLE

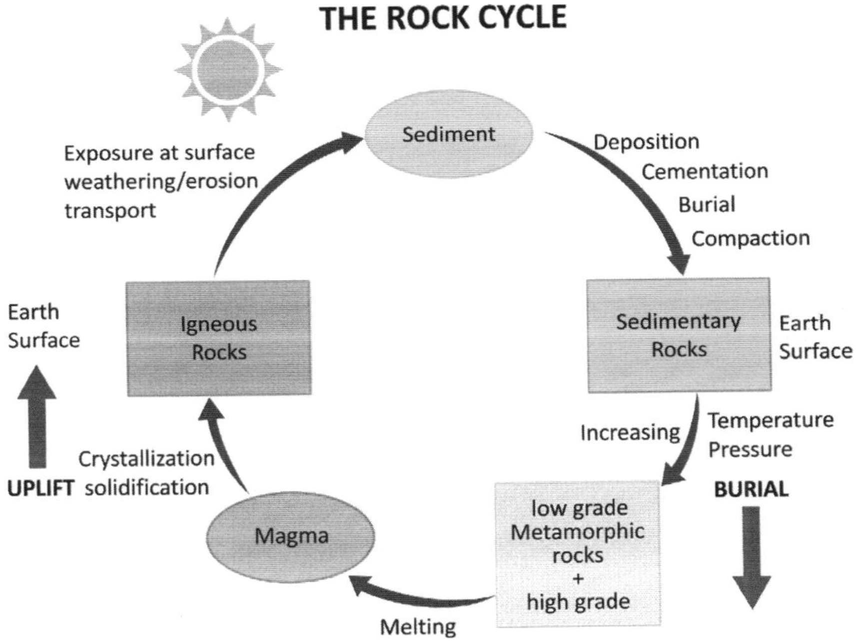

4. How are igneous rocks formed in the rock cycle?

a. Years of sediment are laid down on top of each other and forced together.
b. Acid rain caused by pollution creates holes in metamorphic rocks.
c. Dust and pebbles are pressed together underground from Earth's heat and pressure.
d. Magma from a volcanic eruption cools and hardens.

Refer to the following for question 5:

A biome featuring scrubby plants and small evergreen trees has a hot, dry summer followed by a wetter winter. The following food chain exists in the biome:

$$tree \rightarrow caterpillar \rightarrow frog \rightarrow snake \rightarrow hawk \rightarrow vulture \rightarrow worm$$

5. What trophic level contains the greatest amount of energy?

a. Tree
b. Caterpillar
c. Hawk
d. Worm

6. What happens to gas particles as temperature increases?

a. The average kinetic energy decreases while the intermolecular forces increase.
b. The average kinetic energy increases while the intermolecular forces decrease.
c. Both the average kinetic energy and the intermolecular forces decrease.
d. Both the average kinetic energy and the intermolecular forces increase.

7. Which of the following represents a chemical change?

a. Water sublimating
b. An apple turning brown
c. Salt dissolving in water
d. Rock being pulverized

8. What type of compound is formed by the combination of two or more nonmetallic elements with one another?

a. Organic
b. Ionic
c. Covalent
d. Chemical

9. Which of the following is an example of chemical weathering?

a. Rain freezing on the roadway
b. Ivy growing on the side of a wooden house
c. Vinegar fizzing when poured on a rock
d. A river carrying sediment downstream

10. Which of the following is an example of a descriptive study?

a. Comparing the average height of male vs female penguins of a particular species
b. Investigating the growth rate of fungi in various synthetic media
c. Testing the effectiveness of a drug with a double-blind study
d. Split-testing the impact on sales of a new description of menu items.

11. What happens to the temperature of a substance as it is changing phase from a liquid to a solid?

a. Its temperature increases due to the absorption of latent heat.
b. Its temperature decreases due to the heat of vaporization.
c. Its temperature decreases due to the latent heat of fusion.
d. Its temperature remains the same due to the latent heat of fusion.

12. Which of the following is NOT true of a chemical reaction?

a. Matter is neither gained nor lost.
b. Heat is absorbed or released.
c. The rate of the reaction increases with temperature.
d. The products have a different number of atoms than the reactants.

13. Fossils are least likely to be found in which type of rock?

a. Sedimentary rock
b. Metamorphic rock
c. Igneous rock
d. Fossils are commonly found in all types of rock

14. Which of the following statements correctly compares rocks and minerals?

a. Minerals may contain traces of organic compounds, while rocks do not.
b. Rocks are classified by their formation and the minerals they contain, while minerals are classified by their chemical composition and physical properties.
c. Both rocks and minerals can be polymorphs.
d. Both rocks and minerals may contain mineraloids.

15. Which of the following is true of different isotopes of the same element?

a. It has a different number of protons than its element.
b. It has a different number of electrons than its element.
c. It has a different charge as compared to its element.
d. It has a different number of neutrons than other isotopes of the same element.

16. Which action will help dissolve a gas in a liquid if the gas and liquid are placed in a sealed container?

a. Heat the liquid.
b. Cool the liquid.
c. Shake the container.
d. Decrease the pressure on the lid.

17. How does the freezing point of sea water compare to that of fresh water?

a. Sea water has a higher freezing point.
b. Sea water has a lower freezing point.
c. They are the same.
d. Sea water does not freeze.

18. Tropical climate zones are characterized by:

a. Extreme temperature variations between night and day
b. Extreme temperature variations between seasons
c. Frequent rainfall
d. All of the above

19. The process whereby a radioactive element releases energy slowly over a long period of time to lower its energy and become more stable is best described as which of the following?

a. Combustion
b. Fission
c. Fusion
d. Decay

20. This organelle contains digestive enzymes that break down food and unneeded substances. They are also thought to be linked to the aging process. What part of a cell does this describe?

a. Lysosomes
b. Chromatin
c. Plastids
d. Golgi apparatus

21. On a topographic map, an area where the contour lines are very close together indicates which of the following?

a. A stream is present.
b. The slope is very gentle.
c. The slope is very steep.
d. The area surrounds a depression.

22. The distance from the earth to the sun is equal to which of the following?

a. One astronomical unit
b. One light-year
c. One parsec
d. One arcsecond

23. Which of the following observations provides the best evidence that sound can travel through solid objects?

a. Sound waves cannot travel through a vacuum.
b. The atoms of a solid are packed tightly together.
c. If you knock on a solid object, it makes a sound.
d. You can hear a sound on the other side of a solid wall.

24. Which of the following divisions of plants produces seeds for reproduction?

a. Anthophyta
b. Lycophyta
c. Sphenophyta
d. Pterophyta

25. Which of the following creates a magnetic field?

a. The spinning and rotating of electrons in atoms
b. The separation of charged particles in atoms
c. The vibrational and translational motion of atoms
d. Loosely held valence electrons surrounding an atom

26. The asteroid belt in our solar system is located between:

a. Earth and Mars
b. Neptune and Pluto
c. Uranus and Saturn
d. Mars and Jupiter

27. In a parallel circuit, there are three paths: A, B, and C. Path A has a resistance of 10 ohms, path B a resistance of 5 ohms, and path C a resistance of 2 ohms. How do the voltage and current change for each path?

a. Voltage and current are kept the same in each path.
b. Voltage is greatest in path A and current is greatest in path C.
c. Voltage is lowest in path C and current is greatest in path C.
d. Voltage is the same for each path and current is greatest in path C.

28. Which of the following statements about the physical properties of liquids and gases are true?

I. Liquids and gases are both compressible.
II. Liquids flow, but gases do not.
III. Liquids flow and gases are incompressible.
IV. Liquids flow and gases are compressible.
V. Gases flow and liquids are incompressible.

a. I and III
b. II and IV
c. III and V
d. IV and V

29. World weather patterns are most influenced by which of the following?

a. Wind belts
b. The Earth's orbit
c. Ocean currents
d. Atmospheric conditions

30. For what reason is repetition important to scientific inquiry?

a. It is the only way to prove that an experiment is reliable.
b. It adds to the number of statistics supporting the concept.
c. It assists the scientist in determining which data to consider.
d. It requires many groups of investigators working on a project.

31. In the technological design process, after the problem has been identified and a possible solution selected, what is the next step?

a. Propose designs.
b. Evaluate the solution.
c. Try out the proposed solution.
d. Report results.

32. Young children develop many basic science concepts through everyday activities. Of the following, which activity is most related to the development of measurement concepts?

a. Fitting wooden pegs into holes with matching shapes in a toy
b. Pouring sand from one container into a differently sized one
c. Seeing how many coins they have accrued in their piggy bank
d. Separating toys into piles of cars, trucks, animals, people, etc.

33. Of the following actions, which best represents the science process skill of Inference?

a. Formulating new hypotheses based on experimental results
b. Finding patterns and meaning in the results of experiments
c. Identifying properties of things/situations using the senses
d. Reporting experimental results and conclusions to others

34. Which statement is correct regarding the phenomenon of magnetism?

a. Opposite poles of magnets repel each other.
b. The like poles of magnets attract each other.
c. Magnets can attract/repel without touching.
d. Magnets work beyond their magnetic fields.

35. What is the difference between mass and weight?

a. There is no difference; they are the same.
b. Mass is the amount of matter in an object; weight is the pull of gravity on the object.
c. Mass determines the amount of volume of an object; weight does not.
d. Mass is the amount of cubic space that an object occupies. Cubic space is not related to weight.

36. Heat is transmitted through solid materials via:

a. Conduction
b. Convection
c. Radiation
d. All three

37. Which of the following is not an advantage angiosperms show over other types of plants?

a. Larger leaves
b. Double fertilization
c. Dormant seeds
d. Lower seed dispersal

38. If you were testing the effectiveness of a cream that reduced the signs of wrinkles around women's eyes, which of the following would be a good control group?

a. Rats with no wrinkles
b. A group of women with no wrinkles around their eyes who are given the cream
c. A group of women with wrinkles who are given a cream that has no effect
d. A group of women with wrinkles who are given a similar cream that's already on the market

39. Which of the following are required by all typical organisms in order to survive?

a. Water, cells, shelter, and space
b. Food, water, cellular growth, nurturing
c. Food, water, sunlight, and air
d. Air, shelter, space, and companionship

40. What steps should precede drawing a conclusion about a hypothesis?

a. Testing, observing, and recording data
b. Communicating the hypothesis to others
c. Comparing data with data of other groups
d. Reporting the results so they can be replicated

Social Studies

1. Which of the following BEST describes the significance of the US Supreme Court's decision in the Dred Scott case?

a. The ruling effectively declared slavery to be a violation of the Constitution.
b. The ruling guaranteed full citizenship rights to freed slaves.
c. The ruling turned many Southerners against the Supreme Court.
d. The ruling furthered the gap between North and South and hastened the Civil War.

2. Which of the following is true regarding the Tropic of Capricorn?

a. It separates the northern and southern hemispheres.
b. It separates the eastern and western hemispheres.
c. It is the southernmost latitude at which the sun can appear directly overhead at noon.
d. It is the northernmost latitude at which the sun can appear directly overhead at noon.

3. The Seven Years' War, called the French and Indian War by the Colonists:

a. Was the precursor to the American Revolution
b. Was a conflict related to European colonization
c. Primarily took place in Canada
d. Ended European conquests

4. Which of the following statements is NOT an accurate statement about the Puritans in England?

a. The Puritans unconditionally gave all their support to the English Reformation.
b. The Puritans saw the Church of England as too much like the Catholic Church.
c. The Puritans became a chief political power because of the English Civil War.
d. The Puritans' clergy mainly departed from the Church of England after 1662.

5. During the early Medieval period in Europe, before the 5th century, where were the main centers of literacy found?

a. They were in the homes of the wealthy.
b. They were in the churches and monasteries.
c. They were in the local artisan and craft guilds.
d. There were no centers of literacy.

6. Most federal judges have served as local judges, lawyers, and law professors. These are ________ qualifications.

a. Formal
b. Required
c. Informal
d. Recommended

7. Of the following, who was NOT a dispatch rider notifying Americans of British troop movements reported by American surveillance in 1775?

a. Paul Revere
b. William Dawes
c. John Parker
d. Samuel Prescott

8. The physical geography of a region most directly affects which of the following?

a. The religious beliefs of the native population
b. The family structure of the native population
c. The dietary preferences of the native population
d. The language spoken by the native population

9. The price of oil drops dramatically, saving soda pop manufacturers great amounts of money spent on making soda pop and delivering their product to market. Prices for soda pop, however, stay the same. This is an example of what?

a. Sticky prices
b. Indiscriminate costs
c. Stable demand
d. Aggregate expenditure

10. What does the 10th Amendment establish?

a. Any power not given to the federal government belongs to the states or the people.
b. The president is responsible for executing and enforcing laws created by Congress.
c. Congress has the authority to declare war.
d. The Supreme Court has the authority to interpret the Constitution.

11. What did the Mason-Dixon Line divide?

a. The East from the West before the western states were incorporated
b. The East from the West along the Mississippi River
c. The North from the South before the Civil War
d. The Senate from the House of Representatives

12. The philosophy of the late 17th-18th centuries that influenced the Constitution was from the Age of:

a. Enlightenment
b. Empire
c. Discovery
d. Industry

13. Which geographic features were most conducive to the development of early civilizations?

a. Rivers
b. Deserts
c. Forests
d. Mountains

14. What portion of the federal budget is dedicated to transportation, education, national resources, the environment, and international affairs?

a. Mandatory spending
b. Discretionary spending
c. Undistributed offsetting receipts
d. Official budget outlays

15. Thomas Jefferson embraced a theological philosophy called deism, which promotes which of the following?

a. Abolition
b. Atheism
c. Separation of church and state
d. A theocratic central government

16. When the Senate held an impeachment hearing against Andrew Johnson for overstepping his authority, what did they invoke?

a. Checks and balances
b. Bicameralism
c. Legislative oversight
d. Supremacy

17. What are the first ten amendments to the Constitution more commonly known as?

a. The Civil Rights Act
b. Common law
c. The Equal Protection clause
d. The Bill of Rights

18. A country's currency increases in value on foreign currency exchange markets. What will happen as a result?

I. Exports will drop
II. Imports will rise
III. The balance of payments will rise

a. I only
b. II only
c. I and II
d. II and III

19. Which statement about factors related to the growth of the US economy between 1945 and 1970 is NOT correct?

a. The Baby Boom's greatly increased birth rates contributed to economic growth during this time.
b. The reduction in military spending after World War II contributed to the stronger US economy.
c. Government programs and growing affluence nearly quadrupled college enrollments in 20 years.
d. Increased mobility and bigger families caused fast suburban expansion, especially in the Sunbelt.

20. The civil rights act that outlawed segregation in schools and public places also did which of the following?

a. Gave minorities the right to vote
b. Established women's right to vote
c. Outlawed unequal voter registration
d. Provided protection for children

21. Which of the following world religions is the oldest?

a. Greek Stoicism
b. Confucianism
c. Christianity
d. Judaism

22. Which of the following is associated with market failure?

I. When a firm in a non-competitive industry hires labor at a lower wage
II. When the firms in a non-competitive industry create less than the efficient amount of a good or service
III. When production of a good creates negative externalities born by third parties
IV. Public goods

a. I and II only
b. I and III only
c. I, II, and III only
d. I, II, III, and IV

23. Which of the following statements is NOT correct regarding these religions under the Roman Empire?

a. The Romans generally protected the Jews until the rebellion in Judea (66 AD).
b. Julius Caesar circumvented Roman law to help Jews have freedom of worship.
c. The Druids were a religious group that the Romans ignored but also tolerated.
d. Romans viewed Christianity as a Jewish sect for its first two centuries.

24. Which of the following was a major cause of the Great Depression of the 1930s?

a. The overproduction and underconsumption of consumer goods
b. The failure of industry to produce sufficient consumer goods
c. Underproduction and rising prices in the agricultural sector
d. The reduction of import tariffs

25. The concept of checks and balances is evident in which of the following?

a. Federal judiciary appeals
b. Presidential veto
c. States' rights
d. The House and the Senate

26. Ivy loses her job because her skills as a seamstress are no longer required due to a new piece of machinery that does the work of a seamstress more quickly and for less money. Which type of unemployment is this?

a. Frictional
b. Structural
c. Cyclical
d. Careless

27. Of the following statements, which is true about the March on Versailles during the French Revolution?

a. The March on Versailles was an action undertaken by equal numbers of both men and women.
b. The March on Versailles was an action undertaken primarily by women.
c. The March on Versailles happened prior to the storming of the Bastille.
d. The March on Versailles was not effective in accomplishing its purpose.

28. What judicial system did America borrow from England?

a. Due process
b. Federal law
c. Commerce law
d. Common law

29. Who established the precedent for the two-term limit for the US presidency?

a. Abraham Lincoln
b. Alexander Hamilton
c. George Washington
d. Thomas Jefferson

30. The presidential veto of legislation passed by Congress illustrates which principal in American government?

a. Checks and balances
b. Federal regulation
c. Freedom of speech
d. Separation of church and state

31. To be President of the United States, one must meet these three requirements:

a. The President must be college educated, at least 30 years old, and a natural citizen.
b. The President must be a natural citizen, have lived in the US for 14 years, and have a college education.
c. The President must be a natural citizen, be at least 35 years old, and have lived in the US for 14 years.
d. The President must be at least 30 years old, be a natural citizen, and have lived in the US for 14 years.

32. After the Civil War, urban populations increased. This growth was likely due to:

a. An increased reliance on agriculture
b. The Industrial Revolution
c. Prohibition
d. Slavery persisting in some areas

33. The Trail of Tears was:

a. The forced removal of British soldiers after the American Revolution
b. The forced evacuation of Cherokee peoples into Oklahoma
c. The forced evacuation of freed slaves from the South after the Civil War
d. The tears of Betsy Ross while she sewed the first American flag

Refer to the following for question 34:

A first-grade teacher is planning a geography unit focused on how the weather impacts the way that people live. This unit will focus on how weather differs in the regions near the poles, the tropical regions, and the mid-latitudes.

34. What should the teacher tell students that the main reason that tropical regions near the Equator tend to experience relatively constant year-round temperatures is?

a. They are usually located near the ocean.
b. The angle at which sunlight hits them remains relatively constant throughout the year.
c. They are located along the "Ring of Fire."
d. They do not have seasons.

35. Which scientist first proposed the heliocentric universe instead of a geocentric one?

a. Galileo
b. Ptolemy
c. Copernicus
d. Isaac Newton

36. Congressional elections are held every ___________ years.

a. four
b. two
c. six
d. three

37. All else being equal, which of the following locations is likely to have the coolest climate?

a. A city located at 6,000 feet above sea level
b. A city located at 500 feet above sea level
c. A city that receives less than 10 inches of precipitation per year
d. A city that receives more than 50 inches of precipitation per year

38. Which Italian Renaissance figure was best known as a political philosopher?

a. Dante Alighieri
b. Leonardo Da Vinci
c. Francesco Petrarca
d. Niccolò Machiavelli

39. Emily West, a multiracial woman, who was captured by Santa Anna prior to the battle of San Jacinto and thought to have contributed to the Texans victory, is associated with which of the following symbols of Texas:

a. The Lone Star
b. The Yellow Rose
c. The Blue Lacy
d. The Bluebonnet

40. Which of the following statements is NOT true about the Gilded Age in America?

a. The Gilded Age was the era of the "robber barons" in the business world.
b. The Gilded Age got its name from the excesses of the wealthy upper class.
c. The Gilded Age had philanthropy Carnegie called the "Gospel of Wealth".
d. The Gilded Age is a term whose origins have not been identified clearly.

Answer Key and Explanations for Test #2

English

1. B: Researchers have found that the writing process both forms a hierarchy and is observably recursive. Moreover, they find that when students continually revise their writing, they are able to consider new ideas and to incorporate these ideas into their work. Therefore, choice B is correct. Students who are rewriting and revising do not merely correct mechanical errors (A); they also add to the content and quality of their writing. Furthermore, research shows that writers (including students) not only revise their actual writing during rewrites, but they also reconsider their original writing goals rather than always retaining them (C), and they revisit their prewriting plans rather than leaving these unaffected (D).

2. C: Once the students' notecards have been checked and edited for accuracy, they can easily be used to demonstrate the process of organizing ideas in an essay or research paper. Students can use their notecards as aids for making their outlines. They simply have to arrange the notecards in an appropriate order and add pertinent information to bridge the ideas together in their writing.

3. D: Fluent readers are able to read smoothly and comfortably at a steady pace (rate). The more quickly a child reads, the greater the chance of leaving out a word or substituting one word for another (for example, *sink* instead of *shrink*). Fluent readers are able to maintain accuracy without sacrificing rate. Fluent readers also stress important words in a text, group words into rhythmic phrases, and read with intonation (prosody).

4. C: Homophones are words that are pronounced the same but differ in meaning. For example, a bride wears a 2-carat ring, but a horse eats a carrot. These words are not all nouns or monosyllabic, and none of them are diphthongs. Diphthongs (D) are a single-syllable sound made up by combining two vowels, such as in the words *weird*, *applause*, and *boy*.

5. A: It is a standard of Information Literacy that students must use their own critical thinking skills to evaluate the quality of the information and its sources before they use it, so choice A is correct. Another standard of Information Literacy is that the student should ascertain how much information he or she needs before seeking out the information, as identifying what information is necessary after uncovering excessive information is inefficient (B). Instead of acquiring as much information as possible, students should determine how much information is needed to achieve a reasonable goal. An additional Information Literacy standard is to access necessary information in an efficient and effective way. However, none of these standards include the idea that students will sacrifice any incidental learning by being efficient in their accessing of information, so choice C is incorrect. Another part of Information Literacy Standards is the principle that students should use the information they find in ways that are effective for their specific purposes; this does not require that students avoid using information for purposes that it was not meant to serve, so choice D is incorrect.

6. B: Spelling is often taught in a systematic way. Students receive words and memorize them for quizzes and tests. However, spelling is related to many aspects of language and must be treated as a dynamic subject. Integrating the words into other parts of language instruction will help students not only learn how to spell correctly, but also to recall meanings of words and various rules of English spelling and grammar. By using the same words in different subjects, the students will retain the information more readily than if they study the words intensely for one week in only one context.

7. C: Tier-two words are words that are used with high frequency across a variety of disciplines or words with multiple meanings. They are characteristic of mature language users. Knowing these words is crucial to attaining an acceptable level of reading comprehension and communication skills.

8. D: Teachers will observe a variety of developmental arcs when teaching reading, since all students learn differently. It is very important to understand which instances are normal in the course of learning and which signal a learning difficulty. Barrett is still exhibiting confusion over certain letter-sounds, typically when the letters look similar. At his age, this difficulty could suggest that Barrett has an issue with reading that could be addressed by a reading specialist. The other three choices describe normal behaviors that are commonly exhibited by children when they are learning to read. Choice C, Noelle, may describe an instance in which a student is having a learning problem. However, the teacher will need more information about Noelle's reading skills besides her reluctance to read before making a determination about how to proceed.

9. C: The MLA guidelines for citing sources in research papers advise that multiple authors of the same work can be cited in in-text citations by using the first author's name plus *et al*, where *et al* refers to all the other authors. However, this convention is only advised for situations where there are three or more authors, so choice C is correct. The guidelines also say that in cases where there are two or three authors, each author should be named in a serial list, either in a signal phrase or in a parenthetical reference. For example, authors Smith and Jones could be cited with "Smith and Jones note that ... (45)" or "(Smith and Jones 45)," and authors Smith, Jones, and Gray could be cited with "Smith, Jones, and Gray note that ... (45)" or simply "(Smith, Jones, and Gray 45)." Therefore, choices A, B, and D are incorrect.

10. A: The /p/ sound is among the earliest phonemes to develop, from ages 1.5 to 3 years old. The /ʒ/ phoneme (B) has the oldest age norm for normal development—5.5 years to 8.5 years old is a typical range for children to acquire correct production of this sound. The /v/ sound (C) typically develops in most children from the ages of 4 to 8 years. Most children develop correct articulation of the /s/ sound (D) by 2.5 to 4 years old. Hence, not all kindergarteners, who are typically around 5 years old, are expected to master phonemes with acquisition norm ranges older than 5-8 years. A 5-year-old is most likely to be referred for SLP evaluation if s/he does not correctly produce /p/, which children normally develop by around 3 years old.

11. B: Prior knowledge, which rises from experience and previous learning, provides a framework by which new knowledge gained from the act of reading can be integrated. Every act of reading enriches a student's store of prior knowledge and increases that student's future ability to comprehend more fully any new knowledge acquired through reading.

12. B: Writing haikus will promote students' vocabularies. The tightly controlled syllabic requirements will cause students to search for words outside their normal vocabularies that will fit the rigid framework and still express the writer's intended meanings. Often, students will rediscover a word whose meaning they know, but they don't often use.

13. A: Mnemonic devices are a way to aid in memorization. The concept to be memorized is linked to a device: an easily remembered song, saying, or image. To remember the concept, one needs only to remember the device.

14. A: While there is no consensus among experts as to any universal sequence of instruction for teaching the alphabetic principle through phonics instruction, they do agree that, to enable children to start reading words as soon as possible, the highest-utility relationships should be introduced earliest. For example, the letters *m, a, p, t,* and *s* are all used frequently, whereas the *x* in *box*, the sound of *ey* in *they*, and the letter *a* when pronounced as it is in *want* have lower-utility letter-sound correspondences. Important considerations for the alphabetic principle are to teach letter-sound correspondences in isolation, not in word contexts; to teach them explicitly; to give students opportunities to practice letter-sound relationships within their other daily lessons, not only separately; and to include cumulative reviews of relationships taught earlier along with new ones in practice opportunities.

15. A: Letter–sound correspondence relies on the relationship between a spoken sound or group of sounds and the letters conventionally used in English to write them.

16. A: Explicit instruction involves clarifying the goal, modeling strategies, and offering explanations geared to a student's level of understanding. Explicit instruction is well organized and structured. It offers easily understood steps and depends in part on frequent reference to previously learned materials.

17. C: *Diction* refers to the overall choice of language a writer or speaker makes. *Jargon* is a specialized terminology, used in a discipline, that is not readily understood by readers outside of that discipline. Choice C fills in the blanks correctly. *Style* (A and D) refers to the effect a writer achieves through language. It encompasses diction, which encompasses word choice. *Vocabulary* (D) refers to any set of words in a language.

18. B: Students must be able to distinguish between printed words and the spaces between them to identify the first and last letters of each word, as spaces are the boundaries between words. It is not true that all normally developing students can tell words from spaces: those not exposed to or familiar with print media may need to be taught this distinction. Although left-to-right directionality is more of a problem for ELL students whose L1s have different writing or printing directions (e.g., some Asian languages are written vertically, some can be written vertically or horizontally, and some Semitic languages like Hebrew and Arabic are written right-to-left), again, children unfamiliar with print or writing may also not know writing, print, or book directionality either. Identifying basic punctuation is important to reading comprehension as it affects meaning. For example, consider "Let's eat, Grandma" vs. "Let's eat Grandma"—one comma differentiates an invitation to dinner from a cannibalistic proposal.

19. A: At the beginning of the school year, second-grade students should be able to read 50–80 words per minute. By the time they are well into the school year, second-grade level reading is tracked at 85 words per minute.

20. A: Teachers of English language learners should not employ idioms and slang in their instruction because these informal uses of speech are likely to confuse the students. Involving students in hands-on activities such as group reading and language play makes the experience both more meaningful and more immediate. New knowledge can only be absorbed by attaching it to prior knowledge; referencing what students already know is essential. Speaking slowly to English language learners is important, because they are processing what is being said at a slower rate than a native speaker.

21. A: Choice A is correct as evaluation (i.e., making critical judgments about some information) commonly incorporates the processes that the other answer choices refer to and is therefore more complex than they are. Application (B) requires taking information learned and using it in new or different circumstances. Comprehension (C) requires showing understanding of the information learned. Knowledge recall (D) involves showing proficiency in information learned.

22. D: To instruct students in word analysis following a sequence progressing from simpler to more complex, teachers would first introduce individual phonemes (speech sounds); then the blending of two or more individual phonemes; then onsets and rimes (i.e., phonograms and word families) such as *-ack*, *-ide*, *-ay*, *-ight*, *-ine*, etc.; then the easier short vowels, followed by the more difficult long vowels; then blends of individual consonants; then CVC (consonant-vowel-consonant) words (e.g., *bag*, *hot*, *red*, *sit*) and other common patterns of consonants and vowels in words; and then the six most common types of syllables (i.e., closed, VCe, open, vowel team, *r*-controlled, and C-*le*).

23. C: Students can easily become bored or disinterested in reading if they are not exposed to a variety of reading texts. Also, reading can be overwhelming or frustrating for students who are still learning to read fluently or to comprehend what they read. By incorporating media, oral stories, and various types of print, students of all ability levels can build both fluency and comprehension skills. This approach also enables the teacher and students to discuss the relationship between all aspects of literacy—including speaking, listening, thinking, viewing, and reading.

24. B: Coarticulation affects phonemic awareness. Vocalizing words involves arranging a series of continuous, voiced, unvoiced, and stop sounds. As one sound is being uttered, the tongue and lips are already assuming the shape required by the next sound in the word. This process, which is not conscious, can distort individual sounds. One sound can slur into another, clip the end of the previous sound, or flatten or heighten a sound. For children who have difficulty hearing distinct phonemic sounds, individual instruction may be required.

25. B: This prompt focuses not only on reading fluency skills, but also on the issue of the young reader's confidence. It is very common for students who feel unsuccessful at reading to avoid the skill altogether. The teacher in this question realizes something important: it is vital to build a student's confidence with reading as he or she builds skill. In choice A there is a faulty assumption that a student could ever memorize enough words to eliminate the need to decode. While some students with processing disorders or different learning styles do rely more heavily on sight words, this practice should not be solely relied upon. In choice C the students will likely feel negatively about being asked to read young children's books; their lack of confidence may be reinforced by this plan. In choice D students may also be frustrated by the extra work they are required to do without any evidence of success with this practice. In choice B, students can build their fluency skills by creating words with various sounds, which is often easier for students than decoding as they are learning to read. As their knowledge of letter-sound relationships grows, they will become better at decoding words they see on the page. Allowing students to encode will also provide them with more chances to feel successful as they learn.

26. B: Identifying point of view (A) is an example of literal reading comprehension. Explaining the point of view (B) is an example of evaluative reading comprehension. Identifying the main idea of a text passage (C) is an example of literal reading comprehension. Making predictions about what will happen in a text (D) is an example of inferential reading comprehension.

27. C: Signal words give the reader hints about the purpose of a particular passage. Some signal words are concerned with comparing/contrasting, some with cause and effect, some with temporal sequencing, some with physical location, and some with a problem and its solution. The words since, therefore, and accordingly are words used when describing an outcome; outcomes have causes.

28. C: Graphophonic cues are based on the speech sounds in words and their alphabetic representations in print, so choice C is correct. Syntactic cues (A) are based on how words are arranged and ordered to create meaningful phrases, clauses and sentences. Semantic cues (B) are based on the meanings of morphemes and words and how they combine to create additional meanings. Pragmatic cues (D) are based on the readers' purposes for reading and their understanding of how textual structures function in the texts that they read.

29. B: There are many different adults who can assist children in acquiring various types of language. If a child inconsistently mispronounces certain sounds in reading, he or she may simply need a reminder or instruction from a teacher. Often, children will not acquire knowledge of certain letters or sounds until a certain age. However, the child in this scenario mispronounces words consistently both in reading and in conversation. This combination suggests that the child is not physically able to make certain speech sounds. A speech-language pathologist can assist in determining whether or not the child's mispronunciations indicate the need for therapy. A speech pathologist can also work directly with the child to help him or her learn how to make certain sounds.

30. B: Indirect ways in which students receive instruction and learn vocabulary include through daily conversations, reading on their own, and being read aloud to by adults. Direct instruction and learning in vocabulary include teachers providing extended instruction exposing students repeatedly to vocabulary words in multiple teaching contexts, teachers pre-teaching specific words found in text prior to students reading it, and teachers instructing students over extended time periods and having them actively work with vocabulary words.

31. C: Analogizing is based on recognizing the pattern of letters in words that share phonological and orthographical similarities. In phonology and in spelling, the initial sound of a word is called an *onset*, whereas the sounds that follow the onset are called the *rime*. The following words each have a different onset sound, but share the same rime: *rent*, *sent*, *bent*, and *dent*. Rime analogies are an explicit teaching method that helps draw attention to patterns in rime and onset spellings. As students become more familiar with these patterns, they should be able to decode common rime patterns in words faster and with greater accuracy, contributing to higher reading fluency.

32. A: The student making this observation is connecting a reading about mythological gods to the world—in this instance, to human nature—by noting that despite greater powers, the gods' emotional reactions and behaviors are like those of humans. Since this is an example of connecting text to what the student knows about the world choice A is correct. The student statements in choices B and D reflect connections of text to text—fiction (a novel) to historical accounts of a period, and a character description to another story with a similar character. The student statement in option C reflects a connection of text to self; the student can relate to the feelings of a character in the text.

33. B: Reading responses can take various forms. The most common form of reading response is likely to be targeted student writing. Students may use journals, worksheets, or other formats to construct written responses to something they have read. The purpose of this type of assignment can range from fostering an appreciation of written text to helping a student prepare for an activity in class. Students may also engage in creating an oral reading response in the form of a presentation or debate. Ultimately, reading response increases a student's capacity to understand what is read and to analyze personal responses to the text.

34. C: Depending on their type, graphs can be used to compare quantities or values at the same point in time (or irrespective of time), or to show changes in quantities or values over time. For example, a bar graph can show different numbers of students in different categories or different test scores next to each other for comparison, or different numbers presented yearly, monthly, weekly, daily, etc. Line graphs only show changes in values over time. Tables are good for organizing information into categories but do not show linear changes over time. Maps, when cartographic (actual maps), depict geographical locations and can include other information (e.g., population totals, percentages, income, domestic or national product figures, annual rainfall, temperatures) via color-coding and other graphics. Other map types used in education, including concept maps for students, curriculum maps and resource maps for educators, etc., do not show linear chronological change. Charts like pie charts, which show percentages or proportions of a whole quantity divided by categories, do not show change over time.

35. C: By considering the other words in the story, the student can determine the missing words. The student is depending on the information supplied by the rest of the story. This information puts the story into context.

36. C: Second languages can be learned in a number of educational contexts. For example, they can be segregated from the L1, formally taught via the medium of the L1, taught through submersion, or taught within the language classroom but not used to communicate outside of it. The L2 can also be learned in several natural contexts. Because of these variations, L2 learners may acquire different elements of the language or may vary in how much of the language they acquire, so choice C is correct. Just like an L2, an L1 can also be learned in an education or natural context, so choice A is incorrect. While many L1s are learned naturally at first, they are learned in educational contexts as well, so choice B is incorrect. Just like L1s, L2s can be learned and used naturally, so choice D is incorrect.

37. B: In this project, students will engage in almost every aspect of literacy in a group context. Students must first accurately read and comprehend a short play; they will also use their writing skills to adapt the play to their specific purposes by cutting or adding text. The teacher can gauge the students' interpretive skills by the way they perform their play. By splitting the students into groups, the teacher can provide each student the chance to interpret and perform, as well as to experience the performances. Audience members receive additional practice with listening and interpreting when they generate responses to the performances. Group members can evaluate the effectiveness of their performances based on responses from the audience.

38. D: Teachers should instruct students in writing not in isolation, not relating writing only to reading or reading and speaking, but by showing students the interrelationships of listening, speaking, reading, and writing. In addition, teachers should not just teach writing as a rote chore or drill, but give students lessons and assignments that demonstrate legitimate purposes for writing and provide topics to write about that are meaningful to students.

39. C: Until the teacher monitors the child's verbal abilities and habits, she cannot determine if the lack of interaction suggests a learning disability, an emotional problem, or simply a shy personality. The teacher should informally observe the child over a period of time, noting if and when she initiates or responds to oral language, if she is reading with apparent comprehension, if her vocabulary is limited, and the degree to which the child is interested in understanding.

40. C: The root of the modern English word *debt* is the Latin word *debitum*, which is also the source of the *b*, so choice C is correct. Early scribes and printers, described by some as "inkhorn scholars," introduced many silent letters to English spellings to indicate their Latin or Greek roots, as in this case. Since the origin of the word is in Latin and not Greek, choice B is incorrect. The word came into English during the Middle English form of the language. Therefore, it did not exist in Old English, so choice C is incorrect, and it was not originally a Middle English word, so choice D is incorrect.

Mathematics

1. D: The expression $(x-2)^2$ may be expanded as $x^2 - 4x + 4$. Multiplication of $-3x$ by this expression gives $-3x^3 + 12x^2 - 12x$.

2. B: The sequence $\frac{1}{5} \frac{1}{25} \frac{1}{125} \frac{1}{625}$ ... may be used to represent the situation. Substituting the initial value of $\frac{1}{5}$ and the common ratio of $\frac{1}{5}$ into the formula $S = \frac{a}{1-r}$:

$$S = \frac{\frac{1}{5}}{1-\frac{1}{5}} = \frac{\frac{1}{5}}{\frac{4}{5}} = \frac{1}{4}$$

3. A: The net of a triangular prism has three rectangular faces and two triangular faces, and the rectangular faces must all be able to connect to each other directly. This is shown in choice A.

4. B: Since they are not mutually exclusive events, $P(4 \text{ or } E) = P(4) + P(E) - P(4 \text{ and } E)$. Substituting the probability of each event gives $P(4 \text{ or } E) = \frac{1}{6} + \frac{1}{2} - \frac{1}{6} = \frac{1}{2}$.

5. A: Choice A is correct because second grade students should be able to calculate how money saved can accumulate into a larger amount over time. Choice D, which is expected of first grade students, is too basic for second grade. Choice C is expected of third grade students. Choice B is expected of fifth grade students. Therefore, the correct choice is A.

6. C: Apply the order of operations.

$16 \div (6-4)^2 = 64$	$8 - 2(7-4) = 18$	$2^3 \div 2 - 2(2) = 0$	$2 + 3(2^2) = 20$
$16 \div 2^2 = 64$	$8 - 2(3) = 18$	$8 \div 2 - 2(2) = 0$	$2 + 3(4) = 20$
$16 \div 4 = 64$	$8 - 6 = 18$	$4 - 4 = 0$	$2 + 12 = 20$
$4 \neq 64$	$2 \neq 18$	$0 = 0$	$14 \neq 20$

7. B: Claus has \$20 to spend, so the amount he spends must be less than or equal to ($\leq$) \$20. The entrance fee of \$2.50 is only charged once, so it should not be multiplied by x. The cost of a ticket multiplied by x represents the cost of buying x tickets. The entrance fee plus the cost of the tickets is Claus's total cost: $2.50 + 2x \leq 20$.

8. A: Since area is two dimensional, the units for area have an exponent of 2, such as in^2, yd^2, cm^2, or m^2. Choice B includes a unit of length (yd) and a unit of volume (yd^3). Choice C includes only units of length. Choice C includes a square unit of time (s^2). Therefore, the correct choice is A.

9. B: Since the events are mutually exclusive, the sum of their individual probabilities is 1.0. Subtracting 0.6 from 1.0 yields 0.4. Therefore, the correct choice is B.

10. A: The teacher is using a concrete representation of the concept in question, since the dice she is using are physical objects which help communicate the concept. Verbal, graphic, and pictorial are not correct since the student is not merely observing a discussion about the concept or looking at a graphic representation. Concrete representations often lead to more depth of knowledge and better retention of the concepts.

11. D: We can use the table to find the linear equation in slope-intercept form, $y = mx + b$, where m is the slope and b is the y-intercept. The table shows the y-intercept (the y-value at $x = 0$) to be

−5. The slope is the ratio of the change in y-values to the corresponding change in x-values. As the x-value increases by 1, the y-value increases by 3. Thus, the slope is $\frac{3}{1}$, or 3. So the equation is $y = 3x - 5$.

Only the graphs in choices B and D have a y-intercept at −5. Of these two graphs, only choice D has a y-value increase of 3 for each x-value increase of 1, indicating a slope of 3.

12. C: A line segment with endpoints (x_1, y_1) and (x_2, y_2) has the midpoint $\left(\frac{x_1+x_2}{2}, \frac{y_1+y_2}{2}\right)$. The line segment shown has endpoints (1,2) and (8,8), so its midpoint is $\left(\frac{1+8}{2}, \frac{2+8}{2}\right)$, or (4.5,5).

13. D: The perimeter of the triangle is equal to the sum of the side lengths. The length of the longer diagonal side may be represented as $d = \sqrt{(4-1)^2 + (5-2)^2}$, which simplifies to $d = \sqrt{18}$. The length of the shorter diagonal side may be represented as $d = \sqrt{(6-4)^2 + (2-5)^2}$, which simplifies to $d = \sqrt{13}$. The base length is 5 units. Thus, the perimeter is equal to $5 + \sqrt{18} + \sqrt{13}$, which is approximately 12.85 units. Since each unit represents 5 miles, the total distance she will have walked is equal to the product of 12.85 and 5, or approximately 64 miles.

14. B: The slope of a straight line is a vital concept to understanding linear equations.

15. C: The expression representing the monthly charge for Company A is $\$25 + \$0.05m$, where m is the time in minutes spent talking on the phone. Set this expression equal to the monthly charge for Company B, which is $50. Solve for m to find the number of minutes the two companies charge the same amount.

$$\begin{aligned} \$25 + \$0.05m &= \$50 \\ \$0.05m &= \$25 \\ m &= 500 \end{aligned}$$

Notice that the answer choices are given in hours, not in minutes. Since there are 60 minutes in an hour, $m = \frac{500}{60}$ hours $= 8\frac{1}{3}$ hours. One-third of an hour is 20 minutes, so m is 8 hours and 20 minutes.

16. C: A system of linear equations can be solved by using matrices or by using the graphing, substitution, or elimination (also called linear combination) method. The elimination method is shown here:

$$\begin{aligned} 3x + 4y &= 2 \\ 2x + 6y &= -2 \end{aligned}$$

In order to eliminate x by linear combination, multiply the top equation by 2 and the bottom equation by −3 so that the coefficients of the x-terms will be additive inverses.

$$\begin{aligned} 2(3x + 4y &= 2) \\ -3(2x + 6y &= -2) \end{aligned}$$

Then, add the two equations and solve for y.

$$\begin{aligned} 6x + 8y &= 4 \\ \underline{-6x - 18y} &\underline{= 6} \\ -10y &= 10 \\ y &= -1 \end{aligned}$$

Substitute −1 for y in either of the given equations and solve for x.

$$\begin{aligned} 3x + 4y &= 2 \\ 3x + 4(-1) &= 2 \\ 3x - 4 &= 2 \\ 3x &= 6 \\ x &= 2 \end{aligned}$$

The solution to the system of equations is $(2, -1)$.

17. D: The cross-section is a hexagon.

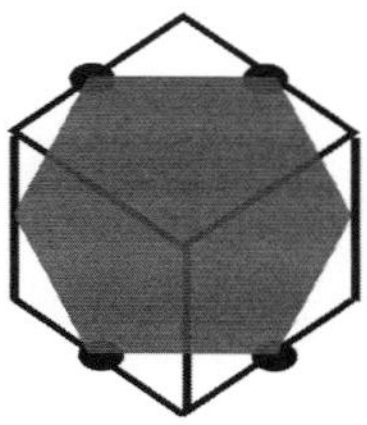

18. D: Since there are 100 homes' market times represented in each set, the median time a home spends on the market is between the 50th and 51st data point in each set. The 50th and 51st data points for Zip Code 1 are six months and seven months, respectively, so the median time a house in Zip Code 1 spends on the market is between six and seven months (6.5 months), which by the realtor's definition of market time is a seven-month market time. The 50th and 51st data points for Zip Code 2 are both thirteen months, so the median time a house in Zip Code 2 spends on the market is thirteen months. Therefore, there is a six-month difference between the median of Zip Code 1 and the median of Zip Code 2.

To find the mean market time for 100 houses, find the sum of the market times and divide by 100. If the frequency of a one-month market time is 9, the number 1 is added nine times (1×9), if the frequency of a two-month market time is 10, the number 2 is added ten times (2×10), and so on. So, to find the average market time, divide by 100 the sum of the products of each market time and its corresponding frequency. For Zip Code 1, the mean market time is 7.38 months, which, by the realtor's definition of market time, is an eight-month market time. For Zip Code 2, the mean market time is 12.74, which, by the realtor's definition of market time, is a thirteen-month market time. Therefore, the difference between the mean of Zip Code 1 and the mean of Zip Code 2 is 5 months.

The mode market time is the market time for which the frequency is the highest. For Zip Code 1, the mode market time is three months, and for Zip Code 2, the mode market time is eleven months. Therefore, the median time a house spends on the market in Zip Code 1 is less than the mean time a house spends on the market in Zip Code 1.

19. C: The amount he donates is equal to 1% of \$45,000. To calculate this value, multiply the two numbers. To multiply a percentage by another number, first convert the percentage to a decimal by changing the percentage sign to a decimal point and moving the decimal point two places to the left. Therefore, $1\% = 0.01$. Now the two numbers can be multiplied: $0.01 \times \$45{,}000 = 1 \times \$450 = \$450$. Thus, he donates \$450.

20. D: This situation may be modeled by an arithmetic sequence, with a common difference of 4 and an initial value of 3. Substituting the common difference and initial value into the formula, $a_n = a_1 + (n-1)d$, gives $a_n = 3 + (n-1)(4)$, which simplifies to $a_n = 4n - 1$.

21. B: The following proportion may be written and solved for x: $\frac{15\text{ ft}}{5\text{ ft}} = \frac{6\text{ ft}}{x\text{ ft}}$. Cross multiplying results in $15x = 30$. Dividing by 15 gives $x = 2$. Thus, the shadow cast by the man is 2 feet in length.

22. C: The probability of tossing a coin and getting heads is $\frac{1}{2}$. Multiply the probability by the number of coin tosses: $\frac{1}{2} \times 300 = 150$. You would expect to get heads about 150 times.

23. B: Since Mr. Mancelli has eight candy bars, he can make at most eight identical bags, each containing a single candy bar and a single package of gum; in this case, however, he will have four packages of gum remaining. To determine the greatest number of prize bags he can make so that no candy bars or packages of gum remain, he needs to find the largest number of groups that both 8 and 12 can be split into. In other words, he must find the greatest common divisor (or greatest common factor) of 8 and 12. The factors of 8 are 1, 2, 4, and 8. The factors of 12 are 1, 2, 3, 4, 6, and 12. The greatest common divisor of 8 and 12 is 4. He can make four prize bags, each of which contains two candy bars and three packages of gum. Therefore, the correct choice is B.

24. C: Addition and subtraction of whole numbers up to 20 using concrete and pictorial models and number sentences is the appropriate level for first-grade students. Numbers up to 1,000 and number pairs are appropriate for third-grade students. Counting by ones and tens is appropriate for kindergarten.

25. A: A hexagon has six sides. A hexagonal prism has 8 faces consisting of two hexagonal bases and six rectangular lateral faces. This results in 18 edges and 12 vertices. Therefore, the correct choice is A.

26. D: The theoretical probability of tossing any particular number is $\frac{1}{6}$. Since she tosses a two $\frac{3}{12}$, or $\frac{1}{4}$ times, the experimental probability of tossing a 2 is greater than the theoretical probability. The experimental probability should grow closer to the experimental probability as she tosses the die more times.

27. C: Substitute 2 for each x and simplify.

$$f(2) = \frac{(2)^3 - 2(2) + 1}{3(2)} = \frac{8 - 4 + 1}{6} = \frac{5}{6}$$

28. C: The distance may be calculated using the distance formula, $d = \sqrt{(x_2 - x_1)^2 + (y_2 - y_1)^2}$. Substitute the given coordinates into the formula.

$$d = \sqrt{\left(4 - (-8)\right)^2 + (3 - 6)^2}$$
$$d = \sqrt{(12)^2 + (-3)^2}$$
$$d = \sqrt{144 + 9}$$
$$d = \sqrt{153}$$

Therefore, the distance between the two points is $\sqrt{153}$.

29. B: $A \cup B$ means "*A* union *B*," or all of the elements in either of the two sets. "*A* union *B*" represents "*A* or *B*," that is, an element is in the union of *A* and *B* if it is in *A* *or* it is in *B*. The elements in sets *A* or *B* are 9, 4, -3, 8, 6, 0, -4, and 2.

30. D: Since there are 100 cm in a meter, on a 1 : 100 scale drawing, each centimeter represents one meter. Therefore, an area of one square centimeter on the drawing represents one square meter in actuality. Since the area of the room in the scale drawing is 30 cm^2, the room's actual area is 30 m^2.

Another way to determine the area of the room is to write and solve an equation, such as this one: $\frac{l}{100} \times \frac{w}{100} = 30 \text{ cm}^2$, where l and w are the dimensions of the actual room.

$$\frac{lw}{10{,}000} = 30 \text{ cm}^2$$
$$\text{Area} = 300{,}000 \text{ cm}^2$$

Since this is not one of the answer choices, convert cm^2 to m^2.

$$300{,}000 \text{ cm}^2 \times \frac{1 \text{ m}}{100 \text{ cm}} \times \frac{1 \text{ m}}{100 \text{ cm}} = 30 \text{ m}^2$$

31. C: If l and w represent the length and width of the enclosed area, its perimeter is equal to $2l + 2w$; since the fence is positioned x feet from the lot's edges on each side, the perimeter of the lot is $2(l + 2x) + 2(w + 2x)$. Since the amount of money saved by fencing the smaller area is \$432, and since the fencing material costs \$12 per linear foot, 36 fewer feet of material are used to fence around the playground than would have been used to fence around the lot. This can be expressed as the following equation.

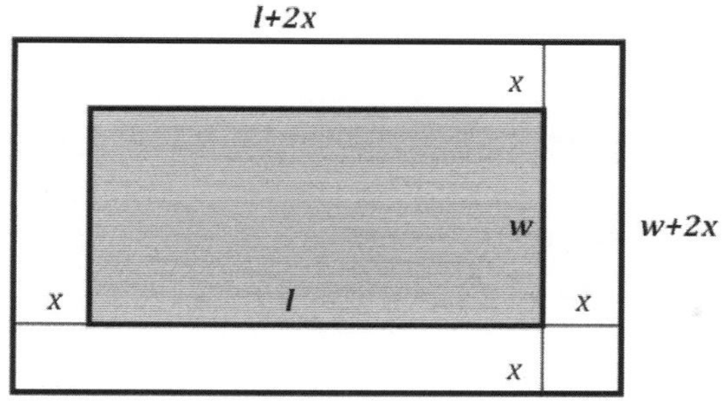

$$2(l + 2x) + 2(w + 2x) - (2l + 2w) = 36$$
$$2l + 4x + 2w + 4x - 2l - 2w = 36$$
$$8x = 36$$
$$x = 4.5 \text{ ft}$$

The difference in the area of the lot and the enclosed space is 141 yd^2, which is the same as 1,269 ft^2. So, $(l + 2x)(w + 2x) - lw = 1{,}269$. Substituting 4.5 for x, we get the following equation that we can solve for $l + w$.

$$(l + 9)(w + 9) - lw = 1{,}269$$
$$lw + 9l + 9w + 81 - lw = 1{,}269$$
$$9l + 9w = 1{,}188$$
$$9(l + w) = 1{,}188$$
$$l + w = 132 \text{ ft}$$

Therefore, the perimeter of the enclosed space, $2(l + w)$, is $2(132) = 264$ ft. The cost of 264 ft of fencing is $264 \times \$12 = \$3{,}168$.

32. C: The line through the center of the box represents the median. The median test score for classes 1 and 2 is 82.

Note that for class 1, the median is a better representation of the data than the mean. There are two low outliers, points which lie outside of two standard deviations from the mean, which bring down the average test score. In cases such as this, the mean is not the best measure of central tendency.

33. B: The problem does not give any information about the size of the bracelet or the spacing between any of the charms. Nevertheless, creating a simple illustration which shows the order of the charms will help when approaching this problem. For example, the circle below represents the bracelet, and the dotted line between A and B represents the clasp. On the right, the line shows the stretched-out bracelet and possible positions of charms C, D, and E based on the parameters.

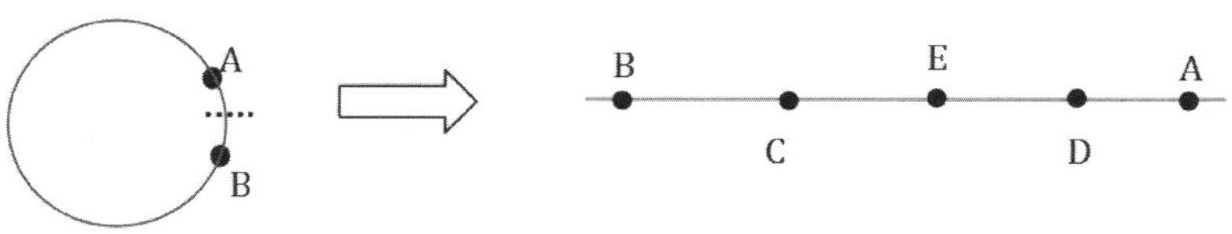

From the drawing above, it appears that statement I is true, but it is not necessarily so. The alternative drawing below also shows the charms ordered correctly, but the distance between B and E is now less than that between D and A.

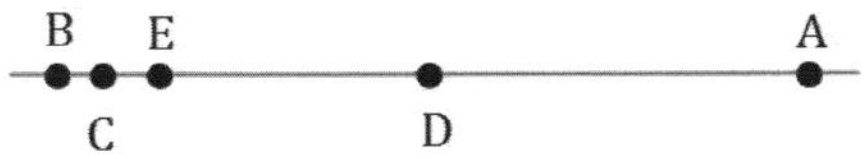

Statement II must be true: charm E must lie between B and D. Statement III must also be true: the distance between charms E and D must be less than that between C and A, which includes charms E and D in the space between them.

34. C: The surface area of a rectangular prism may be calculated using the formula $SA = 2lw + 2wh + 2hl$. Substituting the dimensions of 14 inches, 6 inches, and 8 inches gives $SA = 2(14)(6) + 2(6)(8) + 2(8)(14)$. Thus, the surface area is 488 square inches.

35. D: Let $P(T)$ represent the probability of getting tails on the coin toss. We can see that $P(T) = \frac{1}{2}$. Let $P(P)$ be the chance of getting a prime number on the die. Of the possible outcomes (1 through 6), three are prime (2, 3, and 5), so $P(P) = \frac{3}{6} = \frac{1}{2}$.

Since $P(P)$ and $P(T)$ are not mutually exclusive, $P(P \text{ or } T) = P(P) + P(T) - P(P \text{ and } T)$. Because the events are independent, $P(P \text{ and } T) = P(P) \times P(T)$. Substituting the probability of each event gives $P(P \text{ or } T) = \frac{1}{2} + \frac{1}{2} - \left(\frac{1}{2} \times \frac{1}{2}\right) = \frac{1}{2} + \frac{1}{2} - \frac{1}{4} = \frac{3}{4}$.

36. C: A number that is divisible by 6 is divisible by 2 and 3. A number is divisible by 2 if it is even, and it is divisible by 3 if the sum of the digits is divisible by 3. For example, the number 12 is divisible by 2 and 3, so it is also divisible by 6.

37. A: Marcus needs $325 for the new gaming system. If he earns $6.50 an hour, the number of hours he needs to work can be determined by dividing $325 by $6.50 which is written as $\frac{325}{6.50} = x$. Multiplying both sides of the equation by 6.50 yields $6.50x = 325$.

38. B: The perimeter is equal to the sum of the lengths of the two bases, 2 and 6 units, and the diagonal distances of the other two sides. Using the distance formula, each side length may be represented as $d = \sqrt{20} = 2\sqrt{5}$. Thus, the sum of the two sides is equal to $2\sqrt{20}$, or $4\sqrt{5}$. The whole perimeter is equal to $8 + 4\sqrt{5}$.

39. B: Notice that $x = 1$ results in a zero in the denominator, so choice C cannot be correct since $x \neq 1$. To solve, subtract $\frac{2}{x-1}$ from both sides, then cross-multiply.

$\frac{x-2}{x-1} = \frac{x-1}{x+1} + \frac{2}{x-1}$	Write out the original equation.
$\frac{x-4}{x-1} = \frac{x-1}{x+1}$	Subtract $\frac{2}{x-1}$ from both sides.
$(x+1)(x-4) = (x-1)(x-1)$	Cross multiply.
$x^2 - 3x - 4 = x^2 - 2x + 1$	Multiply the binomials on both sides.
$-3x - 4 = -2x + 1$	Subtract x^2 from both sides.
$-4 = x + 1$	Add $3x$ to both sides.
$-5 = x$	Subtract 1 from both sides.

40. D: Since the pentagon is regular, all the sides are equal, and the shape is convex. Because of this, there are enough constraints to determine the area as a function of the side length of the pentagon.

Science

1. A: Animals of the phylum Mollusca or mollusks, respire (breathe) through gills. Respiration is the process of taking in oxygen and releasing carbon dioxide. Mollusca consists of several classes that include species as diverse as chitons, clams, land and marine snails, and squid. This represents a diverse range of body structures. Many mollusks have a mantle that includes a cavity that is used for both breathing and excretion. Within the mantle are gills (ctenidia). Mollusks do not have tracheas. Some land snails have a respiratory cavity that is often called a lung but is not a true lung. Spiders, which are not mollusks (they are arachnids), have a type of lungs called book lungs. Muscle contraction is not required for the gills to function. Other structures, such as cilia, work to pass water over the gills.

2. D: The equation for power, $power = \frac{work}{time}$, can be utilized. The mass of the object (10 kg) and the distance (10 m) can be used to calculate work, $work = mass \times (gravitational\ acceleration) \times distance$. The value for time is provided.

3. B: Gradualism states that evolution occurs slowly, with organisms exhibiting small changes over long periods of time. According to gradualism, the fossil record should show gradual changes over time. Punctuated equilibrium states that evolution occurs in spurts of sudden change. According to punctuated equilibrium, the fossil record should have large gaps.

4. D: Igneous rocks are formed when magma in the Earth erupts through cracks in the crust. There, the lava cools, creating a hard structure with many air pockets or holes.

5. A: In the food chain of tree → caterpillar → frog → snake → hawk → worm, the tree is at the trophic level with the greatest amount of energy. Trophic level refers to the position of an organism in a food chain. Energy is lost according to the laws of thermodynamics as one moves up the food chain because it is converted to heat when consumers consume. Primary producers, such as autotrophs, are organisms who are at the base and capture solar energy. Primary consumers are herbivores that feed on the producers. Secondary consumers consume primary consumers and so on. Decomposers get their energy from the consumption of dead plants and animals.

6. B: Temperature is a measure of the kinetic energy of particles. As temperature increases, the average kinetic energy also increases. As the gas particles move more rapidly, they occupy a larger volume. The increase in speed of the individual particles combined with the greater distance over which any intermolecular forces must act results in a decrease in the intermolecular forces.

7. B: An apple turning brown is an example of a chemical change; in this case, oxidation. During a chemical change, one substance is changed into another. Sublimation of water refers to the conversion between the solid and the gaseous phases of matter, with no intermediate liquid stage. This is a phase change, not a chemical reaction. Dissolution of salt in water refers to a physical change since the salt and water can be separated again by evaporating the water. Pulverized rock is an example of a physical change where the form has changed but not the substance itself.

8. C: Covalent compounds are usually formed by the combination of two or more non-metallic elements with one another. In these compounds, atoms share electrons. Ionic compounds are most often formed between a metal and a nonmetal. Organic compounds are covalent compounds that contain carbon and hydrogen atoms. Some of the compounds formed by non-metallic elements are polar, but not all of them.

9. C: Vinegar fizzing when poured on a rock is an example of chemical weathering. Mechanical and chemical weathering are processes that break down rocks. Mechanical weathering breaks down rocks physically but does not change their chemical composition. Frost and abrasion are examples. Water, oxygen, carbon dioxide, and living organisms can lead to the chemical weathering of rock. Vinegar is a weak acid and will undergo a chemical reaction, evidenced by fizzing, with the rock. Choice A, rain freezing on the roadway, is an example of the phase change of water from a liquid to a solid and may lead to physical weathering. Choice B, ivy growing on the side of a wooden house, is incorrect since the house is not a rock. Choice D, a river carrying sediment downstream, is an example of erosion.

10. A: Descriptive studies look at and analyze the characteristics of a population or compare aspects across multiple populations. These studies seek information about the state of a population as it is rather than experimentally investigating cause-and-effect relationships by manipulating variables and observing outcomes. Comparing the heights of male and female penguins is an example of a descriptive study. The subject is strictly an observable measure (height) of established populations (male and female). For the other studies, the focus is on the cause-and-effect relationship between a manipulated variable (different media, drug vs. placebo, and old vs. new descriptions) and a result of interest (growth rate, drug efficacy, sales).

11. D: The temperature of a substance during the time of any phase change remains the same. In this case, the phase change was from liquid to solid, or freezing. Latent heat of fusion, in this case, is energy that is released from the substance as it reforms its solid form. This energy will be released and the liquid will turn to solid before the temperature of the substance will decrease further. If the substance were changing from solid to liquid, the heat of fusion would be the amount of heat required to break apart the attractions between the molecules in the solid form to change to the liquid form. The latent heat of fusion is exactly the same quantity of energy for a substance for either melting or freezing. Depending on the process, this amount of heat would either be absorbed by the substance (melting) or released (freezing).

12. D: Chemical equations must be balanced on each side of the reaction. Balancing means the total number of atoms stays the same, but their arrangement within specific reactants and products can change. The law of conservation of matter states that matter can never be created or destroyed. Heat may be absorbed or released in a reaction; these are classified as endothermic and exothermic reactions, respectively. The rate of the reaction increases with temperature for most reactions.

13. C: Fossils are least likely to be found in igneous rock. Igneous rock is formed by extreme heat as magma escapes through the Earth's crust and cools. The remains of plants and animals in fossil form are not usually preserved under these conditions. Sedimentary rock (A) is where most fossils are found. Sedimentary rock is formed more slowly and is very abundant. Since soft mud and silts compress into layers, organisms can also be deposited. Metamorphic rock (B) is rock that has undergone change by heat and pressure. This usually destroys any fossils, but occasionally fossil remains are simply distorted and can be found in metamorphic rock.

14. B: It is true that rocks are classified by their formation and the minerals they contain, while minerals are classified by their chemical composition and physical properties. Choice A is incorrect because rocks may contain traces of organic compounds. Choices C and D are incorrect because only minerals can be polymorphs and only rocks contain mineraloids.

15. D: Isotopes are variations of an element that have different numbers of neutrons. The various isotopes of an element have the same numbers of protons and electrons. For example, carbon has three naturally occurring isotopes: carbon-12, carbon-13 and carbon-14 (which is radioactive). Isotopes of an element differ in mass number, which is the number of protons and neutrons added together, but have the same atomic number, or number of protons.

16. B: If a gas and a liquid are placed in a sealed container, cooling the liquid will help dissolve the gas into the liquid. Gases have higher solubility in liquids at lower temperatures. At higher temperatures, the gas molecules will have more kinetic energy and will have enough energy to overcome intermolecular interactions with the liquid solvent and leave the solution. This also explains why heating the liquid is incorrect. Shaking the container is also incorrect as this would give the gas energy to escape. Decreasing the pressure on the lid may or may not significantly affect the pressure inside the vessel depending on the nature of the vessel, but decreasing the pressure inside the vessel would decrease the solubility of the gas in the liquid.

17. B: The freezing point of sea water is lower than that of fresh water as sea water is denser. It is denser because it has more dissolved salts. The freezing point changes with salinity, pressure, and density, but can be as low as –2 °C (28.4 °F), compared with 0 °C (32 °F) for fresh water.

18. C: Tropical climate zones are characterized by frequent rainfall, especially during the monsoon season, and by moderate temperatures that vary little from season to season or between night and day. Tropical zones do experience frequent rainfall, which leads to abundant vegetation.

19. D: The process whereby a radioactive element releases energy slowly over a long period of time to lower its energy and become more stable is best described as decay. The nucleus undergoing decay, known as the parent nuclide, spontaneously releases energy most commonly through the emission of an alpha particle, a beta particle, or a gamma ray. The changed nucleus, called the daughter nuclide, is now more stable than the parent nuclide, although the daughter nuclide may undergo another decay to an even more stable nucleus. A decay chain is a series of decays of a radioactive element into different elements.

20. A: A lysosome is an organelle that is thought to be linked to the aging process and contains digestive enzymes that break down food and unneeded substances. Chromatin is the structure created by DNA and various proteins in the cell's nucleus during interphase and condenses to form chromosomes. Plastids are found in plants and algae. They often contain pigments and usually help make chemical compounds for the plant. The Golgi apparatus prepares macromolecules like proteins and lipids for transport.

21. C: On a topographic map, an area where the contour lines are very close together indicates that the slope is very steep. Lines very far apart would indicate a more gradual change in elevation. Contour lines help represent the actual shape of the Earth's surface features and geographic landmarks like rivers, lakes, and vegetation. Topographic maps also show man-made features such as roads, dams, and major buildings. They are based on aerial photography, and the quadrangle maps are produced in various scales. The 7.5-minute quadrangle is very common and provides a 1:24,000 scale, where 1 inch represents 2,000 feet.

22. A: The average distance from the earth to the sun is equal to one astronomical unit (AU). An AU is equal to 93 million miles and is far smaller than a light-year or a parsec. A light-year is defined as the distance light can travel in a vacuum in one year, and is equal to roughly 63,241 AU. A parsec is the parallax of one arcsecond and is equal to 2.0626×10^5 astronomical units.

23. D: Sound cannot travel through a vacuum, though it doesn't necessarily suggest that it *can* travel through solids. Nor does the fact that atoms are packed tightly together demonstrate the fact that sound can travel through a solid. The fact that a sound is produced by knocking on a solid object also does not prove sound can pass through the object. However, if you hear a sound on the other side of a solid wall, the sound must have traveled through the wall.

24. A: Anthophyta is a division of plants that produces seeds as part of reproduction. Spermatopyta is the broader group that includes all plants that produce seeds for reproduction, which includes gymnosperms and angiosperms (the same group as anthophyta). Anthophyta are also known as the group that contains flowering plants. It is the largest and most diverse grouping of plants and includes many food, clothing, and medicinal uses for humans. Grains, beans, nuts, fruits, vegetables, spices, tea, coffee, chocolate, cotton, linen, and aspirin are all derived from plants from anthophyta. Lycophyta is a small group of plants including club mosses and scale trees. Sphenophyta contains about thirty species including horsetails, foxtails, or scouring rushes. Pterophyta contains non-seed plants like ferns. Lycophyta, sphenophyta, and pterophyta all use spores to reproduce sexually.

25. A: A magnetic field is created by a spin magnetic dipole moment and the orbital magnetic dipole moment of the electrons in atoms. Therefore, it is the spinning and rotating of electrons in atoms that creates a magnetic field. The separation of charged particles in atoms describes the nucleus and electron clouds within an atom. The vibrational and translational motion of atoms creates thermal energy. Loosely held valence electrons surrounding an atom indicates a good electrical conductor.

26. D: The asteroid belt in our solar system is located between Mars and Jupiter. The asteroid belt is populated by asteroids and dwarf planets that are distributed thinly enough that spacecraft can pass through the belt with relative ease.

27. D: In a parallel circuit, the voltage is the same for all three paths. Because the resistance is different on each path but the voltage is the same, Ohm's law dictates that the current will also be different for each path. Ohm's law says that current is inversely related to resistance. Therefore, the current will be greatest in path C as it has the least resistance, 2 ohms.

28. D: Both liquids and gases are fluids and therefore flow, but only gases are compressible. The molecules that make up a gas are very far apart, allowing the gas to be compressed into a smaller volume.

29. C: The Sun's energy is the energy source behind Earth's weather patterns, but since the Sun's energy only directly reaches a fraction of Earth's landmass, other factors play an enormous role in distributing the energy globally. The ocean absorbs the Sun's energy and transports it throughout the world, acting as the primary driving force behind global climate and weather. Wind belts, the Earth's orbit, and atmospheric conditions also play a role in driving global weather.

30. A: Repetition is the only way to prove that an experiment is reliable. If an experiment can't be successfully repeated with the same outcome, one cannot determine that the experimental results are valid. Repetition is the key to scientific progress.

31. C: The first step is to identify a problem and propose a solution. Trying the solution comes next, followed by evaluation and reporting the results.

32. B: When young children pour sand, water, rice, etc., from one container to another, differently sized (or shaped) container, they are developing basic measurement concepts. Children fitting pegs into matching holes (A) are developing basic 1:1 correspondence concepts. Seeing how many coins they have put into their piggy bank (C) helps children develop basic counting concepts. Separating toys into piles according to type (D), color, shape, size, or any other characteristic helps children develop basic classification/categorization concepts.

33. B: When scientists and students are able to identify patterns and find meaning in the results of their experiments, they are using the process skill of Inference. When they use the results of their experiments to formulate new hypotheses (A), they are using the process skill of Prediction. When they identify the properties of objects or situations using their senses, they are using the process skill of Observation. When they report the results of their experiments and their conclusions based on these results to others (D), they are using the process skill of Communication. These skills are required for solving both math and science problems.

34. C: Magnets do not have to be touching to attract or repel materials; they are able to do this from a distance. However, magnets do NOT work beyond their magnetic fields (D): the magnetic field is defined as the effective range or area of a magnet, so magnets only work within their magnetic fields by definition. Opposite poles of magnets do NOT repel (A), but instead attract each other. Conversely, the like poles of magnets do NOT attract (B), but instead repel one another.

35. B: Mass is the amount of matter in an object. Weight is the measure of the pull of gravity on an object.

36. A: Three ways of transmitting heat are conduction (A), convection (B), and radiation (C). When heat is transmitted through solids, this is done via conduction. Conduction occurs between solid materials directly contacting one another. Convection (B) is how heat travels through liquids and gases. Heat makes them expand, lowering their density so they rise. When they cool, they recover density and fall. This heating-rising and cooling-falling process creates a current known as convection. Radiation (C), like the heat from the sun, occurs when electromagnetic waves travel through space and transfer heat to objects, like the Earth, that they touch. Therefore, (D) is incorrect.

37. D: Lower seed dispersal is not an advantage that angiosperms show over other types of plants. Gymnosperms, for example, have plentiful amounts of pollen, but it does not always hit its mark.

Angiosperms are the most recently evolved plant division and contain at least 260,000 extant species. They are very diverse and occupy many habitats. Many other species in other plant divisions do not have true leaves. Gymnosperms have modified leaves in the form of needles. Double fertilization refers to how one sperm cell fuses with an ovule, forming the zygote. The second sperm forms into a triploid endosperm that provides energy for the embryo.

38. C: The best control group would be women with wrinkles around their eyes using a cream that has no effect. A scientific control group is used to minimize the unintended influence of other variables on a scientific study. Such extraneous variables include researcher bias, environmental changes, and biological variation. Scientific controls ensure that data are valid and are a vital part of the scientific method.

39. C: All typical living organisms need food, water, sunlight, and air. Shelter, space, and nurturing are essential for most organisms, but they are technically indirect needs that are not crucial to sustaining life.

40. A: Before drawing a conclusion about a hypothesis, one should test it, observe it, and record data about the test results. In the discussion of many scientific papers, scientists will compare and contrast their data to the findings of other groups. The methods of an experiment should be written so an experiment can be replicated.

Social Studies

1. D: In the Dred Scott decision of 1857, the Court ruled that no slave or descendant of slaves could ever be a United States citizen. It also declared the Missouri Compromise of 1820 to be unconstitutional, clearing the way for the expansion of slavery in new American territories. This ruling pleased Southerners and outraged the North, further dividing the nation and setting the stage for war.

2. C: Lying at a little more than 23° south of the equator, the Tropic of Capricorn is the border between the Southern Temperate Zone to the south and the Tropical Zone to the north. The southern hemisphere is tilted toward the sun to its maximum extent each year at the winter solstice in December. The northernmost latitude at which the sun can appear directly overhead is at the Tropic of Cancer during the summer solstice. The northern and southern hemispheres are separated by the equator at 0° latitude. The eastern and western hemispheres are separated by the prime meridian at 0° longitude.

3. B: The Seven Years' War was a global military conflict. In the Americas, the conflict was largely between Western European countries, particularly Great Britain and France.

4. A: The inaccurate statement is the Puritans unconditionally supported the English Reformation. While they agreed with the Reformation in principle, they felt that it had not pursued those principles far enough and should make greater reforms. Similarly, they felt that the Church of England (or Anglican Church), though it had separated from the Catholic Church in the Protestant Reformation, still allowed many practices they found too much like Catholicism. The Puritans did become a chief political power in England because of the first English Civil War between Royalists and Parliamentarians. The Royalists had a profound suspicion of the radical Puritans. Among the Parliament's elements of resistance, the strongest was that of the Puritans. They joined in the battle initially for ostensibly political reasons as others had, but soon they brought more attention to religious issues. Following the Restoration in 1660 and the Uniformity Act of 1662, thereby restoring the Church of England to its pre-English Civil War status, the great majority of Puritan clergy defected from the Church of England. It is also accurate that the Puritans in England disagreed about separating from the Church of England. Some Puritans desired complete separation; they were known first as Separatists and after the Restoration as Dissenters. Others did not want complete separation but instead desired further reform in the Church of England. While they remained part of the Church of England, they were called Non-Separating Puritans, and after the Restoration, they were called Nonconformists.

5. B: During the early Medieval period (or Middle Ages), Europe was characterized by widespread illiteracy, ignorance, and superstition once the unifying influence of the Roman Empire was lost. Few universities, like the university at Constantinople founded in 2 AD and those at Athens, Antioch, and Alexandria around the same time, existed then. Before the 5th and 6th centuries C.E., any education was conducted at cathedral or monastery schools or privately in the homes of wealthy families, which cannot be considered "main centers of literacy." More religious schools were created through Charlemagne's reforms in the 9th century, and early forms of universities began developing in the 11th and 12th centuries.

6. C: There are no formal qualifications for members of the judicial branch. However, having a background in law is an informal qualification that is considered when appointing Article III judges.

7. C: Paul Revere and William Dawes were both dispatch riders who set out on horseback from Massachusetts to spread news of British troop movements across the American countryside around the beginning of the War of Independence. John Parker was the captain of the Minutemen militia, who were waiting for the British at Lexington, Massachusetts. Samuel Prescott, a young physician, joined Paul Revere and William Dawes along their route.

8. C: Physical geography focuses on processes and patterns in the natural environment. What people eat in any given geographic region is largely dependent on such environmental factors as climate and the availability of arable land. Religion, family, and language may all be affected by geographical factors, but they are not as immediately affected as dietary preferences.

9. A: The phenomenon of "sticky prices" refers to prices that stay the same even though it seems they should change (either increasing or decreasing).

10. A: The 10th Amendment establishes that any power not given to the federal government in the Constitution belongs to the states or the people. The federal and local governments share many responsibilities.

11. C: The Mason-Dixon Line was the manifestation of a border dispute between the British colonies of Pennsylvania, Maryland, and Delaware. It effectively separated, or illustrated, a cultural divide between North and South before the Civil War.

12. A: The Age of Enlightenment was a time of scientific and philosophical achievement. Also called the Age of Reason, it was a time when human thought and reason were prized.

13. A: Rivers promoted the development of the ancient river valley civilizations of the world, including in the Middle East, India, and China. Rivers not only supply water for drinking and crop irrigation, but also provide fertile soil, vegetation for shade cover, food, building materials, and animal life. They additionally allow water travel to other locations. Although some peoples have settled and lived in deserts, they are among the most inhospitable climates. Forests also provide plenty of flora and fauna and exist in areas receiving enough rainfall, but rivers have been historically superior in attracting human societies. Mountains near living areas provide protective barriers; however, though some peoples live there, as in deserts, living in the mountains is difficult due to high altitudes, harsh climates, poor soil for planting, and rough terrain.

14. B: Discretionary spending is dedicated to transportation, education, national resources, the environment, and international affairs. State and local governments use this money to help finance programs. Mandatory spending covers entitlements such as Medicare, Social Security, Federal Retirement, and Medicaid.

15. C: Thomas Jefferson embraced John Locke's concept of separation of church and state. Deism posits that a Supernatural force created the world and universe, but that He did not intervene after creation. Jefferson wanted minimal central governing, just as he viewed the Creator's relationship with the universe.

16. A: Checks and balances were established to keep one branch of government from taking too much authority. When Johnson violated the Tenure of Office Act by replacing Secretary of War Edwin Stanton, Johnson was impeached, but the final vote in the Senate trial came up one vote short of the number needed to convict him.

17. D: The Bill of Rights was drafted by Congress to limit the authority of the government and protect the rights of individual citizens from abuse by the federal government. It was the first document to detail the rights of private citizens.

18. C: If a country's currency increases in value, foreigners will have to give up more of their own currency to get the original country's currency in order to buy the original country's goods and services. This will cause a drop in exports. At the same time, it will be less expensive for people in the original country to exchange their currency for foreign currencies, causing the price of imported goods to drop and the total value of imports to rise.

19. B: There was not a reduction in military spending after the war. Although the manufacturing demand for war supplies and the size of the military decreased, the government had increased military spending from $10 billion in 1947 to more than $50 billion by 1953—a more than fivefold increase. This increase strengthened the American economy. Other factors contributing to the strengthened economy included the significantly higher birth rates during the Baby Boom from 1946 to 1957, which stimulated the growth of the building and automotive industries by increased demand. Government programs, such as the GI Bill (the Servicemen's Readjustment Act of 1944), other veterans' benefits, and the National Defense Education Act all encouraged college enrollments, which increased by nearly four times. Additionally, larger families, increased mobility and low-interest loans offered to veterans led to suburban development and growth as well as increased home construction. Improvements in public health were also results of the new affluence; the rate of infant deaths decreased significantly, and as a result, from 1946–1957, the American life span rose from 67 to 71 years. Moreover, Dr. Jonas Salk developed the polio vaccine in 1955, which virtually wiped out poliomyelitis, preventing many deaths and disabilities in children.

20. C: The Civil Rights Act of 1964 affected the Jim Crow laws in the Southern states. Many minorities suffered under unfair voting laws and segregation. President Lyndon Johnson signed the Civil Rights Act of 1964 into law after the 1963 assassination of President Kennedy, who championed the reform.

21. D: Judaism has existed since around 1300 BC according to historians' estimates. The Greek religion of Stoicism was founded by Zeno in Athens around 313 BC, almost 1,000 years later than Judaism. Confucianism was founded in China by Confucius, who lived from 551 to 479 BC, around 800 years after Judaism. Christianity dates to approximately 30 AD in Israel.

22. D: A market failure is any situation in which the production of a good or service is not efficient. In the cases listed, non-competitive markets allow for the underpayment of labor and the underproduction of a good or service; externalities are negative consequences assumed by parties not involved in a transaction; and public goods are an example of a good the market will not produce at all, or at efficient levels.

23. C: The Druids were neither ignored nor tolerated by the Romans. Conversely, the Druids were viewed as "non-Roman" and therefore were suppressed. Augustus (63 BC–14 AD) forbade Romans to practice Druid rites. According to Pliny, the Senate under Tiberius (42 BC–37 AD) issued a decree suppressing Druids, and in 54 AD, Claudius outlawed Druid rites entirely. It is correct that the Romans generally protected the Jews up until the rebellion in Judea in 66 AD. In fact, Julius Caesar circumvented the Roman laws against "secret societies" by designating Jewish synagogues as "colleges," which in essence permitted Jews to have freedom of worship. After the rebellion in Judea, according to Suetonius, the Emperor Claudius appeared to have expelled all Jews, probably including early Christians, from Rome. The Roman Empire viewed Christianity as a Jewish sect, which was how Christianity began, for 200 years following its emergence. It is also correct that according to Tacitus, when much of the public saw the Emperor Nero as responsible for the Great Fire of Rome in 64 AD, Nero blamed the Christians for the fire in order to deflect guilt from himself. Following their persecution of Jews, the Roman Empire would continue to persecute Christians for the next two centuries.

24. A: Along with stock market speculation, a major cause of the Great Depression was an increased supply of cars, radios, and other goods that was not matched by consumer demand. Industrial production far exceeded the population's purchasing power. Farmers were plagued by overproduction and falling prices while international trade suffered from rising tariffs.

25. B: The President may veto legislation passed by Congress. The executive branch has this "check" on the legislative branch.

26. B: Structural unemployment is unemployment that results from a mismatch of job skills or location. In this case, Ivy's job skill—her ability to work as a seamstress—is no longer desired by employers. Frictional and cyclical are other forms of unemployment; economists do not use the term careless unemployment.

27. B: The only true statement is the March on Versailles was made primarily by women. Therefore, an equal number of both men and women did not undertake the March on Versailles. The women took action because of the dire economic conditions from which they suffered, especially the high prices on bread and food shortages. The storming of the Bastille occurred on July 14, 1789; the March on Versailles occurred on October 5, 1789, almost three months later, not prior to it. (The date of July 14th is so famous as Bastille Day in France that generally it is familiar in other countries as well.) It is not true that the March on Versailles was not effective in accomplishing its purpose. In fact, the marchers did achieve their goal: They stormed the palace and killed several guards. La Fayette, in charge of the National Guard to control the mob, convinced the royals to move from Versailles to Paris and to stop blocking the National Assembly, and the royal family complied with these demands. The women did not march right to Versailles with no preliminaries. First, they assembled in markets around Paris and marched to the Hôtel de Ville. There they made their demands of the Paris city officials. When those officials did not give acceptable responses, the women then joined a march to the palace at Versailles. While the march to Versailles included men and weapons, some 7,000 women made up the majority of the marchers.

28. D: America is a common law country because English common law was adopted in all states except Louisiana. Common law is based on precedent and changes over time. Each state develops its own common laws.

29. C: George Washington served 2 four-year terms as president. This interval of time was not specified in the Constitution, but future presidents followed suit (until FDR).

30. A: Presidents may veto legislation passed by both houses of Congress, and in turn Congress can override a presidential veto with a 2/3 majority. These governmental practices are a further manifestation that each branch of government is watched by the other branches and, when necessary, can undo a decision it deems ill-advised or unconstitutional.

31. C: The President must be a natural citizen, be at least 35 years old, and have lived in the US for 14 years. There is no education requirement for becoming President. Truman did not have a college education, but most Presidents have had college degrees.

32. B: Growth of industry was concentrated in urban areas, which cyclically drew laborers into cities, growing the population of cities and increasing efficiency and quality in industry.

33. B: The Trail of Tears was the forcible removal of Native American tribes from their homes in the Southeastern US to Oklahoma. The name came due to the high number of Native Americans who died on the journey.

34. B: Tropical regions near the Equator tend to experience relatively constant temperatures year-round because the angle at which sunlight hits them remains relatively constant throughout the year. In regions that are farther north or south, the angle at which sunlight hits them changes much more drastically due to the changing angle of the Earth's axis relative to the Sun. This results in greater variations in the length of daylight and in temperatures. Tropical regions do have seasons (usually a "wet" season and a "dry" season), but temperature fluctuations are less pronounced than those in regions farther from the Equator.

35. C: Copernicus's *De Revolutionibus Orbium Coelestium (On the Revolutions of the Heavenly Spheres)* was published in 1543, almost simultaneously with his death. He was the first to contradict the then-accepted belief that the Earth was the center of the universe and the Sun and other bodies moved around it. This geocentric model was associated with Ptolemy and hence called the Ptolemaic system. Galileo Galilei published Siderius Nuncius (Starry Messenger) in 1610. In it, he revealed his observations, made through his improvements to the telescope, which corroborated Copernicus's theory. Sir Isaac Newton (1642–1727) built the first usable reflecting telescope and erased any lingering doubts about a heliocentric universe by describing universal gravitation and showing its congruence with Kepler's laws of planetary motion.

36. B: Members of the House are elected for two-year terms. Senators serve six-year terms, but the elections are staggered so roughly one-third of the Senate is elected every two years.

37. A: A city located at 6,000 feet above sea level is likely to have a cooler climate, all other things being equal. Since air is less dense at higher altitudes, it holds heat less effectively, and temperatures tend to be lower as a result. Precipitation is not as strong an indicator of temperature. Some areas that receive moderate or large amounts of precipitation are cooler (temperate and continental climates), while some areas that receive lots of precipitation, like the tropics, are warmer.

38. D: Niccolò Machiavelli, perhaps best known for his book The Prince, was an Italian Renaissance political philosopher noted for writing more realistic representations and rational interpretations of politics. In The Prince, he popularized the political concept of "the ends justify the means." Dante Alighieri was a great poet famous for his Commedia (additionally labeled Divina by contemporary poet and author Boccaccio, who wrote the Decameron and other works) or Divine Comedy, a trilogy consisting of Inferno, Purgatorio, and Paradiso (Hell, Purgatory, and Heaven). Dante's work helped propel the transition from the Medieval period to the Renaissance. Francesco Petrarca, known in English as Petrarch, was famous for his lyrical poetry, particularly sonnets.

39. B: The Bluebonnet is the state flower of Texas. The Blue Lacy is the state dog and the Lone Star is the state symbol. The song Yellow Rose of Texas dates back to at least the 1850s though its true origins are unknown. In approximately the 1950's Emily West, a folk hero from the Texas revolution, came to be associated with the song.

40. D: It is not true that the Gilded Age is a term whose origins have not been identified clearly. In 1873, Mark Twain and Charles Dudley Warner co-authored a book entitled *The Gilded Age: A Tale of Today*. Twain and Warner first coined this term to describe the extravagance and excesses of America's wealthy upper class, who became richer than ever due to industrialization. Furthermore, the Gilded Age was the era of the "robber barons" such as John D. Rockefeller, Cornelius Vanderbilt, J.P. Morgan, and others. Because they accumulated enormous wealth through extremely aggressive and occasionally unethical monetary manipulations, critics dubbed them "robber barons" because they seemed to be elite lords of robbery. While these business tycoons grasped huge fortunes, some of them—such as Andrew Carnegie and Andrew Mellon—were also philanthropists, using their wealth to support and further worthy causes such as literacy, education, health care, charities, and the arts. They donated millions of dollars to fund social improvements. Carnegie himself dubbed this large philanthropic movement the "Gospel of Wealth." Another characteristic of the Gilded Age was the Beaux Arts architectural style, a neo-Renaissance style modeled after the great architectural designs of the European Renaissance. The Panic of 1893 ended the Gilded Age and began a severe four-year economic depression. The Progressive Era followed these events.

Practice Test #3

English

Refer to the following for question 1:

Ms. Baird assigns students a historical fiction short story to read. She wants to check her students' individual comprehension skills, specifically their ability to support an idea with evidence from the text. However, one student appears to be struggling with the story. Ms. Baird gives this student a graphic organizer containing the following sentence stems: *Someone, Wanted, But, So, Then.*

1. Which scenario is the best way to accomplish Ms. Baird's goals of assessing individual comprehension skills?

a. Split the students into groups after reading the text as a class and allow them to work together on a worksheet activity she has designed.
b. Play a game in which Ms. Baird posts a card with a main idea. Students read silently and independently and raise their hands to answer when they have found a transition in the plot.
c. As a class, brainstorm main ideas, topics, or concepts from a text. Allow students to choose a select number of these ideas and copy them onto separate index cards. The students then should individually review the text, recording any supporting evidence on the notecard with the applicable main idea.
d. Administer a comprehension quiz during class. Allow students to switch papers and grade each other's work. Next, students can spend the remainder of the class period discussing the answers so that each one understands the text fully.

2. Another name for a persuasive essay is:

a. Dynamic essay
b. Convincing essay
c. Argumentative essay
d. Position paper

3. The teacher and her students brainstorm a list of talents, skills, and specialized knowledge belonging to members of the class. Some of the items on the list include how to make a soufflé, how to juggle, and how to teach a dog to do tricks. One student knows a great deal about spiders, and another knows about motorcycles. The teacher asks the students to each write an essay about something they are good at or know a great deal about. What kind of essay is she asking the students to produce?

a. Cause and effect
b. Compare/contrast
c. Expository
d. Argumentative

4. What is the primary reason the early 21st century has been referred to as the Information Age?

a. Most organizations need more information than ever before.
b. There are more sources and outputs of information than ever before.
c. Privacy and the protection of information are more important than ever before.
d. People are seeking more information about a wider variety of topics than ever before.

5. Which choice constitutes the best method for building conceptual vocabulary?

a. Using word webs to organize thinking about related terms
b. Previewing vocabulary words for upcoming units in other subjects such as science or social studies
c. Implementing a framework for introducing students to various concepts over time
d. Practicing sight words

6. A third-grade teacher has several students reading above grade level. Most of the remaining students are reading at grade level. There are also a few students reading below grade level. She decides to experiment. Her hypothesis is that by giving the entire class a chapter book above grade level, high-level readers will be satisfied, grade-level readers will be challenged in a positive way, and students reading below grade level will be inspired to improve. Her method is most likely to:

a. Succeed, producing students reading at an Instructional reading level. High-level readers will be happy to be given material appropriate to their reading level. Grade-level readers will challenge themselves to improve reading strategies in order to master the text. Because only a few of the students are reading below grade level, the other students, who feel happy and energized, will inspire the slower readers by modeling success.
b. Succeed, producing students reading at an Independent reading level. High-level readers will independently help grade-level readers who will, in turn, independently help those below grade level.
c. Fail, producing students at a Frustration reading level. Those reading below grade level are likely to give up entirely. Those reading at grade level are likely to get frustrated and form habits that will actually slow down their development.
d. Fail, producing students reading at a Chaotic reading level. By nature, children are highly competitive. The teacher has not taken into consideration multiple learning styles. The children who are at grade level will either become bitter and angry at those whose reading level is above grade level or simply give up. The children reading below grade level will not be able to keep up and will in all likelihood act out their frustration or completely shut down.

7. A teacher is working with a group of English language learners. She asks them to take two pieces of paper. At the top of the first paper, they are to write *SAME*, and at the top of the other, *DIFFERENT*. Each child will consider what his native country and the United States have in common, and what distinct features each country possesses. The children are using which method in organizing their ideas?

a. Hunt and peck
b. Consider and persuade
c. Evaluate and contrast
d. Compare and contrast

8. Which of the following reflects MLA guidelines for citing internet sources with regard to page numbers in in-text citations in research papers?

a. A source from the internet should not be used if it does not include page numbers in any form.
b. If a printout from a website has page numbers, citations should include these numbers.
c. In-text citations of online sources in research papers should never include page numbers.
d. If the source is a PDF file, the page numbers from the file should be in citations.

9. English language learner (ELL) students typically are able to develop which type of English language skills the fastest?

a. They typically develop BICS much sooner than CALP.
b. They typically develop CALP more quickly than BICS.
c. They typically develop both at about the same rates.
d. They develop these at individually varying speeds.

Refer to the following for question 10:

A third-grade science teacher gives her students one hour to read an article about penguins, take notes on important information, and use the notes to write a three-paragraph expository essay. Before they begin, the teacher writes the words *Spheniscidae*, *plumage*, and *Aptenodytes forsteri* on the board. She explains the meaning of each word. At the end of the hour, one student, Joshua, only has his notes completed. The teacher examines his notes, part of which are shown below.

> Penguins are animals that live in the Southern Hemisphere.
> Many people believe that penguins live in the Arctic, but that is not true.
> Penguins in Antarctica huddle together to stay warm. They take turns standing on the outside of the huddle, where it is colder.
> Penguins' feathers help protect them from the water and cold air.
> Penguins live in groups called colonies.

10. The words written by the teacher on the board are examples of:

a. Academic words
b. Alliteration
c. Content-specific words
d. Ionization

11. The phrase "pretty as a picture" is best described as a:

a. Metaphor
b. Simile
c. Synecdoche
d. Paradox

12. Which of the following statements is most accurate about writing the introduction of an essay?

a. The introduction should move from the broad and general to the focused and specific.
b. The introduction should save the most attention-getting material for later in the work.
c. The introduction should move from the focused and specific to the broad and general.
d. The introduction should use the technique of starting essays with dictionary definitions.

13. A school has a policy of only permitting administration of its first choice among standardized formal assessments of phonological development twice per school year to conserve money and time. A first-grade teacher wanting to inform her instructional planning, implementation, and adjustments appropriately can do which of these?

a. Stick to the school's policy and do the best she can with the results
b. Lobby administrators to change policy to giving this test more often
c. Use informal assessments continually and exclusively
d. Conduct informal and other formal assessments on an ongoing basis

14. Phonemic awareness is a type of:

a. Phonological awareness. Phonemic awareness is the ability to recognize sounds within words.
b. Phonics. It is a teaching technique whereby readers learn the relationship between letters and sounds.
c. Alphabetization. Unless a reader knows the alphabet, phonemic awareness is useless.
d. Syntactical awareness. Understanding the underlying structure of a sentence is key to understanding meaning.

15. What is the purpose of targeted instruction?

a. Deliver instructions that are precise, clear, and direct so that students understand exactly what is expected.
b. Accurately rank a group of learners from low achievers to high achievers so that the teacher knows from the beginning of the school year which students have less ability and will therefore need support.
c. Teach students how to take information from a text and reorganize it into bulleted lists.
d. Assess and target areas needing improvement as well as areas of greatest strength for each student to ensure that all members of a class are receiving instruction tailored to their specific needs.

16. Which choice most appropriately fills the blanks in this statement? "In writing, _____ is the writer's attitude as evident from the writing, and _____ is the individual way in which the writer expresses themselves through the writing."

a. voice, tone
b. tone, voice
c. style, tone
d. voice, style

17. Which of the following literary elements are most likely to be found in both fictional narratives and nonfictional informational text?

a. The writing style of the author
b. Labeled diagrams and photos
c. Excitement and drama
d. Themes and plots

18. *Train, brain, spring.* The underlined letters are examples of:

a. Consonant digraph
b. Consonant blend
c. Consonant shift
d. Continental shift

19. A student is taking a reading test. The teacher has blocked out a number of words. Each blank is assigned a set of three possible words. The student must select the correct word from each set so that the text makes sense. The student is taking:

a. A cloze test
b. A maze test
c. A multiple-choice quiz
d. A vocabulary test

20. A writing assignment asks the student to do things like organize, plan, formulate, assemble, compose, construct, or arrange some material they have read or learned. Which of the following cognitive (learning) objectives is the teacher aiming to meet with this assignment?

a. Analysis
b. Synthesis
c. Evaluation
d. Application

21. Following a typical developmental sequence, which of the following is expected of second graders in decoding and identifying new or unfamiliar words?

a. Identifying new words and compound words via phonics, roots, suffixes, and analogies
b. Identifying new word meanings through knowledge of familiar synonyms and antonyms
c. Identifying new word meanings by comparing to known homophones and homographs
d. Identifying new word meanings by roots, prefixes, suffixes, idioms, and dictionary markings

22. "Decoding" is also called:

a. Remediation
b. Deciphering
c. Alphabetic principle
d. Deconstruction

23. A teacher has given her students an assignment to write a non-rhyming poem of three lines. The first and last lines each contain five syllables, and the middle line contains seven syllables. The students are writing a:

a. Limerick
b. Metaphor
c. Villanelle
d. Haiku

24. Which of the following would be most useful in assessing and documenting students' language progress throughout a school year?

a. An audio/video recording of each student reading the same text at the beginning of the year and again at the end of the year
b. A portfolio including pre-tests, post-tests, vocabulary work, journal entries, writing assignments, group projects, and other relevant work from throughout the year
c. Score composites and details from state- and national-referenced exams or other standardized tests.
d. A detailed narrative composed by the student's teacher, detailing strengths, weaknesses, and descriptions of the student's work.

25. Of the following statements, which is true about the relationship of reading fluency, word decoding, and reading comprehension?

a. Developing fluency in reading has no relationship to speed and automaticity with decoding words.
b. Students should have strong word recognition foundations established before fluency instruction.
c. Reading fluency shows faster information processing speed, but has no impact on comprehension.
d. Slower, less automatic word decoding decreases reading fluency, but it increases comprehension.

26. A reading teacher is assessing an eighth grader to determine her reading level. Timed at a minute, the student reads with 93% accuracy. She misreads an average of seven words out of 100. What is her reading level?

a. She is reading at a Frustration level.
b. She is reading at a Listening level.
c. She is reading at an Instructional level.
d. She is reading at an Independent level.

27. Which of the following aspects of poetic form is characteristic of haiku?

a. A 5-7-5 syllable pattern
b. An ABA rhyme scheme
c. Perfectly regular meter
d. Lengthy epic narratives

28. Which of the following statements is most true?

a. Introducing oral and written texts from a variety of cultures can enhance students' understanding and appreciation of language.
b. Children typically learn language best when exposed primarily to texts exemplary of their own background or culture, thereby increasing their ability to identify personally with what they are learning.
c. Studying other languages will impair a student's ability to develop his or her own first language.
d. Students should be exposed to one type of text at a time to diminish genre confusion.

29. A teacher writes four sentences on the board and instructs his students to copy the sentences from the board into their notebooks. They must capitalize words with suffixes. Which sentence is correct?

a. The PRINCE declared his undying love for the PRINCESS.
b. Television is a form of MULTIMEDIA.
c. This loud, loud noise is very DISPLEASING.
d. The BOOKKEEPER examined every page of the rare play.

30. Which of the following statements regarding the acquisition of language is FALSE?

a. Young children often have the ability to comprehend written language just as early as they can comprehend or reproduce oral language when given appropriate instruction.
b. Oral language typically develops before a child understands the relationship between spoken and written words.
c. Most young children are first exposed to written language when an adult reads aloud.
d. A child's ability to speak, read, and write depends on a variety of physiological factors, as well as environmental factors.

31. A teacher asks her students to say the word *map*. She then says, "Change the /m/ sound to a /t/ sound. What word do you have now?" Which phonemic awareness skill are students practicing?

a. Alliteration
b. Segmenting
c. Blending onset and rime
d. Phoneme substitution

32. A classroom is comprised of students with varying abilities in language. Some students can read fluently, while others are still just learning. Speech and language abilities also range widely among the students. Which approach best suits this class?

a. Each student begins with reading texts slightly below their ability level and practices reading aloud with partners and teachers to build skills.
b. The teacher consistently presents challenging material for students, knowing that when students are held to high expectations, they typically rise to meet a challenge.
c. The teacher splits the classroom into groups based on ability and appoints a group leader to guide other students.
d. The class is exposed to a variety of "texts," in combination with direct phonetic and vocabulary instruction, including written text, video, song, and spoken stories.

33. To help students understand abstract concepts in the print materials they read, which instructional aids that teachers provide can students always use three-dimensionally?

a. Examples
b. Manipulatives
c. Graphic organizers
d. Charts, tables, and graphs

34. Examples of CVC words include:

a. Add, pad, mad
b. Cat, tack, act
c. Elephant, piano, examine
d. Dog, sit, leg

35. In first-language (L1) and second-language (L2) acquisition, which of the following is true about language acquisition stages?

a. L2 learners do not undergo the first stage, called the "silent period," as L1 learners do.
b. L2 learners undergo all stages, but they are urged to skip the first stage more than L1s.
c. L2 learners do not undergo the second stage, "formulaic speech," as L1 learners do.
d. L2 learners undergo the third stage, "structural and semantic simplifications," later.

36. Which of the following is the best use of technology in a language arts classroom?

a. Providing laptops to students to achieve more effective note-taking, access to word processing programs, and access to the internet
b. Encouraging the use of slide shows or similar programs to support lectures and oral presentations, as well as to organize pertinent class concepts
c. Incorporating a computer-based "language lab" in which students can listen to texts and engage in interactive word-study and comprehension activities
d. Whenever possible, watching film interpretations based on texts studied in class

37. Which of the following is the correct sequence of these phases of spelling development?

a. Semiphonetic, precommunicative, transitional, correct, phonetic
b. Precommunicative, semiphonetic, phonetic, transitional, correct
c. Correct, phonetic, semiphonetic, precommunicative, transitional
d. Phonetic, semiphonetic, transitional, correct, precommunicative

38. Context clues are useful in:

a. Predicting future action
b. Understanding the meaning of words that are not familiar
c. Understanding character motivation
d. Reflecting on a text's theme

39. Which of the following statements is correct regarding Standard English?

a. Standard English does not allow for variations of dialect.
b. Rules from standard English apply to written language.
c. Standard English is universal in English-speaking nations.
d. No standard English exists that is actually used in practice.

40. Which choice is the best method of structuring language arts curriculum and instruction?

a. Examine all state-level or national standardized tests that students will be required to take. Structure the curriculum and lessons to address all concepts included in the tests, with an attempt to proportion the time spent in a way that mirrors the breakdown of the tests.
b. Research the instructional methods used in supplemental education fields. Use those newer methods of introducing and reinforcing concepts in class to ensure that students are receiving consistent and standard instruction.
c. Use the written curriculum provided by the school district or specific campus as a foundation for instruction. Schedule regular planning sessions to incorporate a variety of texts and instruction methods, as well as to coordinate instruction with teachers of other subjects.
d. Plan sequential units of study that focus on isolated skills such as word and vocabulary study, comprehension strategies, listening, viewing, and speaking. Design lessons to focus on the mastery of one skill at a time with the goal of studying the relationship between skills toward the end of the school year.

Mathematics

1. A dartboard consists of two concentric circles with radii of 3 inches and 6 inches. If a dart is thrown onto the board, what is the probability the dart will land in the inner circle?

a. $\frac{1}{4}$

b. $\frac{1}{2}$

c. $\frac{1}{3}$

d. $\frac{1}{5}$

2. A ball has a diameter of 7 inches. Which of the following best represents the volume?

a. 165.7 in^3
b. 179.6 in^3
c. 184.5 in^3
d. 192.3 in^3

3. Which of the following pairs of equations represents the lines of symmetry in the figure below?

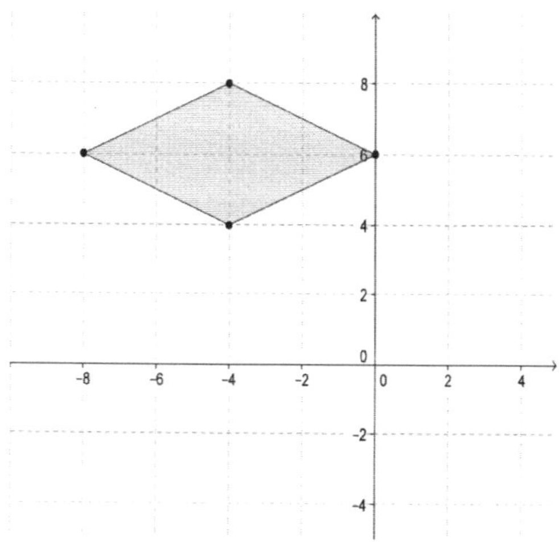

a. $x = -4, y = 6$
b. $x = 4, y = 6$
c. $y = -4, x = 6$
d. $y = 4, x = -6$

4. Which of these graphs is NOT representative of the data set shown below?

3	6799
4	23889
5	011158
6	00123

Key
$2|123 = 21, 22, 23$

a.

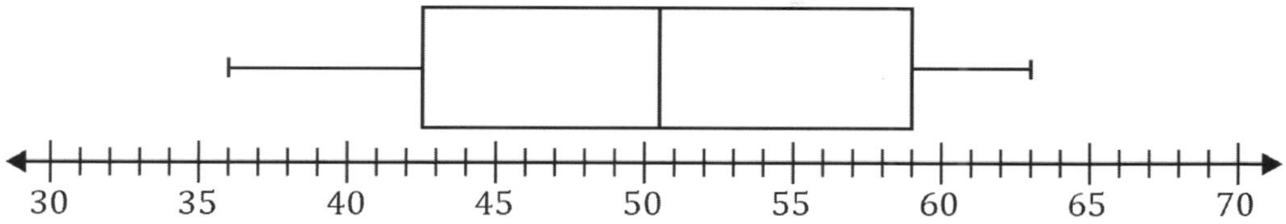

b.

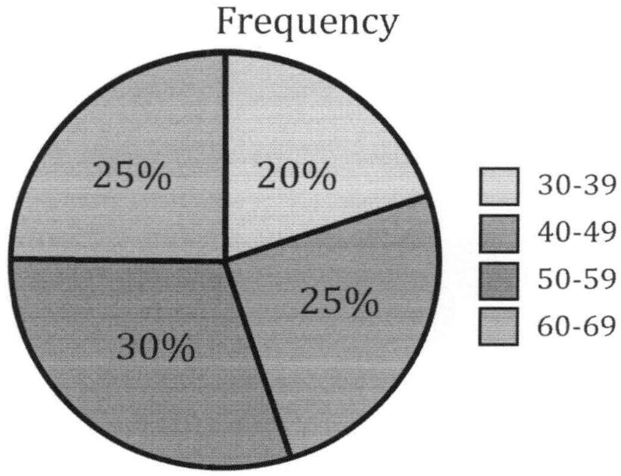

c.

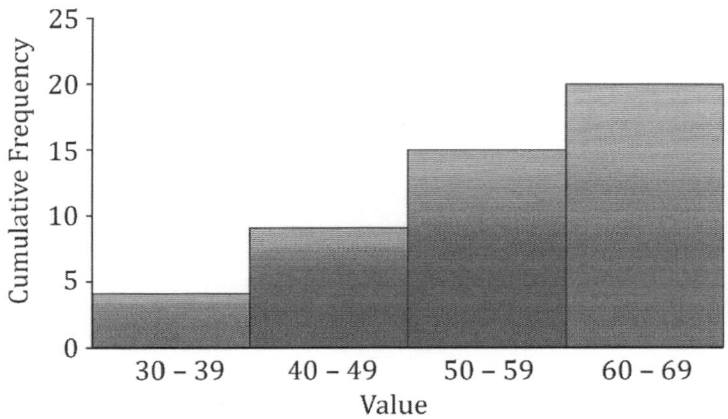

d. All of these graphs represent the data set.

5. Zeke drove from his house to a furniture store in Atlanta and then back home along the same route. It took Zeke three hours to drive to the store. By driving an average of 20 mph faster on his return trip, Zeke was able to save an hour of driving time. What was Zeke's average driving speed on his round trip?

a. 24 mph
b. 48 mph
c. 50 mph
d. 60 mph

6. For which of these does a rotation of 120° about the center of the polygon map the polygon onto itself?

a. Square
b. Regular hexagon
c. Regular octagon
d. Regular decagon

7. Marlon pays $45 for a jacket that has been marked down 25%. What was the original cost of the jacket?

a. $80
b. $75
c. $65
d. $60

8. Aidan has a plastic container in the shape of a square pyramid. He wants to fill the container with chocolate candies. If the base has a side length of 6 inches and the height of the container is 9 inches, how many cubic inches of space may be filled with candies?

a. 98
b. 102
c. 108
d. 112

9. Mr. Sarver, a second-grade teacher, notices that a few of his students are struggling with the concept of borrowing when subtracting two-digit numbers. Which of the following activities would best help students understand this concept of borrowing?

a. The teacher works subtraction problems on the whiteboard.
b. The students watch a children's video about borrowing.
c. The students complete a worksheet with subtraction problems.
d. The students use cardboard manipulatives to model subtraction problems.

10. Coach Weybright's 6th-grade basketball team has played 36 games this season. The ratio of wins to losses is 2 : 1. If x represents the number of wins, which of the following proportions can be used to determine the number of wins?

a. $\frac{x}{36} = \frac{2}{1}$
b. $\frac{x}{2} = \frac{1}{36}$
c. $\frac{x}{3} = \frac{36}{2}$
d. $\frac{x}{36} = \frac{2}{3}$

11. Mr. Orr asks his class to use inductive reasoning to determine the pattern in this sequence of numbers. Which number is next in this series?

2, 5, 10, 17, __

a. 22
b. 24
c. 25
d. 26

12. Given that the two horizontal lines in the diagram below are parallel, which pair of angles is congruent?

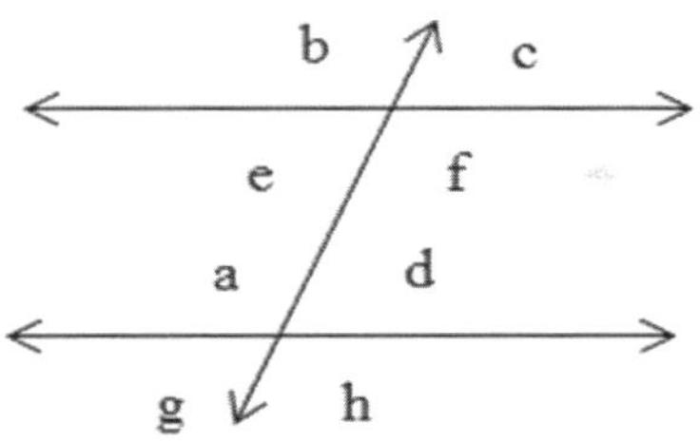

a. ∠e and ∠b
b. ∠d and ∠h
c. ∠g and ∠c
d. ∠d and ∠f

13. Which number comes next in the sequence?

16, 24, 34, 46, 60

a. 56
b. 72
c. 74
d. 76

14. The set $\{a, b, c, d\}$ forms a group under operation #. Which of these statements is (are) true about the group?

#	***a***	***b***	***c***	***d***
a	*c*	*d*	*b*	*a*
b	*d*	*c*	*a*	*b*
c	*b*	*a*	*d*	*c*
d	*a*	*b*	*c*	*d*

I. The identity element of the group is *d*.
II. The inverse of *c* is *c*.
III. The operation # is commutative.

a. I
b. III
c. I, III
d. I, II, III

15. In how many distinguishable ways can a family of five be seated at a circular table with five chairs if Tasha and Mac must be kept separated by at least one chair?

a. 6
b. 12
c. 24
d. 60

16. Which of the following steps were applied to ΔABC?

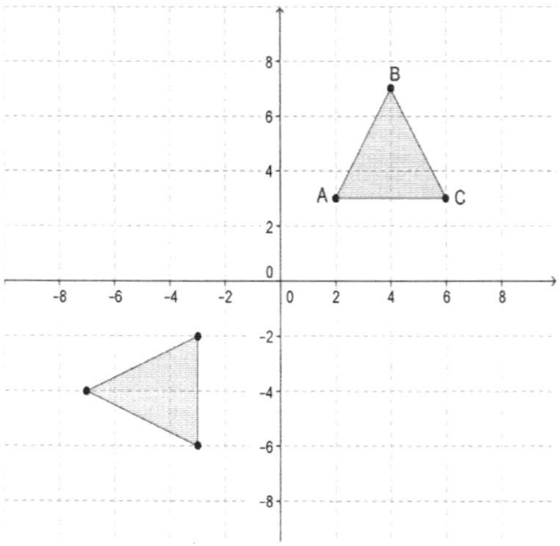

a. Reflection across the x-axis and counterclockwise rotation of 90 degrees about the origin
b. Reflection across the x-axis and counterclockwise rotation of 180 degrees about the origin
c. Reflection across the x-axis and counterclockwise rotation of 270 degrees about the origin
d. Reflection across the y-axis and counterclockwise rotation of 180 degrees about the origin

17. Miss Wise asks her students to work in pairs to construct Venn diagrams which classify rational numbers, irrational numbers, real numbers, and integers. As she walks around the room to observe their progress, which of the following criterion could she use to assess the students' understanding of these sets of numbers?

a. The set of integers should include the other three sets.
b. The set of rational numbers should include the other three sets.
c. The set of irrational numbers should include the other three sets.
d. The set of real numbers should include the other three sets.

18. During a unit on geometry, Ms. Nifong instructs her students to sketch two congruent polygons. Which of the following sketches completes this task correctly?

a. Two rectangles with the same perimeter
b. Two polygons with the same shape
c. Two polygons with the same side lengths
d. Two squares with the same area

19. What is the area of the figure graphed below?

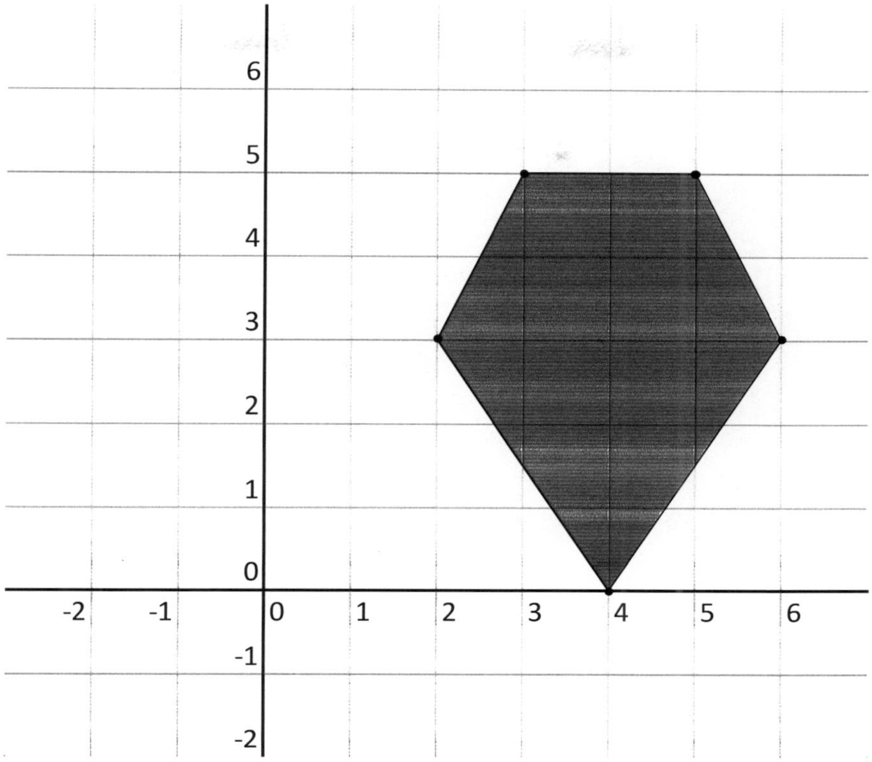

a. 11 units^2
b. 11.5 units^2
c. 12 units^2
d. 12.5 units^2

20. Kayla has a $75 budget to purchase gifts for her colleagues. She wants to buy coffee mugs and note pads. She may purchase a maximum of 30 items. Each coffee mug costs $6 and each note pad costs $3. Which of the following graphs correctly shows the possible combinations of coffee mugs and note pads that she may buy?

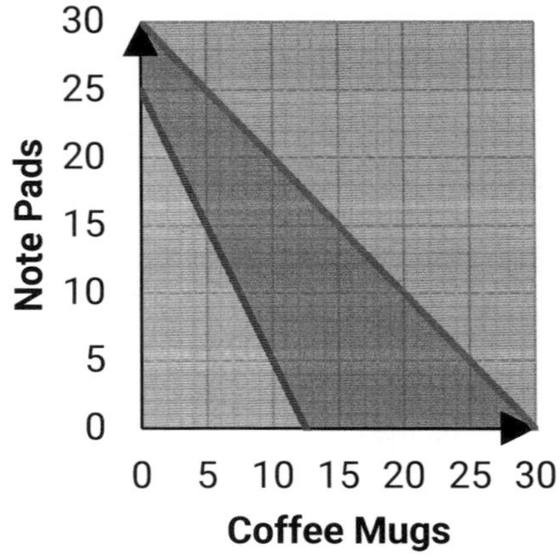

a.

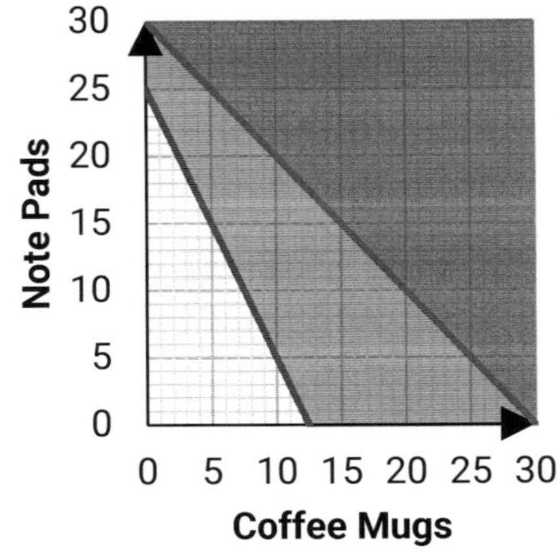

b.

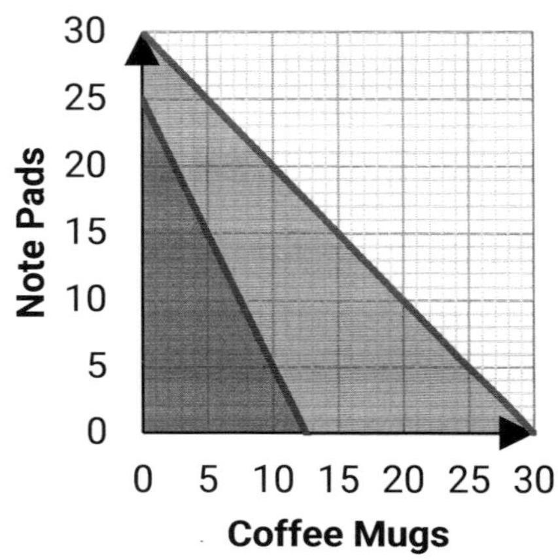

c.

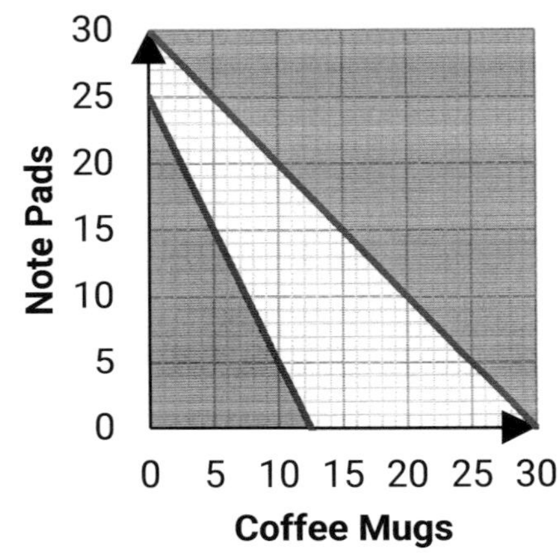

d.

21. What is the constant of proportionality represented by the table below?

x	y
2	−8
5	−20
7	−28
10	−40
11	−44

a. −12
b. −8
c. −6
d. −4

22. Ms. Alejo is teaching a unit on fractions to her third-grade class. Some students are completing an activity in identifying the parts of a fraction. Others are completing an activity on equivalent fractions. Another group of students is completing an activity on adding and subtracting fractions. Which of the following instruction methods describes the various readiness levels Ms. Alejo is incorporating?

a. Collaborative learning
b. Small group instruction
c. Nonlinguistic representations
d. Differentiated instruction

23. During an activity, Mrs. Schwartz instructs her students to place coins into three groups, where each group gets progressively lower in total value. Which of the following students correctly completed this activity?

a. Henry with Group 1: 2 dimes, 2 nickels, and 4 pennies; Group 2: 1 dime, 3 nickels, 2 pennies; Group 3: 2 dimes, 1 nickel, 4 pennies
b. Graham with Group 1: 1 dime, 5 nickels, and 5 pennies; Group 2: 2 dimes, 2 nickels, 8 pennies; Group 3: 1 dime, 2 nickel, 9 pennies
c. Landon with Group 1: 3 dimes, 4 nickels, and 9 pennies; Group 2: 2 dimes, 4 nickels, 3 pennies; Group 3: 1 dime, 9 nickels, 2 pennies
d. Elizabeth with Group 1: 2 dimes, 2 nickels, and 9 pennies; Group 2: 2 dimes, 4 nickels, 1 penny; Group 3: 1 dime, 1 nickel, 7 pennies

24. What is the length of the hypotenuse in the triangle shown below?

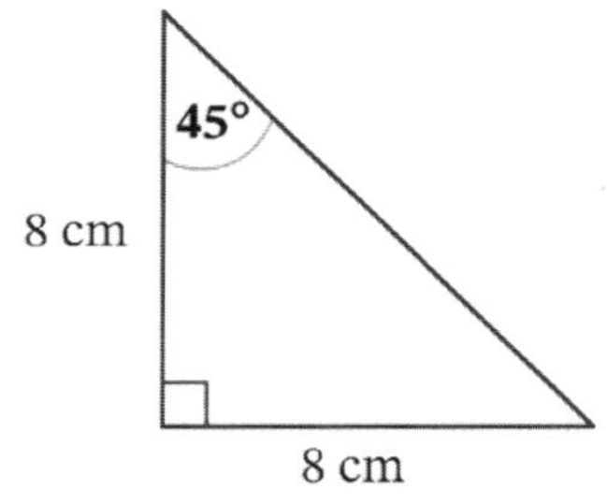

a. 4 cm
b. $8\sqrt{3}$ cm
c. 16 cm
d. $8\sqrt{2}$ cm

25. A cube inscribed in a sphere has a volume of 64 cubic units. What is the volume of the sphere in cubic units?

a. $4\pi\sqrt{3}$
b. $8\pi\sqrt{3}$
c. $32\pi\sqrt{3}$
d. $256\pi\sqrt{3}$

26. Mandy can buy 4 containers of yogurt and 3 boxes of crackers for $9.55. She can buy 2 containers of yogurt and 2 boxes of crackers for $5.90. How much does one box of crackers cost?

a. $1.75
b. $2.00
c. $2.25
d. $2.50

27. Which of the following describes how to find the volume of a regular solid prism?

a. Find the perimeter of the base of the prism and multiply by the height of the prism.
b. Find the area of the base of the prism and multiply by the height of the prism.
c. Find the sum of the areas of the faces and multiply by the length of the prism.
d. Find the sum of the areas of the lateral faces and multiply by the number of faces.

28. $A = \{3, -4, 1\}$ and $B = \{0, 5, 9, 2\}$. What is $A \cap B$?

a. $\{3,-4,1,0,5,9,2\}$
b. $\{-4,2,3\}$
c. $\{0,1,2,3,5,9\}$
d. $\emptyset$

29. Which of these would best illustrate change over time?

a. Pie chart
b. Line graph
c. Box-and-whisker plot
d. Venn diagram

30. Which of the following activities is most appropriate for developing a first-grader's concept of measuring objects?

a. Measuring the height of the pencil sharpener using a meter stick
b. Measuring the length of the chalkboard using a tape measure
c. Measuring the width of their desks using dominoes placed end to end
d. Measuring the circumference of the trash can using a cloth tape

31. The two prisms shown below are similar. What is the measurement of x?

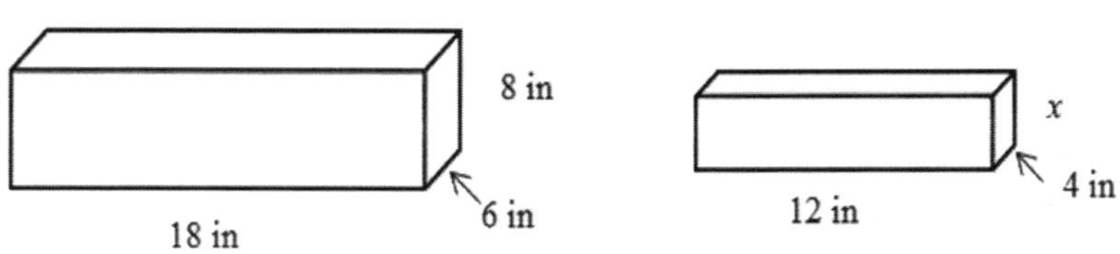

a. $4\frac{3}{4}$ in
b. $5\frac{1}{3}$ in
c. $5\frac{2}{3}$ in
d. $5\frac{3}{4}$ in

32. Kim's current monthly rent is $800. She is moving to another apartment complex, where the monthly rent will be $1,100. What is the percent increase in her monthly rent amount?

a. 25.5%
b. 27%
c. 35%
d. 37.5%

33. A teacher asks her students to find the error in this algebra problem. What is the error?

$$3x + 4x = (2^2 + 1) + 2(2)$$
$$7x = 5 + 2(2)$$
$$7x = 7(2)$$
$$7x = 14$$
$$x = 2$$

a. The student incorrectly added before multiplying.
b. The student incorrectly multiplied before adding.
c. The student incorrectly applied the exponent.
d. The student incorrectly combined like terms.

34. Which of the following is the graph of the equation $y = -4x - 6$?

a.

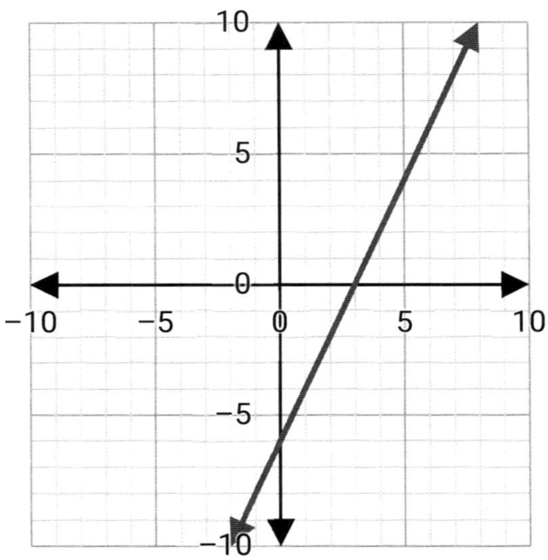

b.

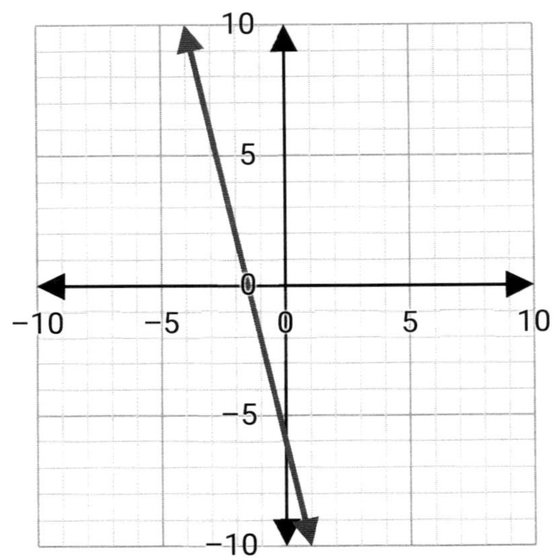

c.

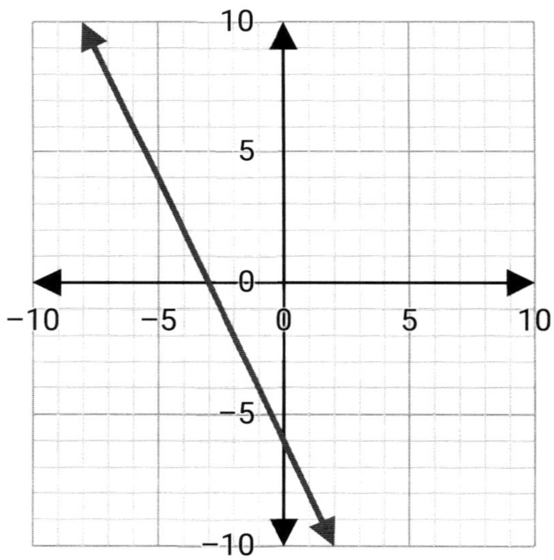

d.

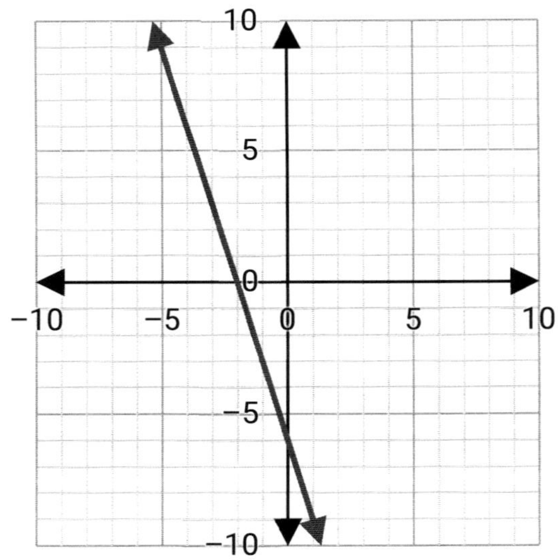

35. Andrea must administer $\frac{1}{12}$ of a medicine bottle to a patient. If the bottle contains $3\frac{4}{10}$ fluid ounces of medicine, how much medicine should be administered?

a. $\frac{17}{60}$ fluid ounces
b. $\frac{15}{62}$ fluid ounces
c. $\frac{3}{19}$ fluid ounces
d. $\frac{17}{67}$ fluid ounces

36. Which of the following options represents equivalency between mathematical expressions?

a. $3 + x + 3x + 3 + x = 5x + 6$
b. $7x - 2x = 9x$
c. $2y + 2y + 2y = 6y^3$
d. $2.5(x + 2) = 2.5x + 2$

37. Kendra uses the pie chart below to represent the allocation of her annual income. Her annual income is $40,000.

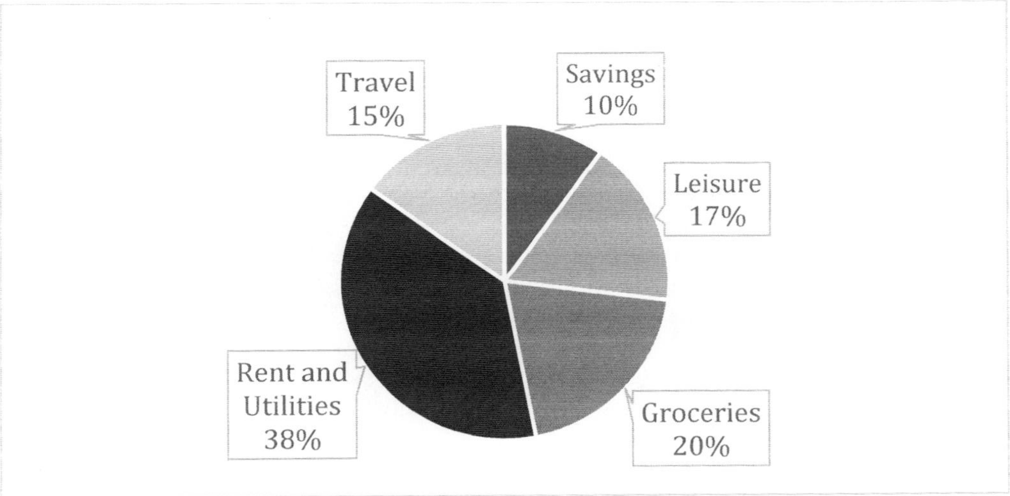

Which of the following statements is true?

a. The amount of money she spends on travel and savings is more than $11,000.
b. The amount of money she spends on rent and utilities is approximately $15,000.
c. The amount of money she spends on groceries and savings is more than $13,000.
d. The amount of money she spends on leisure is less than $5,000.

38. In a pack of 20 jelly beans, there are two licorice- and four cinnamon-flavored jelly beans. What is the probability of choosing a licorice jelly bean followed by a cinnamon jelly bean?

a. $\frac{2}{5}$
b. $\frac{8}{20}$
c. $\frac{2}{95}$
d. $\frac{1}{50}$

39. Amy saves $450 every 3 months. How much does she save after 3 years?

a. $4,800
b. $5,200
c. $5,400
d. $5,800

40. Which of the following equations demonstrates the associative property of multiplication?

a. $2(3 + 4) = 2(3) + 2(4)$
b. $(3 \times 6) \times 2 = (4 \times 3) \times 3$
c. $(2 \times 3) \times 4 = 2 \times (3 \times 4)$
d. $6 \times 4 = 4 \times 6$

Science

1. Which of the following is NOT true about Louis Pasteur?

a. He made the first rabies vaccine.
b. He discovered the medical use for penicillin.
c. His experiments advanced the germ theory of disease.
d. He created the first polio vaccine.

2. Which of the following materials has randomly aligned dipoles?

a. A non-magnetic substance
b. An electromagnet
c. A permanent magnet
d. A horseshoe magnet

3. In the scientific process, which skill do children employ most when they see patterns and meaning in the results of experiments they make?

a. Measurement
b. Classification
c. Inferences
d. Prediction

4. How does the tilt of Earth's axis cause seasons?

a. A hemisphere experiences fall and winter when that half of Earth is tilted away from the sun. It experiences spring and summer when that half of Earth is tilted toward the sun.
b. A hemisphere experiences winter and spring when that half of Earth is tilted away from the sun. It experiences summer and fall when that half of Earth is tilted toward the sun.
c. A hemisphere experiences spring and summer when that half of Earth is tilted away from the sun. It experiences fall and winter when that half of Earth is tilted toward the sun.
d. A hemisphere experiences summer and fall when that half of Earth is tilted away from the sun. It experiences winter and spring when that half of Earth is tilted toward the sun.

5. If a population reaches a maximum size and ceases to grow due to a limited availability of resources, which of the following describes the population?

a. Unstable
b. Shrinking exponentially
c. At carrying capacity
d. Moving towards extinction

6. The center of an atom is called the ____. It is composed of ____.

a. nucleus; protons and neutrons
b. nucleus; protons and electrons
c. electron cloud; electrons and protons
d. electron cloud; electrons and neutrons

7. Of the following insects, which undergo a complete metamorphosis during their life cycle?

a. Mosquitos
b. Butterflies
c. Dragonflies
d. Grasshoppers

8. Most organic molecules have all of the following properties EXCEPT:

a. High solubility in water
b. A low melting point
c. Covalent bonds
d. High flammability

9. Which of the following processes is NOT part of the formation of sedimentary rock?

a. Layering
b. Cementation
c. Compaction
d. Heat

10. Which of the following is usually the first form of study in a new area of scientific inquiry?

a. Descriptive studies
b. Controlled experiments
c. Choosing a method and design
d. Identifying dependent and independent variables

11. The specific heat capacity of ice is half as much as that of liquid water. What is the result of this?

a. It takes half the amount of energy to increase the temperature of a 1 kg sample of ice by 1 °C than a 1 kg sample of water.
b. It takes twice the amount of energy to increase the temperature of a 1 kg sample of ice by 1 °C than a 1 kg sample of water.
c. It takes a quarter the amount of energy to increase the temperature of a 1 kg sample of ice by 1 °C than a 1 kg sample of water.
d. It takes the same amount of energy to increase the temperature of a 1 kg sample of ice and a 1 kg sample of water by 1 °C.

12. Which statement best describes the molecular arrangement of a liquid crystal?

a. The molecular arrangement is random in some directions and regular in others.
b. The molecular arrangement is a regular, repeating pattern in all directions.
c. The molecular arrangement is random in all directions.
d. The molecular arrangement is reduced to one layer with a random pattern.

13. Which statement best describes the process of absolute dating?

a. It compares the amount of radioactive material in a rock to the amount that has decayed into another element.
b. It measures the age of a rock by comparing it to fossils found in the same stratigraphic layer as the rock.
c. It measures the amount of daughter elements that have broken down by half.
d. It measures the mass loss of a rock by estimating the amount of material that has eroded due to catastrophic events.

14. The scientific method is a series of steps to accomplish which of the following?

a. Solve a problem
b. Gather information
c. Ask a scientific question
d. Formulate a hypothesis

15. Enzymes play an important role in the processes that help organisms stay healthy and survive. Which of the following best describes enzymes?

a. Enzymes are protein molecules that act as biological catalysts.
b. Enzymes are fat-soluble organic compounds with specific physiological functions.
c. Enzymes are strong acids that break down large biomolecules.
d. Enzymes are lipids that store energy.

16. Which statement accurately describes an electrolysis reaction?

a. A reaction that changes the charge of the atoms
b. A reaction that uses electricity to drive it
c. A reaction that creates electricity as a by-product
d. A reaction that lowers the pH of the substances

17. Which of the following does NOT control the movement of ocean currents?

a. Wind
b. Landmasses
c. Earth's rotation
d. Phase of the Moon

18. The majority of the solar energy that reaches Earth is absorbed by:

a. Glaciers
b. Landmasses
c. Oceans
d. The Earth's atmosphere

19. Electrons with greater amounts of energy are found _______ the nucleus than electrons with less energy.

a. closer to
b. farther from
c. more often inside
d. more randomly around

20. The main function of _______ is to reduce the number of chromosomes to half the number of parent cells.

a. mitosis
b. telophase
c. meiosis I
d. meiosis II

Refer to the following for question 21:

Many fishermen will watch the tide report for the local area and get up very early or stay out late in order to have the best fishing opportunity. One night while out late fishing, a fisherman noticed that the land temperature cooled rapidly, while the ocean water stayed relatively warm.

21. What type of wind was likely created during these conditions?

a. Sea breeze
b. Land breeze
c. Monsoon
d. Trade wind

22. The structure of the Milky Way galaxy is best described as:

a. Spiral
b. Starburst
c. Elliptical
d. Irregular

23. A ball is resting on the front end of a boat. The boat is moving straight forward toward a dock. According to Newton's first law of motion, when the front of the boat hits the dock, how will the ball's motion change with respect to the boat?

a. The ball will remain at rest.
b. The ball will move backward.
c. The ball will move forward.
d. The ball will move upward.

24. In which taxonomic group are organisms MOST alike?

a. Phylum
b. Family
c. Class
d. Order

25. Which statement best explains the importance of recycling and using alternative sources of energy?

a. It will lead to greater production of goods and consumer spending in the future.
b. It will benefit the health and safety of populations and the long-term sustainability of the environment.
c. It will get rid of human disease and end economic warfare in the future.
d. It will allow fossil fuel supplies to be replenished for their continued use in the future.

26. Which of the following planets in our solar system is NOT a gas giant?

a. Saturn
b. Neptune
c. Venus
d. Jupiter

27. A scientist mixes two chemicals together, and they produce a violent reaction, generating considerable heat. Where did the thermal energy come from to heat up the chemicals?

a. The kinetic energy of the molecules in the chemicals
b. Potential energy inherent in the atomic bonds in the molecules of the chemicals
c. It was absorbed from the surrounding air
d. Nowhere; the energy was completely created by the reaction

28. Plants begin to break down the products of photosynthesis through respiration. What is the result of respiration?

a. Water
b. Oxygen and glucose
c. Carbon dioxide and sugar
d. Carbon dioxide and water

29. Scientists often form hypotheses based on particular observations. Which of the following is NOT true of a good hypothesis?

a. A good hypothesis is complex.
b. A good hypothesis is testable.
c. A good hypothesis is logical.
d. A good hypothesis predicts future events.

30. What type of change occurs when a liquid transitions to a gas?

a. A phase change
b. A chemical change
c. Sublimation
d. Condensation

31. What laboratory practice can increase the precision of a measurement?

a. Repeating the measurement several times
b. Calibrating the equipment each time you use it
c. Using metric measuring devices
d. Reading the laboratory instructions before the lab

32. What will happen to light waves as they hit a convex lens?

a. They will be refracted and converge.
b. They will be refracted and diverge.
c. They will be reflected and converge.
d. They will be reflected and diverge.

33. Which of the following animal structures is NOT paired to its correct function?

a. Muscle System – controls movement through three types of muscle tissue
b. Nervous System – controls sensory responses by carrying impulses away from and toward the cell body
c. Digestive System – breaks down food for absorption into the blood stream where it is delivered to cells for respiration
d. Circulatory System – exchanges gases with the environment by delivering oxygen to the bloodstream and releasing carbon dioxide

34. Which type of nuclear process features atomic nuclei splitting apart to form smaller nuclei?

a. Fission
b. Fusion
c. Decay
d. Ionization

35. Which of the following is considered a non-renewable resource?

a. Glass
b. Wood
c. Cattle
d. Soil

Refer to the following for question 36:

Diagram of a complete, perfect flower

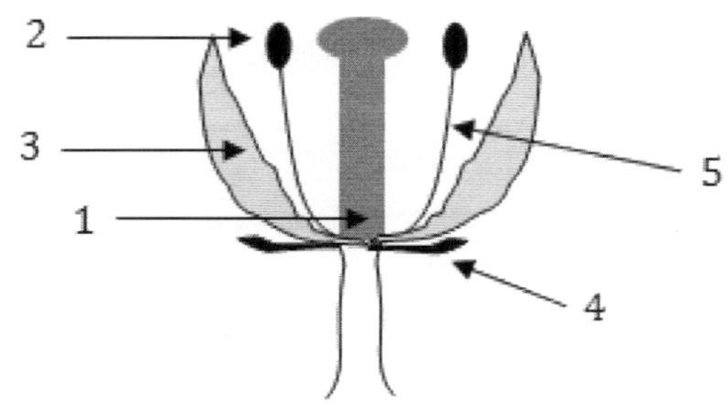

36. Which of the following is NOT considered a reproductive organ of the flower?

a. 1
b. 2
c. 3
d. 4

37. What effect does science have on technology?

a. Science verifies what technology discovers
b. Technology often results from scientific discoveries
c. Science has no effect on technology; each is independent of the other
d. Scientific progress is dependent on technology

38. Which is an example of convection as a method of heat transfer?

a. A person warming his hands by placing them on an electric blanket
b. A person warming his hands by placing them near the sides of an incandescent light bulb
c. A person warming his hands by holding them over a pot of steaming water
d. A person warming his hands by rubbing them together

39. After a science laboratory exercise, some solutions remain unused and are left over. What should be done with these solutions?

a. Dispose of the solutions according to local disposal procedures.
b. Empty the solutions into the sink and rinse with warm water and soap.
c. Ensure the solutions are secured in closed containers and throw away.
d. Store the solutions in a secured, dry place for later use.

40. The most recently formed parts of the Earth's crust can be found at:

a. Subduction zones
b. Compressional boundaries
c. Extensional boundaries
d. Mid-ocean ridges

Social Studies

1. In order to be accepted, amended, or rejected completely, a newly introduced bill is first given to what type of committee?

a. Full committee
b. Conference committee
c. Subcommittee
d. Senate committee

2. Which of the following is NOT true regarding the Virginia Companies?

a. One of these companies, the Virginia Company of Plymouth, made its base in North America.
b. One of these companies, the Virginia Company of London, made its base in Massachusetts.
c. One company had a charter to colonize America between the Hudson and Cape Fear rivers.
d. One company had a charter to colonize America from the Potomac River to north Maine.

3. Why was US industrialization confined to the Northeast until after the Civil War?

a. Because the Civil War delayed the development of water-powered manufacturing
b. Because the Northeast had faster-running rivers than the rivers found in the South
c. Because Slater's first cotton mill with horse-drawn production lost so much money
d. Because the technical innovations for milling textiles had not as yet been invented

4. Unlike slaves, who were considered to be the property of their masters, which of the following was true regarding most indentured servants in colonial times?

a. They received wages for their labor
b. They were generally treated kindly by their employers
c. They were highly educated
d. They voluntarily entered into servitude

5. Which of these was the greatest obstacle to success for the farmers who settled on the Great Plains in the latter part of the nineteenth century?

a. The invention of barbed wire
b. Passage of the Homestead Act
c. Environmental conditions
d. The Grange movement

6. Before the Civil War, to which of the following did Southern states object?

a. An increase in Southern tobacco production
b. An increase in tariffs on Northern manufactured goods
c. An increase in western mining for gold
d. An increase in the voting rights of slaves

7. Which of the following is NOT true about democracy and the formation of the United States?

a. The founding fathers stated in the Constitution that the United States would be a democracy.
b. The Declaration of Independence did not dictate democracy but stated its principles.
c. The United States Constitution stipulated that government be elected by the people.
d. The United States Constitution had terms to protect some, but not all, of the people.

8. According to Karl Marx, which two groups are in continual conflict?

a. Farmers and landowners
b. Workers and owners
c. Kings and nobles
d. Politicians and voters

9. What do the executive, legislative, and judicial branches of government compose?

a. The federal government
b. The democratic process
c. Bicameralism
d. Rule of law

10. Which of the following is NOT correct about the growth of America in the first half of the 19th century?

a. By 1840, two thirds of all Americans resided west of the Allegheny Mountains.
b. The population of America doubled every 25 years during this time period.
c. The trend of westward expansion increased as more people migrated west.
d. Immigration to America from other countries was not substantial prior to 1820.

11. One reason the Articles of Confederation created a weak government was because it limited Congress's ability to do what?

a. Declare war
b. Conduct a census
c. Vote
d. Tax

12. Which of the following ancient civilizations of the Americas lived in Central America?

a. The Incas
b. The Aztecs
c. The Mayans
d. All of these

13. How was the vice president chosen before the 12th Amendment was ratified?

a. The president chose the vice president
b. Congress chose the vice president
c. The vice president came in second in the Electoral College
d. There was no vice president

14. Which list of events is in the correct chronological order?

a. The French and Indian War (Seven Years' War)
The American Revolution
The French Revolution
The War of 1812

b. The American Revolution
The French Revolution
The War of 1812
The French and Indian War (Seven Years' War)

c. The French and Indian War (Seven Years' War)
The French Revolution
The War of 1812
The American Revolution

d. The French and Indian War (Seven Years' War)
The French Revolution
The American Revolution
The War of 1812

15. The Senate and the House of Representatives are an example of:

a. Bicameralism
b. Checks and balances
c. Legislative oversight
d. Federalism

16. If you know the longitude of a city in the United States, what can you determine?

a. The state in which it is located
b. The time zone in which it is located
c. Exactly how far it is from the equator
d. Approximate average winter temperature

17. Which of the following is NOT a direct input in the basic economic concept of a country's gross domestic product (GDP)?

a. The size of its workforce
b. The amount of its capital
c. Technology in place
d. Education of its workforce

18. What was representative democracy likely motivated by?

a. An increase in population
b. Aristocracy
c. The Supreme Court
d. States passing laws that violated federal laws

19. During World War I, which group joined with the Central Powers after it formed?

a. Austria-Hungary
b. Germany
c. Ottoman Empire
d. Italy

20. What is the main purpose of the census?

a. To monitor illegal immigration
b. To apportion seats in the House of Representatives
c. To help determine federal income tax rates
d. To reapportion seats in the United States Senate

21. The impact of a transaction on parties not directly involved in the transaction is known as what?

a. Social cost
b. Social benefit
c. Externality
d. Marginal social cost

22. Which statement is NOT true regarding ancient Greek democracy?

a. Democracy began to develop approximately 500 BC.
b. One of the first, best-known democracies was in Athens.
c. It was a direct democracy, not using any representatives.
d. It was a democracy completely open to all of the public.

Refer to the following for question 23:

During a report on the Industrial Revolution, Mary uses a poster to illustrate cause and effect relationships in the War of 1812.

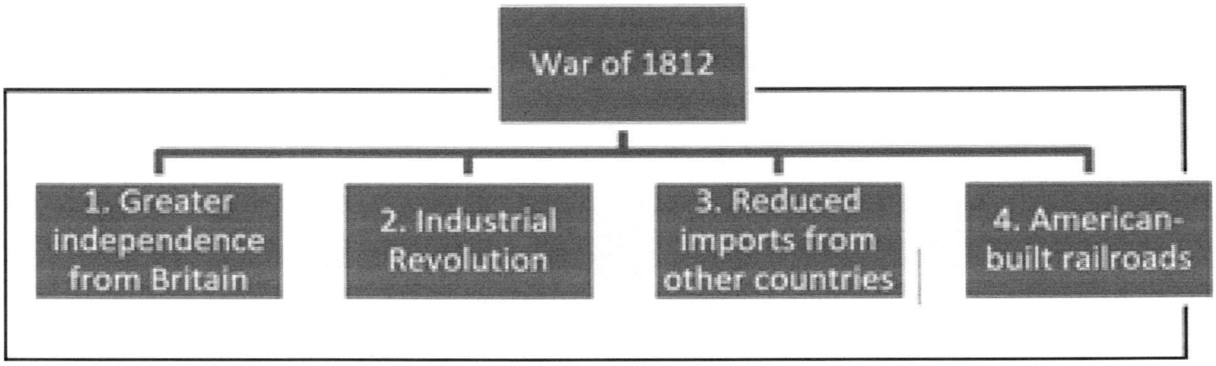

23. Of the following, which should Mary include in her report as more of a cause than an effect of the Industrial Revolution?

a. Emergence of socialism
b. Emergence of capitalism
c. The Romantic movement
d. The Protestant work ethic

24. The Underground Railroad was primarily:

a. A route for abolitionists to smuggle weapons
b. A route for slave owners to traffic slaves
c. A means for slaves to travel to free states
d. A strategy for state control of railway construction

25. What kind of chart would be best for representing the major events of World War I?

a. Timeline
b. Bar graph
c. Pie chart
d. Political map

26. How did World War II influence American society?

a. Consumption decreased in postwar American society.
b. Thousands of people moved to find work in war-related factories.
c. Racially integrated army units helped desegregate American society.
d. Japanese-Americans were banned from serving in the US military.

27. How is a tie broken in the Senate?

a. The president pro tempore casts the deciding vote.
b. The Speaker of the House votes.
c. They vote again.
d. The vice president votes.

28. Which of the following locations would be considered a modern cultural hearth?

a. New York City
b. Baghdad
c. Auckland
d. Edmonton

29. Which map describes the movement of people, trends, or materials across a physical area?

a. Political Map
b. Cartogram
c. Qualitative Map
d. Flow-line Map

30. Which of the following exemplifies the multiplier effect of large cities?

a. The presence of specialized equipment for an industry attracts even more business.
b. The large population lowers the price of goods.
c. Public transportation means more people can commute to work.
d. A local newspaper can afford to give away the Sunday edition.

31. Which entity in American government is the closest to direct democracy?

a. The Electoral College
b. The House of Representatives
c. Committees within the Senate
d. The Supreme Court

32. Which of the following will result if two nations use the theory of comparative advantage when making decisions of which goods to produce and trade?

a. Each nation will make all of their own goods.
b. Both nations will specialize in the production of the same specific goods.
c. Each nation will specialize in the production of different specific goods.
d. Neither nation will trade with one another.

Refer to the following for question 33:

In 1969, 13 African American members of the House of Representatives gathered to form the Congressional Black Caucus (CBC). They felt that a unified voice for minorities was needed. President Richard Nixon met with the group two years later; his weak response to their list of 60 recommendations increased their efforts. These efforts included ending apartheid in South Africa, reforming welfare, expanding educational opportunities, and developing of businesses by minorities. For nearly 20 years, the CBC has proposed an alternative annual budget; it generally varies widely from the budget that the president submits. In 2008, the organization has 43 members from urban and rural areas. The CBC is sometimes called the conscience of Congress.

33. Which of the following statements is an opinion?

a. The Congressional Black Caucus began in 1969.
b. The CBC is often referred to as Congress's conscience.
c. Every year for two decades, the CBC has proposed a national budget.
d. Apartheid was the worst political system of the 20th century.

34. Which of the following is most likely to benefit from inflation?

a. A bond investor who owns fixed-rate bonds
b. A retired widow with no income other than fixed Social Security payments
c. A person who has taken out a fixed-rate loan
d. A local bank who has loaned money out at fixed rate

35. Which of the following is NOT correct regarding assumptions of mercantilism?

a. The money and the wealth of a nation are identical properties.
b. In order to prosper, a nation should try to increase its imports.
c. In order to prosper, a nation should try to increase its exports.
d. Economic protectionism by national governments is advisable.

36. Based on the chart, which of the following statements is NOT accurate?

Jail Inmates by Sex and Race

Year	1990	1995	2000	2005
Male	365,821	448,000	543,120	646,807
Female	37,198	51,300	70,414	93,963
Juveniles	2,301	7,800	7,613	6,759
White	169,600	203,300	260,500	331,000
Black	172,300	220,600	256,300	290,500
Hispanic	58,100	74,400	94,100	111,900

[Source: US Dept. of Justice; does not include federal or state prisons.]

a. Fewer women than men are incarcerated in each year sampled.
b. The rate of jail incarceration rose for every subgroup of prisoner.
c. In 2000 and in 2005, more whites were incarcerated in jails than any other race.
d. Rate of Hispanic jailing has steadily increased over the fifteen years represented.

37. Who negotiates treaties?

a. The President
b. The House of Representatives
c. Ambassadors
d. The Senate

38. How long can members of the Federal Judiciary serve?

a. Four years
b. Eight years
c. For life
d. Six years

39. Three of the nine popularly elected state-wide executive branch officials in Texas are members of the Texas Railroad Commission (TRC). Which of the following explains the importance of the Texas Railroad Commission?

a. As the chief regulator of railroads, the TRC regulates the more than 40 companies that haul almost 300 tons of freight annually over a network of more than 10,000 miles of track.
b. Though the Texas Railroad Commission no longer regulates railroads, the agency regulates the utilities, pipelines, safety and mining operations of the Texas oil and gas industry.
c. Though the Texas Railroad Commission no longer regulates railroads, the agency regulates the economics of livestock (e.g., cattle, sheep, and goats) along with the resources (e.g., water and soil) used by ranches.
d. Though the Texas Railroad Commission no longer regulates railroads, the agency regulates the economics of the agricultural products (e.g., cotton, corn, and wheat) along with the resources (e.g., water and soil) used by farms.

40. What is the correct behaviorist term for strengthening a behavior by taking away something?

a. Positive punishment
b. Negative punishment
c. Positive reinforcement
d. Negative reinforcement

Answer Key and Explanations for Test #3

English

1. C: The question prompt states that Ms. Baird wants to make sure her students understand certain concepts on an individual basis, rather than as a group. This scenario describes a situation in which the students support each other in creating a foundation for the activity. They help each other and are scaffolded by their teacher in determining the main ideas. However, Ms. Baird utilizes the practice of silent reading to ensure that students are practicing the skill of finding supporting evidence on an individual level. She will be able to gauge each student's comprehension levels by checking their notecards after the lesson.

2. C: The goal of a persuasive essay is to convince the reader that the author's position or opinion on a topic is correct. That opinion or position is called the argument. A persuasive essay argues a series of points that are supported by facts and evidence.

3. C: Expository essays are any type of essay in which the writer is providing meaningful information about a topic for the purpose of informing. Most of the topics listed in the example include informational tasks, explaining the process of doing something, such as baking or juggling. Expository essays can use various organizational schemes to help structure the information, such as by comparing and contrasting two things. An expository essay is different from an argumentative essay in that it is not trying to convince the reader of anything, but only trying to inform. Similarly, the purpose of a descriptive essay is to show detail, but not necessarily to inform about how something works.

4. B: Starting in the late 20th century and continuing to today, the current era has been known as the Information Age (as a step forward from the Industrial Age). This is primarily because, with widespread computer and internet use and other innovations in information technology, there are more sources of information and greater output of information than ever before, to such an extent that the amount of information and the power of information technology have caused major shifts in many areas, from how people conduct their lives to how the global economy functions. While some organizations might collect more information that they did before, this is only possible because such information is more readily available now, and it is not necessarily the case that they need the information, so choice A is incorrect. While privacy and the protection of information have come under greater threat recently, they themselves are not more important than they were before, so choice C is incorrect. It is plausible that people are seeking more information about a wider variety of topics than ever before, but this is not the reason that the current era is known as the Information Age, so choice D is incorrect.

5. A: "Conceptual vocabulary" terms are related in meaning and often have complex meanings. For instance, the term *community* may refer simply to a group of people living in close proximity to one another. However, there are many ideas that can be associated with this concept: neighbors, helping, spending time with one another, roles within a community, and so on. Word webs can be used to show a central term and its related concepts, demonstrating the relationship between words based on meaning. Using this type of graphic organizer provides a tangible way to show students that some words have complex meanings and are interconnected with other aspects of language.

6. C: This method is likely to fail, producing students at a Frustration reading level. Those reading below grade level are likely to give up entirely. Those reading at grade level are likely to get frustrated and form habits that will actually slow down their development. Giving students texts that are too far beyond their reach produces frustrated readers. In an effort to succeed, frustrated readers are likely to apply strategies that have worked for them in the past but cannot work in this case because the text is simply beyond them. Looking for contextual clues to understand the meaning of unfamiliar words requires that most of the words in the passage are familiar. Breaking unfamiliar words into individual phonemes or syllables can be effective, but not if the number of such words is excessive. In this case, students below reading level and students at reading level will become frustrated when the skills that have worked for them in the past now fail.

7. D: Asking children to write a list provides them with a visual model that is a side-by-side comparison of the two countries. In creating that visual model, each student first has to organize his or her thoughts mentally, deciding whether each particular item under consideration is shared between both countries or is a difference between them.

8. D: When an online source is in the PDF file format or another file format that has stable pagination, MLA guidelines advise to include applicable page numbers in in-text citations because these numbers are valid and will not change. Therefore, choice D is correct. If an internet source has no pagination, as often happens, the MLA does not advise avoiding the citation, so choice A is incorrect. Rather, it advises simply making the citation without page numbers. Although a printout of an internet source will by necessity have page numbers (for the printed pages), these page numbers will be inconsistent from one printout to another, unlike PDFs. Therefore, the MLA advises not including these page numbers even if you see them, so choice B is incorrect. As already explained, there are cases where an online source will have stable pagination, and the MLA recommends including page numbers in citations of these sources, so choice C is incorrect.

9. A: Basic interpersonal communication skills (BICS) are language skills required in everyday social communication. These are less cognitively demanding, do not involve specialized vocabulary, typically take place in meaningful social contexts, and are necessary for social interaction. Cognitive academic language proficiency (CALP) is formal academic subject content language learning. CALP is more cognitively demanding, involves specialized subject vocabularies, takes place in academic contexts, and is necessary for school success. ELL students typically take 6 months to 2 years to develop adequate BICS, but at least 5-7 years to develop adequate CALP. If they had no formal education in their native languages and/or no second-language acquisition support, development may take 7-10 years.

10. C: These are content-specific words. Because these words are specific to penguins, it's unlikely the students know their meanings. Without understanding what these words mean, the students would not be able to understand the content of the passage they were about to read.

11. B: "Pretty as a picture" is a simile, which is a comparison of two unlike things using the words *like* or *as*. A metaphor is a similar comparison between two unlike things, but metaphors do not use the words *like* or *as*. Synecdoche is a phrase that uses a part to represent the whole of something. For instance, one might refer to "the crown" to refer to a royal family. Finally, a paradox is a statement that appears to contradict itself. All of these are considered figures of speech.

12. A: An introduction should move from broad, general statements about a topic to a focused and specific point regarding the topic. This point is the thesis statement. While the strongest points should come later in the body of an essay, the most attention-grabbing statements should be those in the introduction, as these will serve to engage the reader's interest in the topic and in reading the rest of the essay. Therefore, choice B is incorrect. Starting with focused and specific statements followed by broad and general statements is the opposite of how an introduction should be structured, so choice C is incorrect. Writing experts advise that the technique of beginning an essay with a dictionary definition has become overused and should therefore be avoided, so choice D is incorrect.

13. D: The most practical, thorough, and effective solution is to conduct informal assessments, as well as formal assessments other than the one the school has selected for biannual administration, to obtain continuing data on student phonological development to inform instructional planning, implementation, and adjustments according to student responses. Limiting assessment to the biannual formal test (A) will not provide enough information for individualizing instruction to each student's needs timely enough. Lobbying administrators to change policy (B) could work with some teachers and some administrators, but in many other cases would waste energy and time—and could strain teacher-administrator relations—without succeeding. Using informal assessments continually (C) is a good but not complete solution, whereas using both informal and other formal assessments continually (D) is.

14. A: Phonemic awareness is the ability to recognize sounds within words, so it is a type of phonological awareness. Segmenting words and blending sounds are components of phonemic awareness. Phonological awareness includes an understanding of multiple components of spoken language. The ability to hear individual words within a vocalized stream and the ability to identify spoken syllables are types of phonological awareness.

15. D: Targeted instruction is achieved by assessing areas needing improvement as well as areas of greatest strength for each student, and adjusting instruction to target those areas. This helps to ensure that all members of a class are receiving instruction tailored to their specific needs.

16. B: Tone is the writer's attitude in a given piece of writing, as it is expressed in that writing. Voice can be thought of as the person who the reader "hears"—the particular way an individual writer expresses themselves. Choice B fills in the blanks correctly. Style (C and D) includes both of these and more; it is the effect a writer creates through purposeful use of all the elements of written language, from tone and voice to grammar and structure.

17. A: In both the fictional narrative genre and the nonfictional informational genre, the author will demonstrate some individual writing style; even very factual and objective expositional writing will reveal some personal stylistic characteristics. Labeled diagrams and photos are more likely to be found in informational nonfiction. The majority of books with excitement and drama are fictional narratives (some informational nonfiction books are presented in narrative form and include excitement, especially in children's literature, but these are the minority). Themes and plots are also literary elements associated with fictional narrative.

18. B: Consonant blend refers to a group of consonants in which each letter represents a separate sound.

19. B: A maze test is a specific type of cloze test. In a cloze test, words are deleted, and the reader must supply the missing words using contextual clues and vocabulary that is familiar. A maze test is essentially a multiple-choice application of a cloze test.

20. B: The verbs listed here all refer to taking pieces or parts of information or knowledge and bringing them together to create a whole, and to building relationships among the parts to fit new or different circumstances. Analysis is the opposite of synthesis—breaking information down into its component parts and demonstrating the relationships among those parts. An assignment for analysis would ask the student to compare, distinguish, test, categorize, examine, contrast, or analyze information. Evaluation is making judgments of information based on given criteria, confirming or supporting certain preferences, and persuading the reader. An assignment targeting evaluation would use words like evaluate, predict, appraise, conclude, score, judge, or compare. Application is using knowledge in new contexts. The assignment would ask the student to apply, prepare, practice, use, operate, sketch, calculate, solve, or illustrate.

21. B: According to many academic standards, second graders should be able to determine the meanings of new or unfamiliar words by comparing them to synonyms (words with similar meanings) and antonyms (words with opposite meanings). First graders are expected to use phonics (letter-sound correspondences), word roots, word suffixes, and analogies (A) to decode words for reading. It is expected of third graders to use not only known synonyms and antonyms, but additionally homophones (words sounding the same with different meanings) and homographs (words spelled the same but with different meanings) they know to discern new or unfamiliar word meanings (C). Determining word meanings by referring to word roots, prefixes, suffixes, idiomatic expressions, and familiar diacritical marks used in dictionaries (D) is expected of fourth graders.

22. C: The act of decoding involves first recognizing the sounds individual letters and letter groups make, and then blending the sounds to read the word. A child decoding the word *spin*, for example, would first pronounce *sp/i/n* as individual sound units. She then would repeat the sounds, smoothly blending them. Because decoding involves understanding letters and their sounds, it is sometimes known as the alphabetic principle.

23. D: Based on a Japanese form of poetry, haiku have become popular with students and teachers alike. Reading and writing haiku helps younger students become aware of syllables and helps older students learn about subtleties of vocabulary.

24. B: Assessment is an ongoing process that involves formal testing and a host of other methods. Students are working at any given time in the school year on a multitude of skill sets, and all of these skills are interrelated and developing simultaneously at different rates. It is difficult to provide a complete "snapshot" of a student's abilities, because each student develops in a unique and complex manner. Choice A would only offer insight into a student's reading fluency. Choice C would show how a student could perform on standardized tests; however, many factors such as anxiety and test-taking speed affect those scores. Choice D relies on the teacher to interpret the student's strengths and weaknesses and would require an almost impossible attention to detail. Choice B includes both formal and informal assessments as well as giving insight into writing, vocabulary and other skill sets in a comprehensive portfolio.

25. B: Before beginning fluency instruction, typically not before halfway through the first grade at the earliest, teachers should ensure that students have strong word recognition skills to provide the necessary foundation. Student speed and automaticity in decoding individual words are directly related to developing reading fluency (A): rapid, automatic word decoding is the precursor to fluent reading. Reading fluency not only indicates faster information processing, it also has a direct impact on comprehension (C) because the faster a student can process information, the better the student can comprehend what she reads. When a student must decode words more slowly and less automatically, both reading fluency and comprehension are decreased (D). Slow, conscious decoding does not increase comprehension by being more careful or thoughtful; instead, laborious student efforts to decode separate words for meaning divert the attention they could devote to overall comprehension if they could decode rapidly, effortlessly, and automatically.

26. C: In one minute, a student who misreads one or less than one word per twenty words, or with 95%–100% accuracy, is at an Independent reading level. A student who misreads one or less than one word per ten words, or with 90%–95% accuracy, is at an Instructional level. A student misreading more than one word out of ten, or with less than 90% accuracy, is at a Frustration level.

27. A: The haiku, originating in Japanese poetry and since adopted in English-language poetry, is a short poem of only three lines, often with 17 syllables, with the first and third lines having five syllables and the second line having seven syllables. (In Japanese there are many other rules, which become complicated in comparison to the English version.) Because this syllable pattern is a defining characteristic of English-language haiku, choice A is correct. Haiku are typically unrhymed, so they do not have a rhyme scheme (B). Similarly, they do not employ any regular meter (C). Because haiku are typically 17 syllables or fewer, they do not involve long narratives (D).

28. A: Students are completely capable of understanding and appreciating oral traditions and written texts from other world cultures, as well as those originating from cultures in the students' own community. In fact, introducing a variety of material can increase some students' appreciation of language and literature as it enables them to learn about the world around them. Language skills emerge at a point in most children's development during which students are fascinated with learning new concepts. Introducing a variety of texts also benefits students in a classroom who belong to other cultures; these students are able to learn concepts from texts that represent their family, culture, or country of origin.

29. C: In Choice A, the word prince is capitalized, even though it does not have a suffix. In choice B, the word *multimedia* contains the prefix *multi-*, but no suffix. Choice C contains a word with the root *please*, which also has both a prefix and a suffix. The suffix *-ing* acts as the suffix in *displeasing*, therefore it is correctly capitalized. Choice D correctly has *bookkeeper* capitalized due to the suffix -*er* but neglects to capitalize *examined* even though it also contains a suffix. Choice C is the only correct choice available.

30. A: Most adults can understand the relationship between oral and written language: components of oral language have representational symbols that can be written and decoded. However, most normally-developing children acquire spoken language first and begin to develop reading and writing skills as they approach school-age. Many children are first exposed to the concept of written language when an adult introduces books or other written texts. However, a child's ability to read and write develops over time and is dependent on the development of physiological processes such as hearing, sight, and fine motor skills for writing. Written language development also typically requires direct instruction. Most children must be taught to read and write and rarely learn these skills simply by observing others.

31. D: Phonemes are the smallest units of sound in words. In this activity, students are replacing one phoneme with another, which is known as phoneme substitution. Alliteration refers to a series of words in which most words begin with the same sound. Segmenting refers to breaking a word down into its individual sounds, or phonemes. Onset and rime blending involve blending the beginning sound of a word with the rest of the word.

32. D: Classrooms will most always consist of students at different levels of ability. The physical and psychological processes needed for reading evolve simultaneously over time and do so at different rates for each individual. No two students will match up perfectly with respect to language skills. Language skills also incorporate a variety of other processes, including speaking, listening, thinking, viewing, writing, and reading. By pairing direct instruction with various types of cognitive processes, all students receive varied instruction and will make progress. By being introduced to different types of text, students will develop skills according to their own strengths at that particular time.

33. B: Manipulatives are three-dimensional concrete objects that students can not only look at but also manipulate, as the name indicates (e.g., touch, move, rearrange, dismantle, reassemble). Examples may be three-dimensional objects, demonstrations, or (more often) verbal descriptions given orally, printed, or written. Graphic organizers are diagrams (e.g., Venn diagrams), charts, timelines, concept maps, word webs, etc., which are two-dimensional, visual, graphic materials. Charts, tables, and graphs, though less pictorial and conceptual and more linear and numerical than graphic organizers, are also two-dimensional in print, online, or on screen.

34. D: CVC words, like dog, sit, and leg, are composed of a consonant, a vowel, and a consonant. To learn to read them, students must be familiar with the letters used and their sounds. A teacher can present a word like *sit* to students who also know the consonants *b/f/h/p* and ask them to create a word family of other CVC words. The students will be able to read *bit, fit, hit,* and *pit* because they are similar to the word *sit* that they have just learned.

35. B: Researchers find that both learners a native language (L1 learners) and a learners of a second-language (L2 learners) go through all stages of language acquisition. However, L2 learners are often urged by teachers and others to skip the so-called "silent period" more than their L1 learner counterparts, who are acquiring their native language. Therefore, choice B is correct. Because both L1 learners and L2 learners have been found to go through all the stages, choices A and C are incorrect. L2 learners are not likely to undergo the third stage later, but sooner than or at a similar time as L1 learners, so choice D is incorrect.

36. C: There is currently a wide variety of technology resources available that can support class instruction. However, teachers must choose carefully in order to ensure that the technology is useful and relevant to the intended learning outcomes for the class. The language lab described allows students to experience text through both listening and reading, thereby utilizing different processes in the brain. The interactive modules also support decoding and comprehension skills that go along with the texts. This use of technology reinforces important skills in a way that will be unique and interesting for the students.

37. B: Based on Charles Read's (1975) research into invented and phonetic spelling, Richard Gentry (1982, 2006, 2010) identified five phases of spelling. *Precommunicative*: Alphabetic symbols without letter-sound correspondences, complete alphabet knowledge, spelling directionality, or uppercase and lowercase letter distinctions. *Semiphonetic*: Letter-sound correspondence understanding emerges; students frequently spell words with single letters or abbreviated syllables. *Phonetic*: Not all spellings follow standard conventions, but students systematically represent all phonemes with letters. Misspellings are typically accurate in terms of articulatory placement (*e* for short *i*, *a* for short *e*, *i* for short *o*, etc.) *Transitional*: Students move from phonetic to conventional, visual spellings, informed by their growing understanding of word structure. "Higheked" for "hiked" and "egul" for "eagle" are examples of their more approximate spellings. *Correct*: Students have learned the fundamental rules of English orthography, including irregular and alternative spellings, silent consonants, prefixes and suffixes, etc., and can identify misspellings.

38. B: Context clues offer insight into the probable meaning of unfamiliar words.

39. B: The term standard English refers to a form of English used in an English-speaking country that is reflected in dictionaries and grammar books, taught to English language learners, used in published writing, and so on. Because the rules of standard English are adhered to mainly in edited writing, choice B is correct. Standard English actually includes and allows for a range of dialects, which is exemplified by the fact that what is considered a standard English varies between English-speaking countries, so choice A is incorrect. Standard English is not universal; different English-speaking countries have different standard Englishes, so choice C is incorrect. Choice D is incorrect because edited and published writing generally adheres to some form of standard English.

40. C: All private and public schools will provide some sort of curriculum guidance, which usually takes the form of a list of concepts that must be covered within a certain time frame. Teachers must use this provision as a guideline for planning instruction. However, with time and creativity, teachers can bring these concepts to life using various types of material (e.g., oral, written, media, and performance) and engaging instructional methods. Teachers can also find ways to integrate instruction and concepts with teachers of other subjects to ensure that students understand that language skills are not only interrelated, but also applicable to all areas of learning.

Mathematics

1. A: The probability that the dart will land in the inner circle is equal to the ratio of the area of inner circle to the area of the outer circle, or $\frac{\pi(3)^2}{\pi(6)^2}$. This reduces to $\frac{1}{4}$.

2. B: The volume of a sphere may be calculated using the formula $V = \frac{4}{3}\pi r^3$, where r represents the radius. Substituting 3.5 for r gives $V = \frac{4}{3}\pi(3.5)^3$, which simplifies to $V \approx 179.6 \text{ in}^3$.

3. A: The vertical line of symmetry is represented by an equation of the form $x = a$. The horizontal line of symmetry is represented by an equation of the form $y = b$. One line of symmetry occurs at $x = -4$. The other line of symmetry occurs at $y = 6$.

4. D: To draw a box-and-whisker plot from the data, find the median, quartiles, and upper and lower limits.

3|6 799
4|2|3889   Key
5|0|11158| 2|123 = 21, 22, 23
6|0 0123

The median is $\frac{50+51}{2} = 50.5$, the lower quartile is $\frac{42+43}{2} = 42.5$, and the upper quartile is $\frac{58+60}{2} = 59$. The box of the box-and-whisker plot goes through the quartiles, and a line through the box represents the median of the data. The whiskers extend from the box to the lower and upper limits, unless there are any outliers in the set. In this case, there are no outliers, so the box-and-whisker plot in choice A correctly represents the data set.

To draw a pie chart, find the percentage of data contained in each of the ranges shown. There are four out of twenty numbers between 30 and 39, inclusive, so the percentage shown in the pie chart for that range of data is $\frac{4}{20} \times 100\% = 20\%$; there are five values between 40 to 49, inclusive, so the percentage of data for that sector is $\frac{5}{20} \times 100\% = 25\%$; $\frac{6}{20} \times 100\% = 30\%$ of the data is within the range of 50–59, and $\frac{5}{20} \times 100\% = 25\%$ is within the range of 60–69. The pie chart shows the correct percentage of data in each category.

To draw a cumulative frequency histogram, find the cumulative frequency of the data.

Range	Frequency	Cumulative frequency
30–39	4	4
40–49	5	9
50–59	6	15
60–69	5	20

The histogram shows the correct cumulative frequencies. Therefore, all of the graphs represent the data set.

5. B: Rate in miles per hour can be expressed as, mph $= \frac{\text{distance in miles}}{\text{time in hours}}$. So, Zeke's driving speed on the way to Atlanta and home from Atlanta in mph can be expressed as $\frac{d}{3}$ and $\frac{d}{2}$, respectively, where d is the distance between Zeke's house and his destination. Since Zeke drove 20 mph faster on his way home, (speed home) − (speed to store) = 20. Substitute Zeke's speeds and solve for d.

$$\frac{d}{2} - \frac{d}{3} = 20$$

$$6\left(\frac{d}{2} - \frac{d}{3} = 20\right)$$
$$3d - 2d = 120$$
$$d = 120$$

Since the distance between Zeke's house and the store in Atlanta is 120 miles, Zeke drove a total distance of 240 miles in five hours. Therefore, his average speed was $\frac{240\text{ miles}}{5\text{ hours}} = 48$ mph.

6. B: All regular polygons have rotational symmetry. The angle of rotation is the smallest angle by which the polygon can be rotated such that it maps onto itself; any multiple of this angle will also map the polygon onto itself. The angle of rotation for a regular polygon is the angle formed between two lines drawn from consecutive vertices to the center of the polygon. Since the vertices of a regular polygon lie on a circle, for a regular polygon with n sides, the angle of rotation measures $\frac{360°}{n}$. Therefore, a square has rotational symmetry about the angle 90° and its multiples. A regular hexagon has rotational symmetry about the angle 60° and its multiples. A regular octagon has rotational symmetry about 45° and its multiples. And a regular decagon has rotational symmetry about 36° and its multiples. Since 120° is a multiple of 60°, the correct answer is a regular hexagon.

7. D: The original cost may be represented by the equation $45 = x - 0.25x$ or $45 = 0.75x$. Dividing both sides of the equation by 0.75 gives $x = 60$.

8. C: The volume of a pyramid may be calculated using the formula $V = \frac{1}{3}Bh$, where B represents the area of the base and h represents the height. Since the base is a square, the area of the base is equal to 6^2, or 36 square inches. Substituting 36 for B and 9 for h gives $V = \frac{1}{3}(36)(9)$, which simplifies to $V = 108$ cubic inches.

9. D: Students using cardboard manipulatives is the most learner-centered activity since it includes hands-on activities with the use of manipulatives. Watching a video and completing a worksheet are learner-centered but do not include hands-on activities. The teacher working subtraction problems on the whiteboard is teacher-centered.

10. D: This problem can be represented using the proportion $\frac{number\ of\ wins}{total\ games} = \frac{number\ of\ wins}{total\ games}$. If the ratio of wins to losses is 2 : 1, then the ratio of wins to total games is 2 : 3. The proportion to determine the number of wins is $\frac{x}{36} = \frac{2}{3}$.

11. D: This sequence lists the sum of the squares of natural numbers and 1. For example, $1^2 + 1$ is 2, and $2^2 + 1$ is 5. The next number in the sequence can be determined squaring 5 and adding 1, $5^2 + 1$, which is 26. Note also that the differences between consecutive numbers in the sequence are consecutive odd integers starting at 3. For example, 2 + 3 is 5, 5 + 5 is 10, and 10 + 7 is 17, so the next number in the sequence is 17 + 9, or 26.

12. C: As they are a pair of alternate exterior angles, ∠g and ∠c are congruent.

13. D: The numbers in this sequence progress according to a pattern. Each progressing number can be expressed by the equation $x + 2 = n$, where x is the difference between the previous two numbers and n is the number added to the previous number, to yield the progressing number. For instance, the difference in 24 and 16 is 8. By adding 2 to 8, you know that you must add 10 to 24 in order to yield 34. In the next part of the sequence, $x = 10$ and $n = 12$. 34 + 12 = 46, the next number in the sequence. Therefore, by following this pattern, you would add 16 to 60, which results in 76.

14. D: The identity element is d since $d\#a = a\#d = a, d\#b = b\#d = b, d\#c = c\#d = c$, and $d\#d = d$. The inverse of element c is c since $c\#c = d$, the identity element. The operation # is commutative because $a\#b = b\#a$, $a\#c = c\#a$, etc. Rather than check that the operation is commutative for each pair of elements, note that elements in the table display symmetry about the diagonal elements; this indicates that the operation is indeed commutative.

#	*a*	*b*	*c*	*d*
a	*c*	*d*	*b*	*a*
b	*d*	*c*	*a*	*b*
c	*b*	*a*	*d*	*c*
d	*a*	*b*	*c*	*d*

15. B: One way to approach this problem is to first consider the number of arrangements of the five members of the family if Tasha (T) and Mac (M) must sit together. Treat them as a unit seated in a fixed location at the table; then arrange the other three family members (A, B, and C):

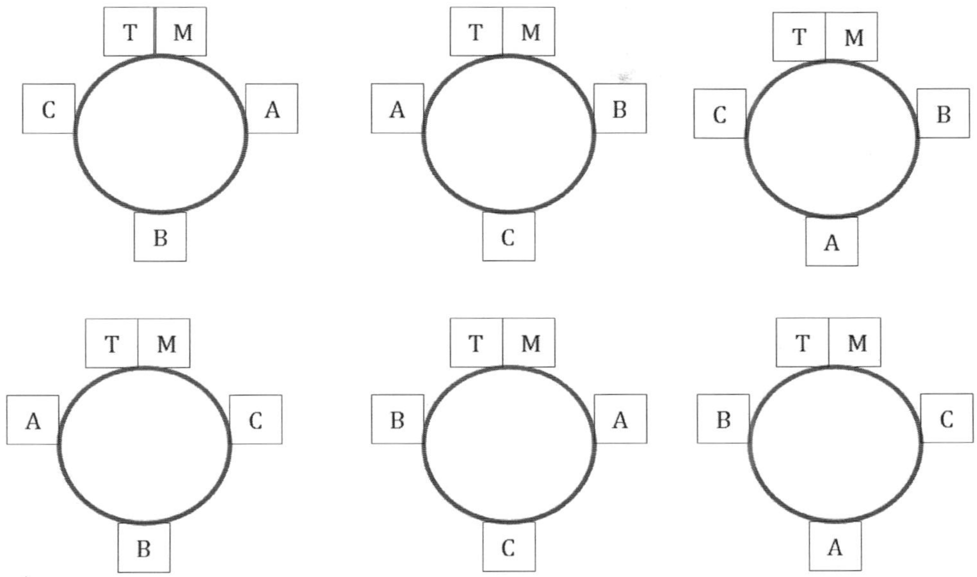

There are six ways to arrange four units around a circle as shown. Any other arrangement would be a rotation in which the elements are in the same order and would therefore not be a unique arrangement. Of course, Mac and Tasha are not actually a single unit. They would still be sitting beside each other if they were to trade seats, so there are 12 arrangements in which the two are seated next to one another. In all other arrangements of the five family members, they are separated. Therefore, to find the number of arrangements in which Tasha and Mac are *not* sitting together, subtract 12 from the possible arrangement of five units around a circle. There are $(n-1)!$ ways to arrange n units around a circle for $n > 1$. So, $(5-1)! - 12 = 24 - 12 = 12$.

16. C: A reflection across the x-axis will result in a triangle with vertices at $(2,-3)$, $(4,-7)$, and $(6,-3)$. A rotation of 270 degrees counterclockwise is denoted by the following: $(x,y) \rightarrow (y,-x)$. Thus, a rotation of the reflected triangle by 270 degrees will result in a figure with vertices at $(-3,-2)$, $(-7,-4)$, and $(-3,-6)$. The transformed triangle indeed has these coordinates as its vertices.

17. D: Real numbers include all rational and irrational numbers. Rational numbers include all integers. The set of real numbers include the other three sets.

18. D: Congruent figures have the same shape and the same size. Two squares have the same shape. If the areas are the same, they also have the same size and are congruent. Choice A is incorrect because two rectangles can have the same perimeter but not the same shape. Choice B is the incorrect because two polygons of the same shape are not necessarily the same size. Choice C is incorrect because two polygons can have the same side lengths but different shapes. Therefore, the correct answer is choice D.

19. C: The area of a trapezoid may be calculated using the formula, $A = \frac{1}{2}(b_1 + b_2)h$. Thus, the area of the trapezoid is represented as $A = \frac{1}{2}(4+2)(2)$, which simplifies to $A = 6$. The area of the triangle is represented as $A = \frac{1}{2}(4)(3)$, which also simplifies to $A = 6$. Thus, the total area is 12 square units.

20. C: The situation may be modeled by the system of inequalities $\begin{cases} 6x + 3y \leq 75 \\ x + y \leq 30 \end{cases}$ where x is the number of coffee mugs and y is the number of note pads. Some algebraic manipulation gives us the inequalities in slope-intercept form: $\begin{cases} y \leq -2x + 25 \\ y \leq -x + 30 \end{cases}$. All four choices graph these lines correctly, but only choice C correctly shades just the region that is below both lines, indicating that both conditions are met.

21. D: The constant of proportionality is equal to the slope. Using the points, $(2, -8)$ and $(5, -20)$, the slope may be written as $\frac{-20-(-8)}{5-2}$, which equals -4.

22. D: Ms. Alejo is using different activities to meet the various readiness levels of her students. This aspect is described as differentiated instruction. Collaborative learning and small group instruction describe the aspect that the students are in groups. The question does not address nonlinguistic representations, such as charts and visual aids. Therefore, the correct answer is choice D.

23. B: Graham has placed Group 1 with 40¢, Group 2 with 38¢, and Group 3 with 29¢. Henry has placed Group 1 with 34¢, Group 2 with 27¢, and Group 3 with 29¢. Landon has placed Group 1 with 59¢, Group 2 with 43¢, and Group 3 with 57¢. Elizabeth has placed Group 1 with 39¢, Group 2 with 41¢, and Group 3 with 22¢.

24. D: The triangle is a 45-45-90 right triangle. Thus, if each leg is represented by x, the hypotenuse is represented by $x\sqrt{2}$. Thus, the hypotenuse is equal to $8\sqrt{2}$ cm.

25. C: The center of the sphere is shared by the center of the cube, and each of the corners of the cube touches the surface of the sphere. Therefore, the diameter of the sphere is the line that passes through the center of the cube and connects one corner of the cube to the opposite corner. In the illustration below, notice that the diameter d of the sphere can be represented as the hypotenuse of a right triangle with a short leg measuring 4 units. (Since the volume of the cube is 64 cubic units, each of its sides measures $\sqrt[3]{64} = 4$ units.) The long leg of the triangle is the diagonal of the base of the cube.

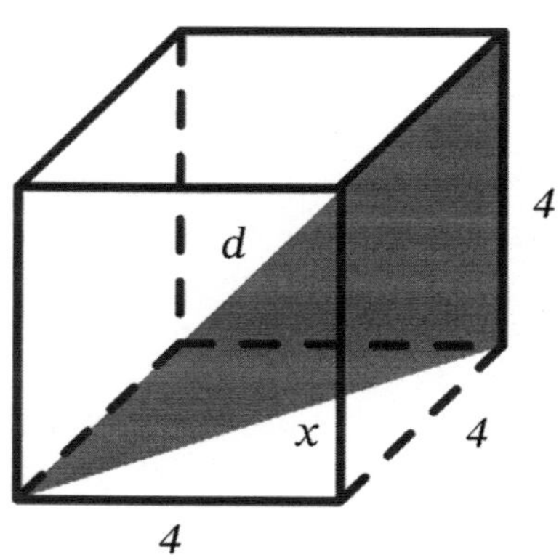

The length of the long leg can be found using the Pythagorean theorem:

$$x^2 = 4^2 + 4^2 = 32$$
$$x = \sqrt{32} = 4\sqrt{2}$$

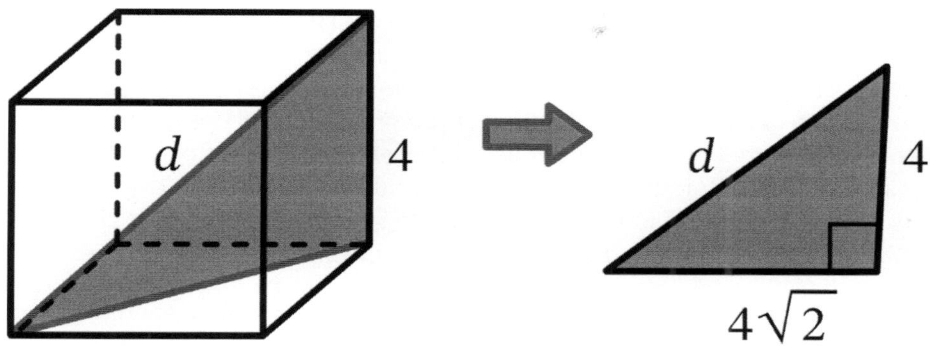

Use the Pythagorean theorem again to find d, the diameter of the sphere:

$$d^2 = \left(4\sqrt{2}\right)^2 + 4^2 = 32 + 16 = 48$$
$$d = \sqrt{48} = 4\sqrt{3}$$

To find the volume of the sphere, use the formula $V = \frac{4}{3}\pi r^3$. Since the radius r of the sphere is half the diameter, $r = 2\sqrt{3}$, and $V = \frac{4}{3}\pi(2\sqrt{3})^3 = \frac{4}{3}\pi\left(24\sqrt{3}\right) = 32\pi\sqrt{3}$ cubic units.

26. C: The situation may be modeled by this system of equations:

$$\begin{cases} 4y + 3c = 9.55 \\ 2y + 2c = 5.90 \end{cases}$$

Multiplying the bottom equation by −2 gives:

$$\begin{cases} 4y + 3c = 9.55 \\ -4y - 4c = -11.80 \end{cases}$$

Adding the two equations gives $-c = -2.25$, or $c = 2.25$. Thus, one box of crackers costs $2.25.

27. B: A regular solid prism is a solid, three-dimensional shape which has length, width, and height. The bases are of the same shape, and the shape of the other faces depend on the shape of the bases. The volume of a regular solid prism can be determined by multiplying the area of the base by the height of the prism.

28. D: The intersection of the two sets is empty, denoted by the symbol, $\emptyset$. There are not any elements common to both sets.

29. B: A line graph is often used to show change over time. A Venn diagram shows the relationships among sets. A box-and-whisker plot displays how numeric data are distributed throughout the range. A pie chart shows the relationship of parts to a whole.

30. C: Students in first grade are generally in Piaget's preoperational stage but are making the transition to the concrete operational stage. In the preoperational stage, children are beginning to think symbolically about concrete objects, but are unlikely to think abstractly. In an activity to develop understanding of measurement, it is best to use concrete, manipulative objects and to avoid measurement tasks involving conservation, as this concept is developed in later stages. Measuring the height of a pencil sharpener with a meter stick and measuring the length of a chalkboard with a tape measure are likely achievable for first graders, but are unlikely to give students the stimulation of individual manipulation with concrete objects. A tape measure would only allow one or two students to participate at a time. Furthermore, it may be beneficial for young children to develop an understanding of units by using various non-standard units. Measuring the circumference of a trash can is also probably developmentally inappropriate as it involves some understanding of later geometry concepts such as circumference and may be confusing to first-graders as they should not understand conservation at this point. Having students measure their desks with units such as dominos is an excellent activity for first graders, as it allows students to work individually with manipulatives and allows them to interact with non-standard units.

31. B: Since the figures are similar, the following proportion may be written and solved for x.

$$\frac{6}{4}=\frac{8}{x}$$
$$6x = 4 \times 8$$
$$6x = 32$$
$$x = \frac{32}{6} = 5\frac{2}{6} = 5\frac{1}{3}$$

Therefore, the measure of x is $5\frac{1}{3}$ in.

32. D: This problem can be solved using the percent change formula: $\%\ change = \frac{new-old}{old} \times 100\%$. Thus, the percentage increase is represented as $\%\ change = \frac{1{,}100-800}{800} \times 100\% = 37.5\%$.

33. A: In the third line of the problem, the student incorrectly added the 5 and 2 rather than multiplying 2(2). According to the order of operations, the student should multiply before adding.

34. B: The equation $y = -4x - 6$ is in slope-intercept form, $y = mx + b$, where m is the slope and b is the y-intercept. All four graphs show the correct y-intercept, –6, but only one shows the correct slope, –4. The slope of a line can be found by picking any two points (x_1, y_1) and (x_2, y_2) on the line and calculating $m = \frac{y_2-y_1}{x_2-x_1}$. For choice B, we can choose points $(0, -6)$ and $(-2,2)$, which gives us $m = \frac{2-(-6)}{-2-0} = -4$. None of the other graphs have a slope of –4.

35. A: The amount to be administered may be written as $\frac{1}{12} \times \frac{34}{10}$, which equals $\frac{17}{60}$. Thus, she should administer $\frac{17}{60}$ fluid ounces of medicine.

36. A: $3 + x + 3x + 3 + x = 5x + 6$ correctly shows how the combination of like terms on the left side of the equation results in the expression on the right side of the equation. $7x - 2x = 9x$ incorrectly combines like terms by adding the coefficients rather than subtracting them. $2y + 2y + 2y = 6y^3$ incorrectly adds the exponents of like terms instead of just adding the coefficients of like terms. $2.5(x + 2) = 2.5x + 2$ incorrectly distributes the 2.5 across the parentheses by neglecting to multiply the 2.5 with the last term in the expression.

37. B: The amount she spends on rent and utilities is equal to 0.38($40,000), or $15,200, which is approximately $15,000.

38. C: To find the probability of an event, divide the number of favorable outcomes by the total number of outcomes. When there are two events in which the first depends on the second, multiply the first ratio by the second ratio. In the first part of the problem, the probability of choosing a licorice jelly bean is two out of twenty possible outcomes, or $\frac{2}{20}$. Then, because one jelly bean has already been chosen, there are four cinnamon beans out of a total of 19, or $\frac{4}{19}$. By multiplying the two ratios and dividing by a common denominator, one arrives at the final probability of $\frac{2}{95}$.

39. C: There are 36 months in 3 years. Since Amy saves $450 every 3 months, the following proportion can be written to find the amount she saves in 36 months: $\frac{450}{3} = \frac{x}{36}$. Cross multiplying gives you the equation $3x = 16{,}200$, which can be solved for x. Dividing both sides of the equation by 3 gives $x = 5{,}400$.

40. C: The associative property of multiplication states that when three or more numbers are multiplied, the product is the same regardless of the way in which the numbers are grouped (i.e., where parentheses are inserted or removed). Choice C shows that the product of 2, 3, and 4 is the same with two different groupings of the factors. Choice A demonstrates the distributive property. Choice B shows grouping, but the factors are different. Choice D demonstrates the commutative property of multiplication. Therefore, the correct choice is C.

Science

1. D: French chemist Louis Pasteur (1822–1895), considered one of the founders of bacteriology, developed a process of heating and cooling food products like milk and wine that reduces the number of pathogenic microbes to a level that will not cause sickness when ingested. This process is named pasteurization after him. Pasteur also made the first vaccines against both rabies and anthrax. All three of these accomplishments were incredible breakthroughs in preventing fatal diseases. Pasteur's experiments advanced the germ theory of disease, which when first proposed, met strong resistance from those who did not believe microorganisms cause sickness. His work supported its acceptance and colleague Robert Koch's proof of it in 1890. However, Pasteur did not create the first polio vaccine.

2. A: Magnetic poles occur in pairs known as magnetic dipoles. Individual atoms can be considered magnetic dipoles due to the spin and rotation of the electrons in the atoms. When the dipoles are aligned, the material is magnetic. Choices B, C, and D are all magnetic materials. Therefore, the magnetic dipoles in these materials are not randomly aligned. Only choice A has randomly aligned dipoles.

3. C: When children conduct simple experiments and are able to see patterns and meanings in the results, they are using the scientific process skill of inference. They use the skill of measurement (A) when they quantify the various physical properties of objects, like length, width, height, weight, etc. They use the skill of classification (B) when they group objects, events, conditions, or situations according to the properties they share in common. They use the skill of prediction (D) when they apply their experiences from experimenting to form new hypotheses to test.

4. A: Heat on Earth is generated by the sun. The more direct sunlight an area on Earth receives from the sun, the warmer it will be. The earth is most tilted toward or away from the sun at the solstices between spring and summer or between fall and winter. When the Northern hemisphere is tilted away from the sun, all of the countries in the Northern hemisphere experience fall and winter. At that same time, the Southern hemisphere experiences spring and summer. The same is true when the Southern hemisphere experiences fall and winter; the Northern hemisphere experiences spring and summer.

5. C: A population that reaches maximum size and ceases to grow due to a limited availability of resources is said to be at carrying capacity. The carrying capacity of a species is influenced by many factors such as the amount of land or water available, food supply, and predators. Unstable and moving towards extinction are not correct as carrying capacity does not necessarily mean it is unstable or becoming extinct. Shrinking exponentially is also incorrect as the question says it has stopped growing, not that it is reducing in size.

6. A: The center of an atom is known as the nucleus. It is composed of protons and neutrons. The nucleus is positively charged due to protons having a positive charge and neutrons being electrically neutral.

7. B: Butterflies undergo a *complete* metamorphosis during their life cycle (i.e., they completely change in form). The stages of a complete metamorphosis are (1) egg, (2) larva, (3) pupa, and (4) imago. Mosquitos (A), dragonflies (C), and grasshoppers (D) all go through an *incomplete* metamorphosis in their life cycles, including the egg, larva, and imago (adult) stages, but not the pupa stage. The butterfly pupa, called a chrysalis, is protected by a cocoon, does not feed, and is inactive until the imago (adult) emerges.

8. A: Most organic molecules are not highly soluble in water. A low melting point, covalent bonds, and high flammability are all characteristics of organic molecules. Organic molecules are those that contain carbon atoms, with a few exceptions. Organic molecules tend to be less soluble in water than inorganic salts. They are good at forming unique structures and there are many organic compounds. Examples of organic compounds include hydrocarbons, carbohydrates, lipids, and proteins.

9. D: The formation of sedimentary rock does not include heat. Of the three types of rock—igneous, sedimentary, and metamorphic—heat is essential to two: igneous and metamorphic. Sedimentary rocks are formed by sediments that get deposited and then compacted or cemented together. Sedimentary rocks are classified into detrital, organic, or chemical sediments. Answer A, layering, is correct since sediments can be deposited or otherwise formed in layers. Answer B, cementation, is also called lithification. Answer C, compaction, refers to the pressure forming sedimentary rock leading to cementation.

10. A: Descriptive studies are usually the first form of study in a new area of scientific inquiry. The other answer options here are also forms of scientific study, but they are typically not employed until after initial descriptive studies have been done.

11. A: Heat capacity refers to the amount of heat or thermal energy required to raise the temperature of a specific substance by a given unit. A substance with a higher heat capacity requires more heat to raise its temperature than a substance with a lower heat capacity. The comparison here is that the specific heat capacity of ice is half as much as that of liquid water, so it takes half the amount of energy to increase the same amount of ice one temperature unit than it would if it were liquid water.

12. A: A liquid crystal is best described as having a molecular arrangement is random in some directions and regular in others. A liquid crystal may seem like a contradiction as it seems to refer to two different states of matter. Liquid crystals have properties of both liquids and solids. The molecules of a liquid crystal are loosely bound, allowing them to flow like a liquid, yet they arrange themselves in a repeating pattern like the molecules of a solid which are rigidly fixed in a pattern. Liquid crystals can also organize into layers, but with randomness in the layers.

13. A: The process of absolute dating compares the amount of radioactive material in a rock to the amount that has decayed into another element. Choice B is not usually done. Usually, the stratigraphic layer of rock is used to date the fossils. This is referred to as relative dating. Choice C is incorrect as this would not lead to a correct date since the daughter elements may have a different half-life than the parent material.

14. A: The scientific method is a series of steps to solve a problem. All of the other choices are steps of the scientific method. The steps of the scientific method in order are to make an observation, ask a scientific question, formulate a hypothesis, make a prediction, and test the hypothesis. After the test or experiment is complete, the question should be addressed with the results and used to ask new questions.

15. A: Enzymes are large protein molecules that act as biological catalysts and play an important role in all bodily processes. They are not fat soluble, are not acids, and are not lipids.

16. B: A reaction that uses electricity to drive it. An electrolysis reaction is a chemical reaction that uses electricity to drive it. Electrolysis reactions take place in an electrolytic cell, where one substance will be oxidized and another will be reduced using electrical energy from a battery or other source. Usually, an electrolytic cell is made up of a battery connected to two metal electrodes which are placed in two separate ionic solutions. A salt bridge connects the two beakers of solution and allows positive or negative ions to flow into the solutions as needed to keep the charge balanced as the reaction takes place. The electrode where oxidation takes place is called the anode, which would be connected to the negative terminal on a battery. The electrode where reduction takes place is called the cathode and is connected to the positive terminal of a battery. These reactions are very important for electroplating metals.

17. D: Ocean currents are not controlled by the phase of the moon. The phases of the moon refer to our viewpoint from Earth of the sun's illumination of the moon. Half the moon is illuminated by the sun at any given time. For example, a new moon is one we do not see because the side being lit by the sun is not facing us. The revolution of the moon around the earth affects the ocean tides, providing two highs and two lows at any given point during the day. Wind affects the surface currents of the ocean, while Earth's rotation affects deep currents. Landmasses affect ocean currents as well.

18. C: The majority of the solar energy that reaches Earth is absorbed by the oceans, which make up 71 percent of the Earth's surface. Because of water's high specific heat capacity, oceans can absorb and store large quantities of heat, thus preventing drastic increases in the overall atmospheric temperature.

19. B: Electrons with greater amounts of energy are found farther from the nucleus than electrons with less energy. The principal quantum number describes the level or shell that an electron is in. The lower the number, the closer the electron is to the nucleus and the lower it is in energy.

20. C: In humans, diploid cells are those that contain 46 chromosomes. There are 23 pairs of chromosomes each made up of one chromosome from the father and one from the mother. In meiosis I, each chromosome replicates itself and lines up, or synapses, with its homologous chromosome, and each of the daughter cells ends up with one copy of each of the chromosomes.

The two daughter cells at the end of meiosis I are haploid because they contain half of the chromosomes of the parent cell. In humans, this would be 23 chromosomes. However, each of these chromosomes are made of two sister chromatids. In meiosis II, the sister chromatids in the daughter cells separate and result in the production of the gametes. These are also haploid cells because they contain one copy of half of the genetic material of the parent cell. Four haploid cells result from meiosis. Choice A, mitosis, can be eliminated as it refers to the process of cell division where each daughter cell contains exactly the same genetic material as the parent cell. Choice B, telophase, refers to phases of both mitosis and meiosis, during which chromosomes move toward the opposite ends of the cell.

21. B: When land cools off rapidly at night and the ocean water stays relatively warm, it creates a land breeze. Sea breeze, or onshore breeze, occurs when the land heats the air above it. This heated, warmer air is less dense and rises. The cooler air from above the sea and higher sea level pressure creates a wind flow in the direction of the land. Coastal areas often have these cooler breezes. A monsoon is a seasonal wind in southern Asia that blows southwest in one season and northeast in another. The southwest winds in the summer bring heavy rain. The trade winds are the steady easterlies about the equator.

22. A: The structure of the Milky Way galaxy is spiral, meaning it has curved "arms" stretching out from a central point. While spiral galaxies have a flat, disc-like appearance, elliptical galaxies are more three-dimensional and appear to be roughly the same shape regardless of the viewing angle.

23. C: The ball will move forward with respect to the boat. Newton's first law of motion states that an object in motion tends to stay in motion until a force acts to change it. The ball is initially at rest with respect to the boat, but the boat is moving forward. When the front of the boat hits the dock, the boat quickly decelerates, but the ball does not. It continues to move forward because the force acting to stop the boat does not significantly affect the ball. With the ball now moving forward faster than the boat, the ball's motion relative to the boat is forward motion.

24. B: Organisms that belong to the same taxonomic group of family are most alike. In biological taxonomy, the ranks in descending order are Domain, Kingdom, Phylum, Class, Order, Family, Genus, and Species. The ranks become more exclusive and specific as the classification descends. Phylum, class, and order are all higher than the family group. The higher the rank, the fewer requirements it takes to be a member. Two mnemonics for taxonomy are Dashing Kings Play Cards On Fat Green Stools or Dear King Philip Cuts Open Five Green Snakes.

25. B: Recycling and using alternative sources of energy reduce the amount of pollutants introduced into the ecosystem, reduce the potential for disease-related human maladies, and reduce the reliance on nonrenewable resources. Greater production of goods and consumer spending in the future would probably be good for the economy, but not necessarily the environment. Fossil fuels are considered to be a nonrenewable energy resource.

26. C: Venus is not a gas giant. The four gas giants are Jupiter, Saturn, Uranus, and Neptune. While these gas giants are larger than Earth and are composed mostly of gases, Venus is a terrestrial planet that is comparable in size to the Earth.

27. B: If the chemicals heat up, their temperatures increase, and their kinetic energies therefore increase, so energy could not have been obtained from kinetic energy. Chemical reactions also do not typically involve absorption of heat from the environment. Instead, chemical bonds contain some amount of potential energy, which may be released in certain chemical reactions.

28. D: Respiration produces carbon dioxide and water. The net equation of respiration is the reverse of the equation for photosynthesis. Respiration is a series of reactions that consume glucose and oxygen to release energy and produce carbon dioxide and water. Oxygen and glucose are the substances that are broken down in respiration.

29. A: A good hypothesis is testable and logical, and can be used to predict future events. A good hypothesis is also simple, not complex.

30. A: The addition of energy causes a phase change. Phase changes are physical changes, not chemical changes. While sublimation is an example of a phase change, it occurs when a solid turns directly into a gas without passing through the liquid state. Condensation, another phase change, occurs when a gas turns to liquid.

31. A: Repeating a measurement several times can increase the precision of the measurement. Calibrating the equipment should only be done once for a whole set of measurements. Calibrating for each use will add a source of error and prevent measurements from being able to be compared. None of the other choices are useful strategies to increase the precision of a measurement.

32. A: When light waves hit a convex lens, they are refracted and converge. A convex lens curves or bulges with the middle being thicker and the edges thinner. A magnifying glass is an example. Light rays are refracted by different amounts as they pass through the lens. After light rays pass through, they converge at a point called the focus. An object viewed with a magnifying glass looks bigger because the lens bends the rays inward. Choice B would indicate a concave lens as it would cause the light to be refracted and diverge. Light is not reflected in this case, so neither choice C nor D would be applicable.

33. D: The circulatory system and gas exchange with the environment is not paired correctly. It is the respiratory system that exchanges gases with the environment by delivering oxygen to the bloodstream and releasing carbon dioxide. The circulatory system transports nutrients, gases, hormones, and blood to and away from cells. The muscle system controls movement through three types of muscle tissue. The nervous system controls sensory responses by carrying impulses away from and toward the cell body. The digestive system breaks down food for absorption into the bloodstream where it is delivered to cells for respiration.

34. A: Fission is a nuclear process where atomic nuclei split apart to form smaller nuclei. Nuclear fission can release large amounts of energy, emit gamma rays, and form daughter products. It is used in nuclear power plants and bombs. Choice B, fusion, refers to a nuclear process whereby atomic nuclei join to form a heavier nucleus, such as with stars. This can release or absorb energy depending upon the original elements. Choice C, decay, refers to an atomic nucleus spontaneously losing energy and emitting ionizing particles and radiation. Choice D, ionization, refers to a process by which atoms obtain a positive or negative charge because the number of electrons does not equal that of protons.

35. A: Glass is manufactured and can be recycled, but is considered a non-renewable resource. Wood is considered a renewable resource because with proper management, an equilibrium can be reached between harvesting trees and planting new ones. Cattle are managed in herds and a balance can be achieved between those consumed and those born. Soil is the result of long-term erosion and includes organic matter and minerals needed by plants. Soil found naturally in the environment is renewed. Crops can be rotated to help maintain a healthy soil composition for farming.

36. D: In the image, the parts of the flower are as follows:

1. Ovary – the pollen-receiving portion of the flower that resides at the base of the pistil.
2. Anther – the pollen-bearing tip of the stamen.
3. Petal – The soft, colorful parts of the flower that attract pollinators and protect the inner parts.
4. Sepal – The outermost part of a flower that protect the developing bud before blooming.
5. Filament – The stalk that supports the anther.

Of the available choices, only choice D, the sepal, is not considered a reproductive organ of the flower.

37. B: Technology often results from scientific discoveries. The relationship between science and technology is evident when scientific discoveries prompt technologic advances.

38. C: Methods of heat transfer include conduction, convection, and radiation. With convection, heat is transferred by moving currents in fluids such as air or water. When a person holds his hands over steaming water, heat is transmitted to his hands by means of convection. With conduction, heat is transferred by direct contact, such as when someone touches an electric blanket. In radiation, heat is transferred by electromagnetic waves, such as when someone places his hands near the sides of an incandescent light bulb. When a person warms his hands by rubbing them together, heat is generated by friction.

39. A: Solutions and compounds used in labs may be hazardous according to state and local regulatory agencies and should be treated with appropriate precaution. Emptying the solutions into the sink and rinsing with warm water and soap does not take into account the hazards associated with a specific solution in terms of vapors or interactions with water, soap, and waste piping systems. Ensuring the solutions are secured in closed containers and throwing them away may allow toxic chemicals into landfills and subsequently into freshwater systems. Storing the solutions in a secured, dry place for later use is incorrect, as chemicals should not be reused due to the possibility of contamination.

40. D: The most recently formed parts of the Earth's crust can be found at mid-ocean ridges. New crust forms here when magma erupts from these ridges and pushes preexisting crust horizontally towards the continental plates. Such ridges include the Mid-Atlantic Ridge and the East Pacific Rise.

Social Studies

1. C: A bill is usually first reviewed by the appropriate subcommittee. The subcommittee can accept the bill, amend the bill, or reject the bill. If the subcommittee accepts or amends the bill, they send it to the full committee for review. Expert witnesses and testimony are all part of committee review.

2. B: The Virginia Company of London was based in London, not Massachusetts. It had a charter to colonize American land between the Hudson and Cape Fear rivers. The other Virginia Company was the Virginia Company of Plymouth, which was based in the American colony of Plymouth, Massachusetts. It had a charter to colonize North America between the Potomac River and the northern boundary of Maine. Both Virginia Companies were joint-stock companies, which had often been used by England for trading with other countries.

3. B: US industrialization was confined to the Northeast until after the Civil War because the Northeast had faster-running rivers than the South. The earliest American factories used horse-drawn machines. When waterpower was developed and proved superior, the Northeast's faster rivers were more suited to water-powered mills than the South's slower rivers. The war did not delay the development of waterpower. Waterpower was developed before the Civil War in the late

1790s. Steam power, a more efficient alternative to waterpower, was developed after the Civil War and eventually replaced waterpower. With steam-powered engines, industry could spread to the South, since steam engines did not depend on rapidly running water like water-powered engines. While British emigré Samuel Slater's first cotton mill using horse-drawn production did lose a lot of money, this was not a reason for industrial delay. In fact, Slater's Beverly Cotton Manufactory in Massachusetts, the first American cotton mill, in spite of its financial problems, was successful in both its volume of cotton production and in developing the water-powered technology that ultimately would succeed the horse-drawn method. Slater's second cotton mill in Pawtucket, Rhode Island, was water-powered. Industrial delay was not because milling technology had not yet been invented. Slater learned of new textile manufacturing techniques as a youth in England, and he brought this knowledge to America in 1789.

4. D: Indentured servants agreed to work for a set period of time in exchange for transportation to the New World and such basic necessities as food and shelter. They did not receive wages and were generally not highly-educated people. Employers often viewed indentured servants with scorn and treated them as harshly as they treated slaves.

5. C: Nature imposed great hardships on farmers. Drought, wind, fires, blizzards, and subzero temperatures made life on the plains very difficult and dangerous. The invention of barbed wire in 1874 allowed farmers to keep livestock from damaging their crops. The Homestead Act of 1862 encouraged settlement of the west and made land available to some 600,000 homesteaders. Founded in 1867, the Grange united farmers in their effort to regulate storage and shipping costs and generally protect their own interests.

6. B: Southern states provided raw materials that were manufactured into commodities in Northern states. Southerners resented paying taxes to Northern states for these products (textiles, furniture, etc.).

7. A: It is not true that the founding fathers specifically stated in the Constitution that the United States would be a democracy. The founding fathers wanted the new United States to be founded on principles of liberty and equality, but they did not specifically describe these principles with the term *democracy*. Thus, the Declaration of Independence, like the Constitution after it, did not stipulate a democracy, although both did state the principles of equality and freedom. The Constitution also provided for the election of the new government, and for protection of the rights of some, but not all, of the people. Notable exceptions at the time were black people and women. Only later were laws passed to protect their rights over the years.

8. B: Marx's focus in *The Communist Manifesto* (1848) and *Das Kapital* (1867) was on the inevitable conflict between the working class and the capitalists who own the means of production. He identified these two opposing forces as the proletariat and the bourgeoisie.

9. A: The federal government has three branches: executive, including the president, the vice president, and the president's cabinet; legislative, including the House of Representatives and the Senate; and judicial, including the Supreme Court and the court system.

10. A: By 1840, more than one third of all Americans lived west of the Alleghenies, but not two thirds. It is correct that in the first half of the 19th century, the American population doubled every 25 years. It is also correct that westward expansion increased as more people moved west during these years. It is correct that there was not a lot of immigration to the US from other countries before 1820. It is also true that foreign immigration to America increased quickly around that time, with most immigrants coming from the British Isles.

11. D: Congress did not have the authority to levy taxes under the Articles of Confederation. Without the ability to levy taxes, there was no way to finance programs, which weakened the government.

12. C: The ancient Mayan civilization was located in Central America. Today, the land of their former empire comprises Guatemala, Belize, Honduras, and El Salvador in Central America and also the Yucatan Peninsula and the south of Mexico. The ancient civilization of the Incas was located in what is now Peru in South America. The ancient civilization of the Aztecs lived in what is Mexico today.

13. C: The 12th Amendment passed in 1804 gave each member of the Electoral College one vote for the president and another for the vice president. Previously, the runner-up in the presidential election became vice president.

14. A: The French and Indian War (Seven Years' War) happened from 1754–1763. The American Revolution happened from 1775–1783. The French Revolution happened from 1789–1799. The War of 1812 happened from 1812–1815.

15. A: The Senate and House of Representatives make up a bicameral legislature. The Great Compromise awarded seats in the Senate equally to each state, while the seats in the House of Representatives were based on population.

16. B: Lines of longitude, which run north-south from pole to pole, are used to separate time zones. Houston, Texas, and Fargo, North Dakota, which are on almost the exact same line of longitude, are both in the Central Time Zone; however, they are not in the same state, do not have the same climate, and are not equidistant from the equator. To calculate distance from the equator, the latitude of the city would need to be known.

17. D: The education of the workforce generally is not treated as a separate, direct input in the basic model of GDP. GDP refers to the value of all goods and services produced by a country in a specific timeframe, and basic models describe that output as depending directly on inputs like labor, capital, and technology. The education of its workforce can impact the quantity of output by increasing worker productivity, but it is usually considered part of labor quality (human capital) rather than a standalone input. GDP is more directly impacted by the size of the workforce, the amount of a country's capital, and the technology already in place. The size of the workforce implies that there are people who are ready and willing to work. The amount of capital means that there is a sufficient number of factories and assets available to create goods and services. Technology refers to the methods, processes, and tools that help labor and capital produce more efficiently.

18. A: Representative government, by which citizens elect officials who share their views and who, in turn, present their views in a democratic system, is not a true democracy in which each individual votes on each issue. As the population of a democracy grows, the practicality of every individual voting on every issue becomes prohibitive to the process.

19. C: The Ottoman Empire joined with the Central Powers in 1914 during World War I. The original Triple Alliance was formed by Austria-Hungary, Germany, and Italy in 1882 and renewed in 1902. The Ottoman Empire signed the Turco-German Alliance in August 1914, joining with the Central Powers. In October 1914, with the bombing of Russian ports on the Black Sea, Turkey formally entered World War I. The Allied Powers of the Triple Entente (Great Britain, France, and Russia) declared war on the Ottoman Empire in November 1914.

20. B: Article I of the Constitution mandates the taking of a census every ten years. The purpose was to be sure that each state was proportionately represented in Congress according to its population as specified in the Constitution. Census data is also used to allocate federal funding for various programs and for shaping economic policies. Individual data collected by the US Bureau of the Census is kept confidential for seventy-two years and does not affect income tax rates. Every state has two seats in the Senate regardless of population.

21. C: The impact of a transaction on third parties not involved in the transaction is known as an externality. An externality can be positive, in which case it's a positive externality or social benefit. An externality can also be negative, in which case it's a negative externality or a social cost.

22. D: Ancient Greek democracy was not completely open to all of the public. However, participating persons were not chosen or excluded based on their respective socioeconomic levels. The city-state of Athens had one of the first and most well-known democracies in ancient Greece. It began around 500 BC. The experiment of Athenian democracy was unique in that it was a direct democracy, meaning people voted directly for or against proposed legislation without any representation such as the House of Representatives and the Senate, as we have in modern democracies.

23. D: The Protestant work ethic is considered by many historians to have contributed to the Industrial Revolution. In Britain, where industrialization started, financial stability encouraged investment in industry, and the eventual dominance of Protestantism is believed to have contributed to a class of entrepreneurs who believed in education, technological progress, and hard work. The other choices are considered effects of industrialization. Mass production enabled the privately owned, for-profit enterprises that characterize capitalist economic systems. Socialism developed as a criticism of capitalism; Karl Marx argued that capitalism polarized societies into owners versus workers. Marx also viewed capitalism as a necessary precursor to socialism within the logical progression of economies. Romanticism also developed in reaction against mechanization and involved using art and literature to contrast nature with the dark side of scientific progress.

24. C: The Underground Railroad was not necessary literally a railroad but a series of clandestine paths to move runaway and freed slaves out of southern states prior to 1865.

25. A: A timeline would be the best way to represent the major events of World War I. Timelines place events in chronological order, with the distance between the events correlated to their interval on the line. A timeline can run in any direction. A thematic map or a flow-line map might also be good at representing this subject, but a political map is restricted to borders and cities; therefore, it would not be able to suggest the changes caused by the war. Bar graphs and pie charts are used to depict quantities and proportions rather than sequences of events.

26. B: Many Americans migrated during World War II, seeking work in war-related factories; boomtowns sprang up as a result. Some Japanese-Americans served in the United States military during World War II; in fact, the all-Japanese 442nd Regimental Combat Team was decorated by the US government for its service. This eliminates choice D. Answer C can be rejected because Caucasian and African-American soldiers served in segregated units. Answer A can be eliminated because consumption actually increased in postwar American society, as production was high and returning US soldiers had income to spend.

27. D: The vice president also serves as the president of the Senate. If a tie occurs in the Senate, the vice president casts his vote to break the tie.

28. A: Of the four answer choices, New York City is the most likely to be considered a modern cultural hearth. A cultural hearth is an area from which cultural trends emanate. Geographers suggest that there were seven original cultural hearths, including Mesoamerica and the Indus River Valley. The modes of living that originated in these areas emanated out into the rest of the world. These days, the cultural hearths tend to be the cities and countries with the most economic power. Of the four answer choices, New York City is clearly the wealthiest and the most influential. The styles and trends that originate in New York City find their way into communities all around the world.

29. D: A flow-line map describes the movement of people, trends, or materials across a physical area. The movements depicted on a flow-line map are typically represented by arrows. In more advanced flow-line maps, the width of the arrow corresponds to the quantity of the motion. Flow-line maps usually declare the span of time that is being represented. A political map depicts the man-made aspects of geography, such as borders and cities. A cartogram adjusts the size of the areas represented according to some variable. For instance, a cartogram of wheat production would depict Iowa as being much larger than Alaska. A qualitative map uses lines, dots, and other symbols to illustrate a particular point. For example, a qualitative map might be used to demonstrate the greatest expansion of the Persian Empire.

30. A: One example of the multiplier effect of large cities would be if the presence of specialized equipment for an industry attracted even more business. Large cities tend to grow even larger for a number of reasons: they have more skilled workers, they have greater concentrations of specialized equipment, and they have already-functioning markets. These factors all make it easier for a business to begin operations in a large city than elsewhere. Thus, the populations and economic productivity of large cities tend to grow quickly. Some governments have sought to mitigate this trend by clustering groups of similar industries in smaller cities.

31. B: Direct democracy is a system in which all members of a population vote directly on the issue at hand. A representative democracy refers to a system in which representatives vote on behalf of the population. The House of Representatives, the Senate, and the Electoral College are all representative democracies. The House of Representatives gives weight to population, whereas the Senate and the Electoral College do not. Members of the House of Representatives are elected in proportion to the population of each state. Representation by senators is not based on population and is therefore skewed in electoral weight. The Electoral College can and has contradicted the popular vote in the Presidential election.

32. C: When a nation follows the theory of comparative advantage, it specializes in producing the goods and services it can make at a lower opportunity cost and then engages in trade to obtain other goods.

33. D: One key to an opinion statement is the use of superlatives. This sentence states that apartheid was the worst political system. This is an opinion that could be challenged, given Nazism and fascism during World War II. All other statements can be verified as fact.

34. C: A person who has taken out a fixed-rate loan can benefit from inflation by paying back the loan with dollars that are less valuable than they were when the loan was taken out. In the other examples, inflation harms the individual or entity.

35. B: In order to prosper, a nation should not try to increase its imports. Mercantilism is an economic theory including the idea that prosperity comes from a positive balance of international trade. For any one nation to prosper, that nation should increase its exports but decrease its imports. Exporting more to other countries while importing less from them will give a country a positive trade balance. This theory assumes that money and wealth are identical assets of a nation. In addition, this theory also assumes that the volume of global trade is an unchangeable quantity. Mercantilism dictates that a nation's government should apply a policy of economic protectionism by stimulating more exports and suppressing imports. Some ways to accomplish this task have included granting subsidies for exports and imposing tariffs on imports. Mercantilism can be regarded as essentially the opposite of the free trade policies that have been encouraged in more recent years.

36. B: The rate of incarceration for juveniles did decrease after 1995. Answer A is a correct statement. Fewer women than men are incarcerated in each year sampled, even though the number of females incarcerated is growing. Response C is also accurate; in the years specified, more whites were incarcerated in jails than any other race. The chart clearly shows an increase in the number of Hispanics being jailed, making response D an accurate statement.

37. A: The president has the authority to negotiate and sign treaties. A two-thirds vote of the Senate, however, is needed to ratify a treaty for it to be upheld.

38. C: Article III judges are appointed for life and can retire at 65. They can only be removed from their posts by impeachment in the House and conviction in the Senate. Having judges serve life terms is meant to allow them to serve without being governed by the changing opinions of the public.

39. B: The Texas Railroad Commission now chiefly concerned with regulating the oil and gas industry.

40. D: In behaviorism, reinforcement is anything strengthening the probability of repeating a behavior. Punishment is anything weakening that probability. In behaviorism, "positive" means presenting a stimulus; "negative" means removing one. Hence positive punishment is presenting a stimulus that makes a given behavior less likely. Negative punishment is removing a stimulus that makes a given behavior less likely. Positive reinforcement is presenting a stimulus that makes a given behavior more likely. Negative reinforcement is removing a stimulus to make the behavior more likely.